Community-Based Tourism in the Developing World

This book analyses community-based approaches to developing and regenerating tourism destinations in the developing world, addressing this central issue in sustainable tourism practices.

It reviews a variety of systems useful for analysing and understanding management issues to offer new insight into the skills and resources that are needed for implementation, ongoing monitoring and review of community-based tourism. Adopting a multidisciplinary approach, this book explores alternatives to the dominant interpretation which argues against tourism as a benefit for community development. International case studies throughout the book illustrate and vouch for tourism as a transformative force while clarifying the need to manage expectations in sustainable tourism for community development, rejuvenation and regeneration. Emphasis is placed on accruing relevant decision-support material, and creating services, products and management approaches that will endure and adapt as change necessitates.

This will be of great interest to upper-level students, researchers and academics in the fields of tourism impacts, sustainability, ethics and development as well as the broader field of geography.

Peter Wiltshier has a PhD which explored responsible development of tourism in a creative and dedicated fashion; creatively supporting communities to provide resources for their welfare and dedicated to the pursuit of a responsible future with a focus on the beautiful and important 'Green Lungs' of rural Britain in the East Midlands and in New Zealand. His role as senior lecturer destination and community tourism management at the University of Derby Buxton is to ensure that the public and private sector work together to develop resources and skills for communities to take charge of their own destinies. He also works with the Diocese of Derby to identify how tourism can benefit churches. He supports the county, the district and parishes within Derbyshire and the Peak District in their endeavours to create a better environment for all through purposeful leisure and recreation.

Alan Clarke is employed at the University of Pannonia in Hungary, where he has been appointed as a full Hungarian professor. His commitment to communities has been marked throughout his career, beginning with his teaching in community education in Sheffield, followed by time with the community education team at the Open University. He has led research in the inner city of Salford and worked with the Roma community in the North West of England. He has been known to say that the best chapter in his PhD was the one on community development (which never appeared). The Derby Jubilee Community Festival crystalised a number of issues – power, hegemony, inclusion, engagement and capacity building – plus the opportunity to develop a lifelong friendship with Allan Jepson. Alan moved to Hungary where communities and festivals are constructed differently. There were hard lessons in coming to terms with this – cultures, structures and stakeholder relations have to be seen through differently sensitised lenses. This opened up an interest with religious and heritage tourism and the ways these belief systems impacted on the cultures in which they are experienced in the communities that give them life. It was here that he made the significant bond with his co-editor, Peter Wiltshier.

Contemporary Geographies of Leisure, Tourism and Mobility

Series Editor: C. Michael Hall

Professor at the Department of Management, College of Business and Economics, University of Canterbury, Christchurch, New Zealand

The aim of this series is to explore and communicate the intersections and relationships between leisure, tourism and human mobility within the social sciences.

It will incorporate both traditional and new perspectives on leisure and tourism from contemporary geography, e.g. notions of identity, representation and culture, while also providing for perspectives from cognate areas such as anthropology, cultural studies, gastronomy and food studies, marketing, policy studies and political economy, regional and urban planning, and sociology, within the development of an integrated field of leisure and tourism studies.

Also, increasingly, tourism and leisure are regarded as steps in a continuum of human mobility. Inclusion of mobility in the series offers the prospect to examine the relationship between tourism and migration, the sojourner, educational travel, and second home and retirement travel phenomena.

The series comprises two strands:

Contemporary Geographies of Leisure, Tourism and Mobility aims to address the needs of students and academics, and the titles will be published in hardback and paperback. Titles include:

Sustainable Tourism Practices in the Mediterranean
Edited by Ipek Kalemci Tüzün, Mehmet Ergül and Colin Johnson

Overtourism
Tourism Management and Solutions
Edited by Harald Pechlaner, Elisa Innerhofer and Greta Erschbamer

Tourism Fictions, Simulacra and Virtualities
Edited by Maria Gravari-Barbas, Nelson Graburn and Jean-François Staszak

Community-Based Tourism in the Developing World
Community Learning, Development and Enterprise
Edited by Peter Wiltshier and Alan Clarke

For more information about this series, please visit: www.routledge.com/Contemporary-Geographies-of-Leisure-Tourism-and-Mobility/book-series/SE0522

Community-Based Tourism in the Developing World

Community Learning, Development and Enterprise

**Edited by Peter Wiltshier
and Alan Clarke**

Routledge
Taylor & Francis Group

LONDON AND NEW YORK

First published 2020 by Routledge

2 Park Square, Milton Park, Abingdon, Oxon OX14 4RN
605 Third Avenue, New York, NY 10017

Routledge is an imprint of the Taylor & Francis Group, an informa business

First issued in paperback 2022

Publisher's Note

The publisher has gone to great lengths to ensure the quality of this reprint but points out that some imperfections in the original copies may be apparent.

British Library Cataloguing-in-Publication Data
A catalogue record for this book is available from the British Library

Library of Congress Cataloging-in-Publication Data
Names: Wiltshier, Peter, editor. | Clarke, Alan, 1956- editor.
Title: Community-based tourism in the developing world : community learning, development & enterprise / edited by Peter Wiltshier and Alan Clarke.
Description: Abingdon, Oxon ; New York, NY : Routledge, 2020. | Series: Contemporary geographies of leisure, tourism and mobility | Includes bibliographical references and index.
Identifiers: LCCN 2019027847 (print) | LCCN 2019027848 (ebook) | ISBN 9781138494305 (hardback) | ISBN 9781351026383 (ebook)
Subjects: LCSH: Sustainable tourism—Developing countries. | Community development—Developing countries. | Tourism—Social aspects—Developing countries. | Tourism—Economic aspects—Developing countries.
Classification: LCC G156.5.S87 C657 2020 (print) | LCC G156.5.S87 (ebook) | DDC 338.4/791—dc23
LC record available at https://lccn.loc.gov/2019027847
LC ebook record available at https://lccn.loc.gov/2019027848

ISBN: 978-1-138-49430-5 (hbk)
ISBN: 978-1-03-233786-9 (pbk)
DOI: 10.4324/9781351026383

Typeset in Times New Roman
by Apex CoVantage, LLC

Contents

Figures

Maps

Tables

Contributors

Adenike Adebayo is Associate Lecturer and Researcher in the Division of Geography, Events, Leisure and Tourism in the School of Human and Life Sciences at Canterbury Christ Church University, Canterbury, UK. Adenike gained her B.A. in mass communication from Babcock University, Nigeria. She then obtained an MSc. in tourism and events management from the University of Bedfordshire, UK. She worked as an assistant lecturer at Elizade University, Nigeria, before she got a scholarship award to research her PhD in tourism studies at Canterbury Christ Church University. Adenike's research interests includes participatory planning approaches in tourism development, tourism policies and governance, and sustainable tourism.

Vitor Ambrósio has a PhD in geography, M.A. in geography, B.A. in modern languages and literatures and B.A. in tourism (tour guiding). He is a senior lecturer of ESHTE – Escola Superior de Hotelaria e Turismo do Estoril (Estoril Higher Institute for Tourism and Hotel Studies), Portugal, since it was founded in 1991. He has also been teaching in bachelor's, master's and doctoral tourism programmes in other national and international institutions. Prior to this, between 1980 and 1995, he worked as a travel agent promoter and tourist guide. He was the director of the doctoral programme in tourism and the director of the master's programme in tourism and communication, both offered by the ESHTE and the University of Lisbon (UL). He was head of the Department of Tourism Planning and also head of the Department of Tourism Practices, both in ESHTE. He has collaborated with some NGOs in the field of religious and sustainable tourism development, taking part in missions within the frame of technical assistance programmes on sustainable religious development. During the last decades he has been publishing (articles, book chapters, a book) in tourism, mainly in religious tourism, his main research interest.

Giovanna Bertella is Associate Professor at the School of Business and Economics, UiT The Arctic University of Norway, Tromsø (Norway). She received her PhD from the Department of Sociology, Political Science and Community Planning at UiT. Her PhD dissertation concerns learning and collaborative approaches to tourism development in rural and peripheral areas. She teaches marketing and organisational studies courses at the bachelor and master level. Her works are published in several international journals. Her research interests are management, marketing, entrepreneurship/innovation, tourism and leisure studies (nature- and animal-based experiences, rural tourism, food tourism, events), food studies (veganism), and futures studies (scenarios).

Alessio Cavicchi is Associate Professor at the Department of Education, Cultural Heritage and Tourism at University of Macerata (Italy). His main fields of interest and research are consumer food choice, economics of food quality and safety, sustainable tourism and innovation in the agro-food sector. He has experience as coordinator of several EU-funded projects, and as an invited expert for several programmes and DGs of the European Commission in the food sector (DG Agri, DG Research, DG Regio-Urbact, Joint Research Center, European Agency for Competitiveness and Innovation).

Alan Clarke is employed at the University of Pannonia in Hungary, where he has been appointed as a full Hungarian professor. His commitment to communities has been marked throughout his career, beginning with his teaching in community education in Sheffield, followed by time with the community education team at the Open University. He has led research in the inner city of Salford and worked with the Roma Community in the North West of England. He has been known to say that the best chapter in his PhD was the one on community development (which never appeared). The Derby Jubilee Community Festival crystalised a number of issues – power, hegemony, inclusion, engagement and capacity building – plus the opportunity to develop a lifelong friendship with Allan Jepson. Alan moved to Hungary where communities and festivals are constructed differently. There were hard lessons in coming to terms with this – cultures, structures and stakeholder relations have to be seen through differently sensitised lenses. This opened up an interest with religious and heritage tourism and the ways these belief systems impacted on the cultures in which they are experienced in the communities that give them life. It was here that he made the significant bond with his co-editor, Peter Wiltshier.

Amran Hamzah (PhD) is a professor in tourism planning at Universiti Teknologi Malaysia. His area of specialisation is the interface between community-based tourism and conservation. Besides his academic duties Amran is active is research and consultancy having led more than 50 consultancy projects for international agencies such as APEC, IUCN, the Ministry of Environment Japan and the ASEAN Secretariat as well as national agencies such as the Ministry of Tourism and Culture Malaysia and Tourism Malaysia. Among others he was the lead consultant for the National Tourism Policy 2019–2050, National Ecotourism Plan 2016–2025 and Business Strategies for Upscaling the Malaysian Homestay Experience 2017 to 2028. Amran is also a regional councillor for the International Union for Conservation of Nature (IUCN) for the term 2016 to 2020.

Nutfillo Ibragimov is a professor at Bukhara State University, Department of Economic Education and Tourism. He obtained his doctorate (PhD) in Economics from the Samarkand Institute for Economics and Service in 2007. His doctoral thesis was "The application of the concept of destination management in the development of internal tourism in Uzbekistan". Nutfillo completed a master's degree in Macroeconomics at Bukhara State University in 2000–2002. Further on, in year 2002 he began to study the discipline of destination management" in Trento Tourism Academy in Italy, under the supervision of Professor Umberto Martini. He is the author of more than twenty articles, including a monograph "Destination Management: the Art of the Management of Internal Tourism with Market Measures". As Co-founder and Director of "Jahongashtatur service" LLC in 2014, he has been leading his company with tour operating (internal tourism) activity. Based on the licence given from "Uzbektourism" national company, which deals with the organisation of cultural-enlightenment tours around Uzbekistan for only Uzbekistan residents, he proposes a variety of professionally arranged tours to different sections.

Tadeja Jere Jakulin (PhD) is Professor of Tourism Systems, Modelling, Simulation, Cultural Events, Social Networks in Tourism and Pilgrimage Tourism in UNESCO's UniTwin Faculty of Tourism Studies-TURISTICA at University of Primorska, Slovenia. She obtained her PhD for research on the systems, modelling and simulation in tourism from the University of Maribor, Slovenia. She researches and teaches in the field of soft systems (organisational networks, social and tourism systems) and consciousness as the evolutionary system. The research work gained her international and national prizes (Prometheus document of gratitude for excellence in scientific communication and teaching excellence. She lectures around the world and has been appointed as a visiting professor at the University of Rijeka, Croatia. She is a member of the UNWTO Panel of Tourism Experts, and a member of Chairs of Cultural Tourism within UNESCO UNITWIN Chair of Culture, Tourism, Development (Paris-Sorbonne). She is an international reviewer for the area of systems approach in tourism and national reviewer for national vocational professions in tourism. She is a "doctor honoris causa" of the IIAS (International Institute for Advanced Studies in Systems Research and Cybernetics) and an active member of Colour Mirrors (chromo practitioners and teachers) network.

Allan Jepson currently works in the Tourism, Hospitality and Event Management Group at The University of Hertfordshire, UK. His research journey began by investigating relationships of hegemony/power in local community festivals (PhD thesis) to demonstrate a lack of cultural inclusion/engagement in community festivals and events. Following this he has undertaken research into: engagement in the festival and event planning process (MOA model/self-efficacy), and knowledge management. He has published four edited books (*Exploring Community Festivals and Events*; *Managing and Developing*

Communities, Festivals and Events; *Power, Construction and Meaning in Festivals*, with Alan Clarke. And: *Events and Marginalisation* with Trudie Walters) to advance knowledge in the field of event studies/critical event studies. His current research is concerned with using innovative methods to better understand communities and well-being, which includes sociological impacts (psychosocial/physiological, and cultural) of localised events upon their communities and in particular research into participatory arts events, emotion, and collective memory. Further details of his research are available here: https://eventsandwellbeing.wordpress.com. Outside of work he is Daddy to three very special little people, and husband to one very special lady. He plays football, runs with his dog, and although the editor may want to discuss this further he supports the greatest football team on the planet (Nottingham Forest FC).

Andrew Jones holds a senior academic post at the University of Malta and has also held positions at The University of Wales, International Faculty Cardiff UK, Swansea Business School, UK and the University of Brunei. Andrew has professional experience in planning, environmental management and tourism at both international, regional and local levels and has been an enthusiastic contributor, for over thirty years, to the academic tourism community within Malta, the UK and internationally. Andrew first qualified in urban and regional planning but joined higher education in the late 1980s where he focused his research on tourism, sustainability and environmental planning. In his most recent work Andrew has focused part of his teaching and research specialising in two distinct areas: i) sustainable tourism – specialising in community and niche market development, coastal tourism and climate change and ii) the development of transnational education (TNE). In this respect he has had the opportunity to work within academic sectors internationally in Europe, Central, South and Southeast Asia. These include assignments in Japan, China, India, Hong Kong, Singapore, Uzbekistan, Malaysia, Japan, Germany Greece. Italy, Bulgaria, Romania and the UK over the last ten years.

Valeria Klitsounova is an associate professor at Belarusian State University, and Chair of the Board, Belarusian Association of Agro and Ecotourism "Country Escape". She introduced the idea of agrotourism in Belarus and is considered there as "agrotourism mother". She specialises in rural development through tourism. She has been working with many Belarusian rural communities trying to implement a tourism cluster model with a clear brand. Her special interest is gastronomy tourism and traditional Belarusian cuisine revival. She has published three books, including a textbook about agro-ecotourism. She developed six individual teaching courses about rural and ecotourism, marketing and promotion in tourism, heritage interpretation, and events promotion. She is active on Facebook and works with popular sites and bloggers.

Lelokwane Lockie Mokgalo is a programme leader in tourism studies at Botswana Accountancy College (BAC). Before he joined BAC, Lelokwane

Lockie started his academic career with the University of Botswana. He holds a BSc in travel and tourism marketing as well as an MSc. in responsible tourism management with the International Centre for Responsible Tourism (ICRT) at Leeds Beckett University (formerly Leeds Metropolitan). He is presently pursuing his PhD studies with North West University in South Africa with a thesis focused on formulating strategies to mitigate the ban of hunting on local communities and conservation. Lelokwane Lockie is passionate about sustainability in the tourism industry and has published articles in the area, cultural heritage as well as domestic tourism in Botswana. His other passion is mentoring and playing an advisory role to young learners in tourism and other business fields. His research interests are; responsible and sustainable tourism, cultural heritage tourism, domestic tourism and operations in tourism businesses.

Daniella S. Marcondes lives in Brazil and is a consultant in tourism planning in protected areas and traditional communities with twelve years of experience.

She holds a master's degree in tourism development from School of Arts, Science and Humanities of University of Sao Paulo (2018) and a bachelor of tourism from the Methodist University of Piracicaba (2002). She attended PG certificate in Brazilian and Portuguese studies (2008) at Kings College London. In public management, she acted as the Director of Ecotourism for the municipality of Ilhabela (2011–2015). This involved working on the related topics of ecotourism, natural resource management and public use in protected areas of natural, environmental heritage and community-based tourism. From 2013 to 2017, she coordinated the Technical Chamber of Ecotourism, was a member of the advisory board of the Tourism Council of Ilhabela and State Park Council, offering as a volunteer technical support for tourism development. She currently works as a consultant at Maembipe Ecoturismo Consultoria acting in traditional caiçara communities using non-formal education to foster local empowerment. Link to resume: http://lattes.cnpq.br/8034334548382667.

Gwinyai Mercy Musikavanhu (Manhotoma) is an accomplished academic and researcher in Botswana. Her experience in education in Botswana spans almost a decade in the tertiary education sector. Gwinyai Mercy has also served in management positions previously in the tourism and hospitality industry in Zimbabwe and then Botswana before joining the tertiary education sector. She has published in the fields of hospitality and tourism. Her research interests include tourism diversification, service experience, service quality and niche tourism. She is mainly a proponent of service experience. Her works comprise peer-reviewed articles in international journals and refereed conference proceedings. She is a fellow of the Higher Education Academy in the UK.

Vikneswaran Nair (PhD) is currently the Dean of Graduate Studies and Research at the University of The Bahamas (UB) in Nassau, Bahamas. Prior to joining

UB in August 2017, Vikneswaran was at Taylor's University, Malaysia, for nineteen years as a full professor of sustainable tourism, at the School of Hospitality, Tourism and Culinary Arts; programme leader for the Responsible Rural Tourism Network; research fellow of the Centre for Research and Innovation in Tourism (CRiT) and the founding Director of the Centre for Research and Development at the university. A consultant with many national and international projects, Vikneswaran's exceptional research achievements with more than 200 publications to his credit have earned him many international and national awards. Between 2001 and 2016, he led a national project worth US$3 million in developing a responsible rural tourism framework for Malaysia. He recently completed his first consultancy work in the Bahamas when he led the project in writing the country report for the Bahamas for UNDP's Sustainable Development Goals. His research specialisation is in sustainable and responsible tourism, rural tourism, ecotourism management, environmental management, community-based tourism and green tourism.

Ade Oriade (PhD) is Senior Lecturer in Tourism and Course Leader for MA Hospitality and Event Management at the University of Wolverhampton. Ade's research interests are in services management and marketing in tourism/hospitality/event. He also focuses on sustainable tourism development and planning, an area in which Ade's work continues to contribute to decision making in the industry and enhance the socio-economic development of destinations. The common thread running through Ade's research is a unique interest in producing impactful output to create theoretical knowledge and help tourism destinations and services sector organisations develop their products and enhance customers' experiences. Ade has a wide range of academic publications in journal articles, books, book chapters and reports. He has published numerous consultancy reports and peer-reviewed articles in journals such as *International Journal of Tourism Research*, *Journal of Destination Marketing & Management* and *Event Management, an International Journal*. Ade's research has been presented at several national and international workshops and peer-refereed conferences. In his numerous scholarly activities and engagements Ade serves as editorial member, guest editor and reviewer for many high-impact journals.

Gigliola Paviotti is a doctoral candidate in education at the University of Macerata. Her research interests include employability, transitions from education to work, and engagement of universities for regional development. She is currently involved in research projects related to pedagogy for employability and co-creation approaches for employment and entrepreneurship purposes.

Akmal Rahmonov is Co-Founder of Jahongashta Tur Servis (a domestic tour operator in Uzbekistan). He is concurrently Chief Executive Officer of Pilgrim Travel System. He has previously been a volunteer in a society of disabled people in Germany, Lebensgemeinschaft Richthof. Akmal has published "The destination marketing tools for Seven Sufi Saints of noble

Bukhara pilgrimage cluster" and "Improvement perspectives in tourism by clustering multi-confessional destinations of Uzbekistan". He is fluent in English, German, Russian, Uzbek and Tadjik.

Peter Robinson (PhD) is Head of the Centre for Tourism and Hospitality Management at Leeds Beckett University. He is a fellow of the Tourism Management Institute and a fellow and director of the Institute for Travel and Tourism. He is a member of the Tourism Society and is a principal fellow of the Higher Education Academy. Peter enjoys working with businesses in the tourism and hospitality sectors and has worked on consultancy projects with First Rate Exchange services, the British Motor Museum, Lichfield Cathedral, Leicester Cathedral, Burlington Slate and The Holker Group, Utopia Leisure and TUI. Peter teaches a broad spectrum of subjects but specialises in tourism business development, destination creation, visitor experience, heritage tourism, dark tourism, destination marketing and urban regeneration. Peter's research interests focus on prosumption within tourist experiences, Cold War tourism, nostalgia, urban exploration and visitor experiences. Peter is a reviewer for several journals and has been a guest editor for the *Journal of Destination Marketing and Management* and the *International Journal of Management Practice*. Peter has written several books, including the first textbook discussing operations management in the travel industry.

Susan L. Slocum is an associate professor at George Mason University in Fairfax, Virginia. She specialises in sustainable economic development through tourism and policy implementation at the regional and national level. Working with communities to enhance backward linkages between tourism and traditional industries, Susan has worked with rural communities in the United States, the UK, and with indigenous populations in emerging tourism destinations in Tanzania. In particular, she is interested in balancing policy development and integration to provide a more bottom-up form of planning within tourism destinations and has approached sustainable tourism from a contemporary view, which includes the addition of institutional reform and social justice. She has published four edited books and authored two books, including a textbook on food and agricultural tourism.

Sabrina Tomasi is a doctoral candidate in human sciences at the Department of Education, Cultural Heritage and Tourism at the University of Macerata (Italy). Her main fields of interest and research are: educational tourism, ecotourism, health tourism and experiential tourism. She is involved in EU research projects (The Wine Lab and FoodBiz) about the role of higher education institutions in promoting bottom-up approaches and stakeholder engagement to facilitate innovation and co-creation in rural areas.

Peter Wiltshier has a PhD which explored responsible development of tourism in a creative and dedicated fashion; creatively supporting communities to provide resources for their welfare and dedicated to the pursuit of a responsible future with a focus on the beautiful and important "Green Lungs" of rural

Britain in the East Midlands and in New Zealand. His role as Senior Lecturer – destination and community tourism management at the University of Derby Buxton is to ensure that the public and private sector work together to develop resources and skills for communities to take charge of their own destinies. He also works with the Diocese of Derby to identify how tourism can benefit churches. He supports the county, the district and parishes within Derbyshire and the Peak District in their endeavours to create a better environment for all through purposeful leisure and recreation.

Julian Zarb is a visiting senior lecturer at the Institute for Tourism Travel and Culture at the University of Malta. He has held positions in tourism and hospitality in various organisations in Malta and internationally. Before his time at the University Julian held the position of Director of Tourism at the Ministry for Tourism: Malta. He is an active and founding member of the Malta Tourism Society and is a fellow of the Tourism Society UK, the Royal Geographical Society and the Institute of Hospitality. Presently he is concluding his doctoral studies. His main research interests are with sustainable and community tourism and local tourism planning.

1 Principles and practices

Case studies in innovation

Peter Wiltshier and Alan Clarke

Introduction

We define emerging tourism destinations in the context of community-based tourism (CBT) as places that have yet to achieve maturity in developed or mass tourism; as spaces that have the capacity to explore, analyse and interpret visitors' responses to an offer; as areas for the application of contemporary and emerging visitor management practices (Coccossis, 2017; Dangi and Jamal, 2016). These emerging destinations have quite likely not reached a crisis in capacity control or exceeded limits of acceptable impacts from tourism according to commentators and as judged perhaps by the academy as well as by visitors.

Furthermore, the warning signs for exceeding these constraints of social environmental responsibility may not yet have been noticed. Contributors to this book have clearly signposted opportunities for future development from tourism; contributors also acknowledge destination strengths to strive for a sustainable future that includes tourism.

The book captures glimpses of opportunity and indicates strengths in destinations from Zambia and Malawi to Uzbekistan and Belarus. Chapters also acknowledge democratic political processes in play from Malaysia to Botswana.

The literature surrounding community-based tourism (CBT) has common features with the literature impacting social welfare systems, health and education. In effect, some of the underpinning concepts that are employed in CBT emerge from the body that concerns communities wishing to develop, rejuvenate and refresh. In this text the underpinning twenty-first century contributions are discourses about resilience, equity, accessibility, wellbeing, affordability, localisation and responsibility. The issues underpinning all of these contributions are emerging from the development and implementation of the sustainable development goals (see Boluk et al., 2017).

Therefore, this text addresses the conceptual contributions and melds methodological and discursive views with the case studies explored by the chapter authors from the dialectics of emerging destinations. To clarify, the editors seek to balance the conceptual starting points for today's stakeholder with the actual practices in emergent destinations and address those needs, expectations and aims of stakeholders deliberately seeking to use tourism as a springboard for community development.

We also see parallels with the debates around the development of sustainable tourism. There are roots into the communities as the rhetoric builds the harmonious development of economy, environment and socio-cultural factors. These areas should not be seen as separable in anything other than an analytical sense. Economics has been considered to be the cornerstone of tourism development as without a profit there is no motive to drive or guide tourism development. More than that, however, CBT allows economics to be valued in more open ways as it allows the exploration of the connections between and through parts of the communities. Similarly, the environment should not be viewed as a canvas on which tourism is to be painted. The environment is an active agent shaping and being shaped by the way communities grew through them, liberating some features and constrained by others. What makes these interconnections possible is the socio-cultural aspects of the communities.

The basic model of the three elements also form the foundations of the triple bottom line – often used in the critiques of capitalist development: people, profit and planet. The triple bottom line lens seems to offer a sharper look at the business activities within the communities. It also offers an alternative way into understanding the construction of stakeholder spaces and places.

We see stakeholders as representatives of demand and supply in a strict input-output economic model (Slack et al., 2013). However, stakeholders are coincidentally filling key roles in demand and supply under the auspices of the sharing economy: the economy of co-creation and co-production in which lines of strategy, operation and control are not mutually exclusive for supplier or consumer. The essence of the 'co' in these terms is embedded in the role the stakeholders have in multi-directional communications. These are the agents who have to be engaged in shifting the direction of development from 'top-down' to 'bottom-up' practices. A phenomenon of shared responsibility in driving community-based tourism is an emerging theme which is further explored in chapters on the Southern African communities.

In addition to an economic focus we take a stance on quality and competitiveness as drivers of success in endeavours to understand and grasp the essentials of CBT in emerging destinations. Quality and competitiveness have a solid contribution in themes of exemplar case studies. Managing systems and business processes must go hand in hand with success in practice (Uzumeri, 1997). Service improvement, quality management, and a customer-relationship orientation accompany more prosaic issues like standards assurance, environmental management practices, knowledge exchange and retention to address needs of resource and skills shortages and management of monitoring and performance data analysis (Dumas et al., 2013). Sharing and creative economies rely on adaptability and human creativity. It is with this creativity and immense zest for life and gratitude for being a gifted and relied-on individual that communities turn into destinations that are distinctive and typical of human creativity (Florida, 2006). Individuals, as part of the larger sharing community, perceive that they give value to all people, organisations and the wider society (den Ouden, 2011). Innovation is typical of experiential services such as tourism in physical, delivery, and support roles and supply chain and is exemplified in these cases (see Voss Zomerdijk, 2007; Pechlaner et al., 2012; Weiermair, 2004). Such destinations are emblematic of continuous improvement and innovation strategies and feature, as we can see from each study, cycles of regular innovation, niche innovation and revolutionary innovation (Pikkemaat and Weiermair, 2003).

Social issues for CBT reflect the withdrawal of resources and policy and planning work from central government with deregulation and decentralisation. The fact that this might not be a surprise probably comes from the way these arguments have been well advanced for almost forty years in Europe and North America, Putnam, 2001.

Outcomes in socially equitable and adaptable communities rely on skills possessed of a wide array of local stakeholders; sometimes termed modernisation and engaged community practices (Hoggett Mayo and Miller, 2008). Such social adaptations rely on creating a locally skilled and resilient community that can capture destination 'habitus' (Bourdieu, 1979) and community image, values and branding without alienating stakeholders nor ignoring the need for an analytical approach supportive of policies addressing equity, sustainability and innovation. Building CBT from inside the community from the bottom upwards builds a healthy repository of new social capital for future aspirations of entrepreneurs and public sector workers intent on renewal in communities (Flaccavento, 2016). Presciently some chapters identify that the empowered elites where wealth has traditionally become concentrated are responding to equity and equality issues by focusing on capital invested to social enterprise (within the shared economy), on small, even micro-, businesses that can be managed by small groups within the community. In order to do this, we do see a focus on narratives that capture unique and distinctive stories for dispersal within the community, and importantly, across boundaries to acknowledge meeting challenges in both mobility and accessibility of the co-created economy.

Our case studies represent what is perceived to be excellence in social adaptability, practices in ambiguity and dilemmas of development that identify, apportion and monitor outcomes from shared responsibility.

Elements of economics, society and the physical representation of destination thus form the basis of a systemic approach to a sustainable community-driven model of good practices (Jamal and Stronza, 2009).

Essentially, on three environmental fronts, and with empowerment as a key theme, authors identify successes in emergent economies where communities can be turned into destinations. Successes feature issues to do with acknowledging the special and unique nature of communities (habitus). Simultaneously these successes reflect the co-creating facility and capacity to innovate, reflect, and acquire deep learning to create repositories of competitiveness, quality and differentiation. Each case study represents the best in product innovation in Belarus, process innovation in Brazil, managerial innovation in Malta and Zambian institutional innovation (Hjalager, 2010).

The editors acknowledge prior research to manage community-based tourism with embedding best practices and therefore recommend the ACES model to destination managers, students of tourism management, practitioners in consultation in community regeneration and renewal, investors in tourism and storytellers willing and able to add unique offers to hosts and guests in emerging destinations worldwide. We commend our eight stage ACES model detailed as follows.

Revitalisation and rejuvenation

A situational analysis of a destination from a participant observation perspective is presented in Part 2 where future directions for that destination are offered. The bottom-up and community-driven aspirations for tourism are presented as a partial salvation to community capacity building (Giampiccoli, 2015; Zahra, 2010; Mair and Reid, 2007; Beeton, 2006). Tourism therefore can be perceived as a conduit for capture of community beliefs and values to be embedded by stakeholders in a variety of business trajectories. Tourism can reflect many stakeholders' concerns for revitalisation, rejuvenation and independence and mirror resilience and the unique nature that local centres of excitement offer. Thirty years' reflections on Philip Putnam's' 'Bowling Alone' illustrate the need for localisation and for individuals to work collectively at grassroots level to elevate their environments and summarise their offer to investors and guests.

Turning a community into a destination: "Why should we adopt tourism?"

Every stakeholder must consider and develop plans for future success in community development and resilience (Swanson and Edgell, 2013). These chapters reflect plans that may include tourism development as themes for future relevance and endurance. Having a substantive plan for tourism development that reflects contemporary political policy guidelines and therefore mirrors a need to be embraced at a local, or even a regional, level is conducive for educators and policy directors to entice tourism business to take a confident approach to development alongside key elements of business development and partnership with negligible fears contradicting start-up business or micro-business. There should be few contraindications for success in return on investment or dubious marketing and branding activity undertaken by new operators in the community. This has been relatively well documented (see for example, Thomas and Thomas, 2006; Getz and Carlsen, 2005; or, Middleton, 2001).

Process of building a destination starts with values, beliefs and identity: "Evidence to support our beliefs in tourism"

A fifteen-year window of relevance to collect inalienable beliefs, values and identities was drawn up for Kangaroo Island, South Australia by Manidis-Roberts in 1997. It appears that all communities must reflect, sift, analyse and blend these values, beliefs and resulting identity over extended periods to joyously produce plans for the future that indicate where the destination journey has taken stakeholders to the current time. Again, we expect to identify and prioritise opportunities for micro-business to cooperate with partners in supply chains and recognise that evolving practices still mirror beliefs and values as they will inevitably change and not feel discouraged to embark on diversification or product development in the context of external negative political or social pressures (Zehrer and Raich, 2013; Wiltshier, 2007).

Resources needed for destination building: "What do we need here"

To undertake an exercise in reflection, an inventory to accompany the values and beliefs statement – a brief document exploring what is relevant and largely agreed to be used in building tourism for the community from this moment – is essential (Tinsley and Lynch, 2007). Simply put, communities must acknowledge resources, an inventory of product, business operators possessed of the skills and aptitudes to capitalise on resources and underlying opportunities and strengths within the community as a whole to produce reliable outcomes and meet key performance indicators (Roberts et al., 2017; Altinay et al., 2016).

Analysis of key markets and prospects – moving beyond Michael Porter: "Who is going to come here next time?"

Operationally stakeholders should gather data to reinforce our knowledge of the suppliers and consumers that are currently using our resources in tourism (Sheehan et al., 2016). The data can be analysed and key markets categorised to identify and continue to collect relevant data for management and monitoring purposes. Such items include infrastructure, accommodation and performance spaces that are building blocks for the tourism industry to carve a profile.

Assigning responsibility for building and tracking progress (how to do it)

Governance and assigning responsibility are key here. Who will manage and monitor progress and report outcomes. There are examples where stakeholders have taken responsibility for tourism development initiatives and assigned tasks to other stakeholders to ensure a smooth transition from planning to operations to monitoring and ongoing management with key performance indicators and outcomes determined (Valente et al., 2015; Gössling et al., 2012; Jamal and Getz, 1995). We can start assigning tasks to key stakeholders where boundaries are crossed in healthcare, education, business development, creative and design elements thereof.

Review and reflection on processes

Sharing new social capital is a key outcome that is expressed at the outset and completion of many projects in CBT (see Moscardo, 2014; Macbeth et al., 2004; Falk and Kilpatrick, 2000). Underpinning new social capital is the enduring identifiable brand, identity and focus for future development (McGehee et al., 2010), linking potentially disparate groups or adversarial parties in community wellbeing through alliances in meetings, publications, shared spaces in social media etc.

As we have demonstrated, our approach to CBT has been influenced by many sources of policy and practical research; we see the world from many perspectives and through lenses which are sometimes difficult to align. This should not be a surprise as one of us matured in the Southern Hemisphere and the other in the Northern Hemisphere. We followed different patterns of study, work and research but found added depth by bringing our experiences and insights together. We believe that the virtue in this coming together is also shared with our contributors – who bring their different knowledge sets to good effect in exploring the complexities of the CBT. Some may argue that we should have standardised both the written English and the references to a single dominant English. We believe that much would have been lost had we done so. We hope that the voices of our authors contribute to the value of their chapters and to sharing their understanding with others to extend our feeling for the nexus of issues which underpin CBT. Whilst it is true and importantly so to admit that we are still learning and developing our analytical techniques, we do have one that we use in our work and will elaborate here.

Transformative tourism through the ACES model: accrual of relevant responses

In understanding and using CBT we posit that new models of development are captured for future application and emulation, enlargement, interpretation and re-investment in nascent as well as maturing visitor destinations.

Cohesion of ideas and themes to explore

The accrual of new knowledge and success in practice will require ongoing reflection and re-working to assure the academy and practitioners that such experiences have largely been beneficial in case studies and productive of performance indicators and outcomes generally beneficial to communities and regions (Giaoutzi, 2017; Roberts et al., 2017).

Enduring networks and partnership between disparate groups

Prior applications of discourse and new worldviews demonstrate that notions and practices of partnership and network have been critical in success for communities and for planning responsible development across the globe (Saarinen et al., 2017).

Sharing input resources and outcome value-added

A democratic approach to new knowledge sharing has been demonstrated to make wise use of scarce resources through various platforms emerging in the current development discourses.

References

Altinay, L., Sigala, M., & Waligo, V. (2016). Social value creation through tourism enterprise. *Tourism Management, 54*, 404–417.

Beeton, S. (2006). *Community development through tourism*. Collingwood: Landlinks Press.

Boluk, K., Cavaliere, C. T., & Higgins-Desbiolles, F. (2017). Critical thinking to realize sustainability in tourism systems: reflecting on the 2030 sustainable development goals: Guest Editors. *Journal of Sustainable Tourism, 25*(9), 1–4.

Bourdieu, P. (1979). Symbolic power. *Critique of Anthropology, 4*(13–14), 77–85.

Coccossis, H. (2017). Sustainable tourism and carrying capacity: a new context. In *The challenge of tourism carrying capacity assessment* (pp. 19–30). Routledge: Abingdon on Thames.

Dangi, T., & Jamal, T. (2016). An integrated approach to "sustainable community-based tourism". *Sustainability, 8*(5), 475.

den Ouden, E. (2011). *Innovation design: Creating value for people, organizations and society*. London: Springer Science & Business Media.

Dumas, M., La Rosa, M., Mendling, J., & Reijers, H. A. (2013). *Fundamentals of business process management* (Vol. 1, p. 2). Heidelberg: Springer.

Falk, I., & Kilpatrick, S. (2000). What is social capital? A study of interaction in a rural community. *Sociologia ruralis, 40*(1), 87–110.

Flaccavento, A. (2016). *Building a healthy economy from the bottom up: harnessing real-world experience for transformative change*. Lexington: University Press of Kentucky.

Florida, R. (2006). The flight of the creative class: the new global competition for talent. *Liberal Education, 92*(3), 22–29.

Getz, D., & Carlsen, J. (2005). Family business in tourism: state of the art. *Annals of Tourism Research, 32*(1), 237–258.

Giampiccoli, A. (2015). Community-based tourism: origins and present trends. *African Journal for Physical Health Education, Recreation and Dance, 21*(2), 675–687.

Giaoutzi, M. (2017). *Tourism and regional development: new pathways*. Abingdon on Thames: Routledge.

Gössling, S., Hall, C. M., Ekström, F., Engeset, A. B., & Aall, C. (2012). Transition management: a tool for implementing sustainable tourism scenarios? *Journal of Sustainable Tourism, 20*(6), 899–916.

Hjalager, A. M. (2010). A review of innovation research in tourism. *Tourism Management, 31*(1), 1–12.

Hoggett, P., Mayo, M., & Miller, C. (2008). *The dilemmas of development work: ethical challenges in regeneration*. Bristol: Policy Press.

Jamal, T., & Stronza, A. (2009). Collaboration theory and tourism practice in protected areas: stakeholders, structuring and sustainability. *Journal of Sustainable tourism*, *17*(2), 169 189.

Jamal, T. B., & Getz, D. (1995). Collaboration theory and community tourism planning. *Annals of Tourism Research*, *22*(1), 186–204.

Macbeth, J., Carson, D., & Northcote, J. (2004). Social capital, tourism and regional development: SPCC as a basis for innovation and sustainability. *Current Issues in Tourism*, *7*(6), 502–522.

Mair, H., & Reid, D. G. (2007). Tourism and community development vs. tourism for community development: conceptualizing planning as power, knowledge, and control. *Leisure/Loisir*, *31*(2), 403–425.

McGehee, N. G., Lee, S., O'Bannon, T. L., & Perdue, R. R. (2010). Tourism-related social capital and its relationship with other forms of capital: an exploratory study. *Journal of Travel Research*, *49*(4), 486–500.

Middleton, V. (2001). The importance of micro-businesses in European tourism. In *Rural tourism and recreation: principles to practice* (pp. 197–201). Egham: CABI.

Moscardo, G. (2014). Social capital, trust and tourism development. In *Trust, tourism development and planning* (pp. 78–99). Abingdon on Thames: Routledge.

Pechlaner, H., Volgger, M., & Herntrei, M. (2012). Destination management organizations as interface between destination governance and corporate governance. *Anatolia*, *23*(2), 151–168.

Pikkemaat, B., & Weiermair, K. (2003, June). The aesthetic (design) orientated customer in tourism-implications for product development. In *EIASM 10th International Product Development Management Conference* (pp. 825–839). EIASM Brussels.

Putnam, R. (2001). Social capital: measurement and consequences. *Canadian Journal of Policy Research*, *2*(1), 41–51.

Roberts, L., Hall, D., & Morag, M. (2017). *New directions in rural tourism*. Abingdon on Thames: Routledge.

Saarinen, J., Rogerson, C. M., & Hall, C. M. (2017). Geographies of tourism development and planning. *Tourism Geographies*, *19*(3), 307–317.

Sheehan, L., Vargas-Sánchez, A., Presenza, A., & Abbate, T. (2016). The use of intelligence in tourism destination management: an emerging role for DMOs. *International Journal of Tourism Research*, *18*(6), 549–557.

Slack, N., Brandon-Jones, A., & Johnston, R. (2013). *Operations management*. Harlow: Pearson.

Swanson, J. R., & Edgell Sr, D. L. (2013). *Tourism policy and planning: yesterday, today, and tomorrow*. Abingdon on Thames: Routledge.

Thomas, R., & Thomas, H. (2006). Micro politics and micro firms: a case study of tourism policy formation and change. *Journal of Small Business and Enterprise Development*, *13*(1), 100–114.

Tinsley, R., & Lynch, P. A. (2007). Small business networking and tourism destination development: a comparative perspective. *The International Journal of Entrepreneurship and Innovation*, *8*(1), 15–27.

Uzumeri, M. V. (1997). ISO 9000 and other metastandards: principles for management practice? *Academy of Management Perspectives*, *11*(1), 21–36.

Valente, F., Dredge, D., & Lohmann, G. (2015). Leadership and governance in regional tourism. *Journal of Destination Marketing & Management*, *4*(2), 127–136.

Voss, C., & Zomerdijk, L. (2007). *Innovation in experiential services: an empirical view*. Hockessin: AIM Research.

Weiermair, K. (2004, June). Product improvement or innovation: what is the key to success in tourism. In *Innovations in tourism UNWTO conference* Madrid.

Wiltshier, P. (2007). Visibility from invisibility: the role of mentoring in community-based tourism. *Turizam: međunarodni znanstveno-stručni časopis, 55*(4), 375–390.

Zahra, A. L. (2010). A historical analysis of tourism policy implementation by local government. *Journal of Tourism History, 2*(2), 83–98.

Zehrer, A., & Raich, F. (2013). Applying a lifecycle perspective to explain tourism network development. In *Advances in service network analysis* (pp. 109–132). Abingdon on Thames: Routledge.

2 A benchmarked step by step community-based tourism (CBT) toolkit for developing countries

Vikneswaran Nair and Amran Hamzah

Introduction

At a United Nations special summit on sustainable development held on the 25th of September of 2015, all countries adopted the 2030 Agenda for Sustainable Development, which includes a set of 17 Sustainable Development Goals (SDGs) and 169 associated targets. The SDGs officially came into force on 1 January 2016. The SDGs are aimed at ending poverty, fighting inequality and injustice, and tackling climate change by 2030. Thus, the impact of these SDGs on community-based tourism (CBT) is important for developing nations. Rural community development is at the heart of the SDGs where there is an aim of leaving no one behind.

In the inaugural Tourism Ministerial Meeting held in Korea in 2000, community-based tourism (CBT) is given importance in the Asia Pacific Economic Cooperation (APEC) Forum's Tourism Charter. The Charter implicitly highlights the significance of CBT through the following three statements (APEC, 2000): (a) an important generator of business opportunity for small and medium-sized enterprises; (b) an effective vehicle for dispersing economic benefits within and among economies, particularly at the provincial level; and (c) a catalyst for partnership between the public and private sectors.

The concept of CBT is not new. For decades it has been applied in developing economies like Vietnam, Indonesia, China and Malaysia, as well as developed member economies such as Canada, New Zealand and Australia (Ashley and Garland, 1994; Bramwell and Sharman, 1999; Canadian Universities Consortium, 2000). Interest in CBT started long before the APEC Forum, which commissioned a review of CBT projects in 1999 with the aim at identifying factors that influenced member economies to implement CBT (Chebuskorn, 2003; Hatton, 1999). The long-term economic viability of CBT in this region carried out via the APEC funding in 2009 resulted in the knowledge transfer and sharing of the study findings in the form of a CBT toolkit for developing countries.

Hence, the aim of this chapter is to provide a methodology using a toolkit to prepare, develop and sustain CBT based on benchmarking of best practices in both the developing and developed nations in responsible rural tourism development. The focus of the chapter will be to provide a better understanding of the long-term viability of CBT as a development tool in rural tourism, and how the best practices from the Asia Pacific region can be used to strategize a nine-stage plan to prepare, develop and sustain it in the long term. The adaptation and adoption of a holistic business model is crucial in dissuading the project from government or donor reliance, as well as to scale up the project as CBT matures (Mitchell and Reid, 2001; Reed, 1997). Thus, in ensuring the long-term sustainability of CBT projects, economically, socio-culturally or environmentally, a flexible toolkit based on the regional best practices is the way forward for knowledge transfer and sharing. The toolkit outlined in this chapter can be used by government officers, planners, industry players and community leaders as a guide to ensuring that CBT is developed in a sustainable and responsible manner. Derived from some of the best practices in Asia Pacific, the recommendations are practical and the suggested actions suit the socio-economic condition of the member country or site. Hence the recommendations are meant to be useful for communities who are on the verge of embarking on CBT projects as well as for those with existing projects which are experiencing either rapid growth, consolidation or an impending decline.

This chapter is formulated using a case study approach based on the lessons learned and the best practices in ten member economies of the Asia Pacific Economic Cooperation (APEC) Forum, namely, Australia, Canada, China, Chinese Taipei, Indonesia, Korea, Malaysia, New Zealand, the Philippines and Vietnam. Based on the analyses of the ten case studies, the chapter reflects the nine steps for preparing, developing and sustaining CBT. These nine steps are divided into three sections – preparing CBT, developing CBT and sustaining CBT. The first two steps relate to preparing and starting CBT initiatives which include assessing community needs and readiness for tourism and also educating and preparing the community for tourism. These steps are fundamental for projects and sites that are embarking on CBT. The next three steps focus on developing the CBT initiatives. This critical phase is important in identifying and establishing leadership/local champion; preparing and developing community organization; and planning and designing quality products. The subsequent final phase of sustaining CBT is the most difficult phase, which results in most CBT failing and shutting down. This phase is more appropriate for mature CBT projects that are gradually moving up the value chain. Thus, the focus here is on developing partnerships; adopting an integrated approach; identifying market demand and developing a marketing strategy; and finally implementing and monitoring performance.

The nine steps are presented and supported by the model developed from the case studies. For each step, a list of actions is recommended to guide the development of CBT for potential destinations. Nonetheless, the development of this toolkit is limited by the ten case studies selected by the researchers. The conditions for these selected case studies may not be identical in other locations, and thus, the proposed nine-step framework developed in the toolkit can be used only as a guide. Each step outlined may vary from one nation to another. As suggested by Bramwell and Sharman (1999), tourism is an important tool for economic regeneration. As such, it is imperative to mainstream the principles and mechanism of developing CBT. Thus, CBT can evolve from an alternative development model to a formal development model (Chebuskorn, 2003).

Contextualizing community-based tourism

CBT can be regarded as a "community development tool" that strengthens the ability of rural communities to manage tourism resources while ensuring the local community's participation (Jamal and Getz, 1995; Responsible Travel, 2000). Further, CBT can also be used as a tool to assist the local community to be more sustainable economically (by diversifying their local economy and generating income), social-culturally (by preserving culture and providing educational opportunities) and environmentally (by conserving the natural and built environment). An APEC (2000) study also showed that CBT can be used as a tool for the local community to generate alternative income, and thus can be considered as a poverty reduction tool. CBT limits the negative impacts of tourism on the community and their environmental resources, if it is managed appropriately and systematically. The study by Kiss (2004) indicated that a study on the suitability of the community to be involved in tourism is critical before the community is introduced to tourism. Through CBT, the community has the opportunity to be involved in tourism; participate in related projects; and get involved in monitoring and controlling the negative impacts. Not all communities may be apt for tourism.

The United Nations Economic Program (UNEP) and United Nations World Tourism Organizations (UNWTO) (World Tourism Organization, 2008), highlighted some fundamental characteristics of CBT. They include the following:

a   involving appreciation not only of nature, but also of indigenous cultures prevailing in natural areas, as part of the visitor experience;
b   containing education and interpretation as part of the tourist offer;
c   generally, but not exclusively, organized for small groups by small, specialized and locally owned businesses;
d   minimizing negative impacts on the natural and socio-cultural environment;
e   supporting the protection of natural and cultural areas by generating economic benefits from it;
f   providing alternative income and employment for local communities; and
g   increasing local and visitor awareness of conservation efforts.

Nonetheless, the gestation period to reap from the benefits of CBT is normally long for the local community. Successful CBT projects go through a product lifecycle (Jones, 2005). In the initial stage, CBT projects can be small scale, low density and are usually operated by the community with some aid from nongovernmental organizations (NGOs). At this stage of development the local community sees the benefit that CBT brings to the community, especially in terms of job opportunity. Good CBT projects attract tour operators who extend their cooperation to form partnerships with the local community. As the number of tourist arrivals increases with changing tourist demand, the local community will be over reliant on the tour operators. As indicated by studies done by The Mountain Institute (2000), gradually, CBT projects will move up the value chain. Their long-term viability will very much depend on how efficient the key stakeholders cope with new and changing expectations.

Hence, in light of the growing importance of tourism as a tool for economic regeneration, it is important that the principles and mechanisms of CBT are mainstreamed. In this light, the development of this toolkit can assist countries in Southeast Asia in incorporating the CBT model as part of their mainstreaming process. By doing so, CBT will no longer be an alternative development model but a formal development tool.

Development of the case studies

This toolkit is formulated based on the main findings and lessons learned from a study on CBT that was funded by the APEC Tourism Working Group. The study on Capacity Building on Community Based Tourism as a Vehicle for Poverty Reduction and Dispersing Economic Benefits at the Local Level was carried out between November 2008 to April 2009 by the Ministry of Tourism Malaysia, in collaboration with the Tourism Planning Research Group (TPRG), Universiti Teknologi Malaysia. Following that, the toolkit was further enhanced through the development of the ASEAN CBT Standard (ASEAN, 2016), and the Long Term Research Grant Scheme project, funded by the Ministry of Higher Education (Nair et al., 2017) to develop a tourism barometer for gauging the health of rural tourism destination in Malaysia.

This toolkit was developed with the aim to incorporate the best practice and long-term viability of CBT, based on the experience of successful CBT models in the APEC region. Thus, ten case studies in member economies were used to develop the toolkit, namely Australia, Canada, China, Chinese Taipei, Indonesia, Korea, Malaysia, New Zealand, Philippines and Vietnam. A series of face-to-face interviews with key stakeholders were carried out at the study sites, employing ranges of research instruments. Stakeholders involved in the study include CBT organizations, government officials, tour operators, NGOs and the local communities themselves. Through a screening process, suitable case studies were selected based on the socio-economic conditions of the member economies. Four types of leading institutions were identified among the ten case studies, namely government agencies, NGOs, the tourism industry and the community itself, as indicated in Table 2.1.

Case studies in ten member economies were selected for this study, namely Australia (Thala Beach Nature Reserve, 2014), Canada (St Jacobs, 2014), China (XinTuo, 2014), Chinese Taipei (Hsiao-Yin Lin, 2009), Indonesia (Saung Angklung Udjo, 2012), Korea (Kang Ki Sook, 2009), Malaysia (KOPEL, 2014; Mohd. Hasim Abd. Hamid, 2009), New Zealand (Whale Watch Kaikoura, 2014); Philippines (Province of Guimaras, 2009) and Vietnam (CBT Vietnam, 2014; Footprint Travel Guides, 2014; Footprint Vietnam Travel, 2014).

Table 2.1 Case studies according to project initiator

Led by	Community-Based Tourism
Government-initiated CBT	• Guisi Community Heritage Based Tourism, Guimaras, Philippines (Province of Guimaras, 2009) • Seongup Folk Village, Jeju Island, Korea (Kang Ki Sook, 2009)
NGO–initiated CBT	• Ta Phin Village, Sapa, Vietnam (CBT Vietnam, 2014; Footprint Travel Guides, 2014; Footprint Vietnam Travel, 2014) • Lashihai Homestay, Lijiang, China (XinTuo, 2014) • Misowalai Homestay, Kinabatangan, Sabah, Malaysia (KOPEL, 2014; Mohd. Hasim Abd. Hamid, 2009)
Industry-initiated CBT	• Saung Angklung Udjo, Bandung, Indonesia (Saung Angklung Udjo, 2012) • St. Jacobs County, Toronto, Canada (St Jacobs, 2014) • Shui-Li Snake Kiln Ceramic Park, Nantou, Chinese Taipei (Hsiao-Yin Lin, 2009)
Community-initiated CBT	• Whale Watch, Kaikoura, New Zealand (Whale Watch Kaikoura, 2014) • Kuku Yalanji Dreamtime Walk, Mossman, Australia (Thala Beach Nature Reserve, 2014)

Analysis is done to identify the critical success factors of these CBT project that can be replicated in other destinations. Although one size does not fit all, the study has shown that there is commonality in the development process and its life cycle. Hence, a toolkit can be developed based on these critical success factors for adaptation in similar economies. Three phases of maturity can be identified in this toolkit – initiating stage, development stage and sustainability stage. The various factors involved in initiating CBT projects will vary from the development stage and sustainable stage. As CBT matures, adaptation of a sophisticated business model becomes essential. The project cannot overly rely on the government for donor reliance as well as to scale up the project. Hence, the long-term sustainability of the CBT project will be impacted.

Recommended actions in the toolkit provide flexible options to suit the socio-economic conditions of destinations using the toolkit. These actions can be useful for communities who are on the verge of embarking on new CBT projects, as well as for existing CBT projects that require assistance because of experiencing either rapid growth, consolidation or an impending decline. On the whole, the approach of the toolkit is to encourage the development of the CBT projects to become mainstream tourism products.

Analysis of case studies for the toolkit

Based on the analysis of the ten case studies, the toolkit was developed by the authors. A nine steps approach is recommended as outlined in Figure 2.1. These nine steps are divided into three phases. The first two steps (Steps 1

Phase III: **Sustaining CBT**	**Step 9**	Implement and monitor performance
	Step 8	Identify market demand and develop marketing strategy
	Step 7	Adopt an integrated approach
	Step 6	Develop partnership
Phase II: **Developing CBT**	**Step 5**	Plan and design quality product
	Step 4	Prepare and develop community organisation
	Step 3	Identify and establish leadership or local champion
Phase I: **Preparing the Community**	**Step 2**	Educate and prepare the community for tourism
	Step 1	Gauge community needs and readiness for tourism

Figure 2.1 Nine steps in understanding, developing and sustaining CBT

Source: Adapted from Nair et al. (2017) and APEC (2009)

and 2) in Phase I of this toolkit are related to activities in preparing the community to understand what CBT is all about; Phase II (Step 3 to 5) focus on developing CBT initiatives, which are useful for projects and sites that are embarking on CBT. The subsequent four steps (Step 6 to 9) in Phase III of this toolkit are meant to address the sustainability of CBT projects, which are more appropriate for mature CBT projects that are gradually moving up the value chain. For each step, a list of actions is recommended to guide the development of CBT, which is summarized in table form at the end of each step. Specific templates are given at the end of each step for the community to adopt and adapt accordingly based on their CBT needs. Each phase in the toolkit will end with links to related websites and resources to guide CBT with more reading materials that can assist them in their project.

Phase I: preparing the community

The aim of this phase is to give exposure, educate and prepare the community on what tourism is and what CBT is all about. The target outcome for this phase is ensure the level of community readiness. Two steps are proposed in this phase (Steps 1 and 2).

a. Step 1: gauge community needs and readiness for tourism

In this first step, the key question that needs to be explored is why the community should be involved in tourism. This is a fundamental question before a community can embrace tourism as highlighted in the case by the Kuku Yalanji indigenous community in Australia, the Guisi community in the Philippines and the case studies used in this project from New Zealand, Indonesia, and Malaysia as reflected in Table 2.1.

Three actions to support this step that came out of the case studies included

i   Action 1: Asking the right questions. What is the community's current source of livelihood? What is their current socio-economic condition? (e.g. level of employment, average income, incidence of poverty, etc.); What are the long-term prospects of their current source of livelihood? (e.g. opportunities and threats); Are they happy with their current socio-economic condition? and Do they want change?

ii Action 2: Determining the role of tourism. Tourism as an alternative and lucrative source of livelihood and income; tourism as a tool to justify conservation efforts; and tourism as a "training ground" for future participation in other economic sectors.

iii Action 3: Carrying out a situational analysis. What does the community expect to gain from CBT? (e.g. increase income, employment opportunity, upgrade the quality of life style, and complement the current physical development); determine community values, attitudes, aspirations and concerns (e.g. pride in community, conserve local culture, sense of ownership, and identify the labour force needs for tourism); and identify the labour force needs for tourism (e.g. level of education, previous occupation, current occupation, and special skills).

The community's level of readiness for tourism can be gauged in terms of resources (culture/heritage/nature/coastal), community attitude, special skills, available capital, and indigenous products.

b. Step 2: educate and prepare the community for tourism

Educating and preparing the community are crucial once a community decides to embrace tourism. The challenges were highlighted in case studies in Kaikura, New Zealand; Ta Phin Villa in Vietnam; Guisi Guimaras, Philippines and Misowalai Homestay, Kinabatangan, Sabah, Malaysia (in capacity building).

For this step, three actions have been identified based on these case studies:

i   Action 1: Conduct preliminary workshops. A series of preliminary workshops should be conducted in the initial stage to achieve the following objectives: identifying potential tourism activities to be developed and promoted; Developing linkages with surrounding tourism attractions; organizing workshop on involvement of different sections of community; identify training needs; and developing and conducting advanced training modules (e.g. interpretation and communication, service skills, marketing strategies, basic computer skills, proficiency in foreign languages and visitor management).

ii Action 2: Study trip and "community to community" training. The study trips can be organized at two phase – study trips to surrounding areas with the country, and study trips to overseas.

iii Action 3: Formulation of training manual. Documentation of the training modules and instructions is critical for the sustainability of all the trainings in the long term.

Phase II: developing CBT

The aim of this phase is to give exposure, educate and prepare the community on what tourism is and what CBT is all about. The target outcome for this phase is ensure the level of community readiness. In this phase, three steps are proposed (Step 3 to 5).

a. Step 3: Identify and establish leadership or local champion

Leadership and organization are fundamental to the success of CBT projects. A strong leader or local champion who commands respects is vital to the continuous support from the community. This is evident from the cases in Kaikoura, New Zealand and Misowalai, Kinabatangan, Malaysia. This leader or "local" champion can be a government-appointed project manager, a dedicated volunteer hired by an NGO or a self-appointed spokesperson for the community. A local champion breeds local champions. Some of the characteristics of this leader or local champion include visionary, good communication skills, disciplined, proactive, innovative, sensible, patient, trustworthy, courageous, never say die attitude, dedication, and commitment.

b. Step 4: prepare and develop community organization

At this stage of the development, the leader or local champion should establish a CBT organization that will take the task to plan, operate and promote this project. All CBT projects will go through a lifecycle similar to any tourism product lifecycle. This will include the exploration, declination, stagnation or rejuvenation phase. When a CBT product matures and the leadership and organization fail to innovate new products, the product will go into the decline phase as seen in in Kaikoura, New Zealand and Saung Angklung Udjo in Indonesia.

Hence, for the three phases of the CBT project (Phases I, II and II), the organization structure has to evolve accordingly. Initially at Phases I and II, the CBT will mainly be organized by the talent within the local community. As the CBT matures in Phase III, a more robust community organization is required and may seek professional help without sacrificing community structure. As indicated in the case studies, the CBT organization plays an important role in:

i Empowering women and youths, as seen in Seongup Folk Village, Jeju Island, Korea and Ta Phin Village, Sapa, Vietnam (e.g. creating specific bureau/association, appointment of office bearers, and designation of roles and type of activities of each bureau);

ii   Formulating a common vision but realistic targets, as experienced by the community in Guisi Guimaras, Philippines and Misowalai Homestay in Kinabatangan, Malaysia (e.g. provide the direction to guide the community, inform the locals about the impact of tourism, formulate the common vision, set realistic targets in considering factors such as level of education, skills and training gaps);

iii Nurturing an anti-handout mentality as seen in Misowalai case study (e.g. encourage self-help sense of ownership); and

iv   Establishing a community fund as successfully administered in Misowalai and Saung Angklung Udjo, Bandung, Indonesia (e.g. set up the community fund to manage the income and expenditure, create revolving fund for community and create microcredit facilities).

c. Step 5: plan and design quality products

In order to complete Phase II of developing CBT projects, the next step is to plan and design the potential quality tourism products in a comprehensive approach. In this step, a formulation of a CBT action plan is required. The CBT action plan will allow the community to detail out the various actions that are required to develop a distinct tourism experience. A detailed inventory of the tourism resources (which include primary and secondary attractions) in the area and surrounding areas will be identified. Techniques like the Product Inventory Matrix and/or Product Competitiveness Index can be used to assist the evaluation as indicated in Table 2.2.

The action plan will include:

i   Product development – Developing and showcasing the core products to differentiate the village/community from other tourism destinations and leveraging off the other attractions in the surrounding areas.

ii   Destination/leisure management – This includes adequate tourist infrastructure and facilities, good interpretation and high level service quality. Hence, this will create a distinct product that offers high quality tourist experience as follows as indicated in the case studies: Authentic (Shui-Li Snake Kiln Ceramic Park, Nantou, Chinese Taipei); Educational (Misowalai Homestay, Kinabatangan, Sabah, Malaysia); Entertaining (Saung Angklung Udjo, Bandung, Indonesia); Enjoyable (Misowalai Homestay, Kinabatangan, Sabah, Malaysia); and Memorable (Whale Watch, Kaikoura, New Zealand).

iii Interpretation and communication – This will include visual interpretation and oral presentation, through the setting up of an interpretive centre and interpretive trails.

iv   Service quality – Capacity building and structured training programmes to enhance service quality of the front liners in operational and communication skills.

Table 2.2 Example of Product Inventory Matrix

Components	Sub Components	VP (1)	P (2)	M (3)	G (4)	E (5)
Uniqueness	Iconic					
	Popularity					
Activities	Variety					
	Quality					
Accessibility & Connectivity	Road access					
	Public transport					
	Signboard					
Basic Facilities	Parking					
Interpretation Facilities	Visitor information centre					
	Toilet					
	Food outlet					
	Souvenir outlet					
	Internal signage					
Accommodation Facilities	Chalet					
	Camping sites					
Maintenance	Physical structures					
	Cleanliness					
	Landscaping					
Service Quality	Front desk					
	Guiding					
	Security					
Marketing & Promotion	Brochure					
	Guide book					
	Website					
Total Audit Rate Ranking						

Note: Very Poor (VP), Poor (P), Moderate (M), G (2) and Excellent (E) (source)

Source: Adapted from Nair et al. (2017) and APEC (2009)

Phase III: sustaining CBT

In this final phase, the aim is to upscale and sustain CBT, with a target outcome of a CBT business plan. In this phase, four important steps are proposed (Steps 6 to 9).

a. Step 6: develop partnerships

As the CBT project evolves further, the business of managing it effectively becomes more complex, as to sustain the expansion of the market segmentation is crucial. The fastest and the more efficient way to overcome this is the establishment of smart partnership amongst the key stakeholders. As shown in the case studies, these stakeholders include

i   Government agencies (Province of Guimaras, 2009; Angeles Gabinete, 2009) – Avoid the "handout" or "subsidy traps". Instead, take a hands-on approach by having field officers stationed onsite to provide consultancy service to the local community and monitoring the project.

ii NGOs (Canadian Universities Consortium, 2000; CBT Vietnam, 2014; Footprint Travel Guides, 2014; Footprint Vietnam Travel, 2014; Dang Xuan Son, 2009; Jenny Shantz, 2009) – Can increase the community's capacity in undertaking conservation projects in which tourism is used as a tool.

iii Universities (Dong Xuan Son, 2009) – Able to educate the local community on the appropriate framework to develop community-based projects, tools/ approaches to improve the quality of the tourist experience, and analyze changing tourist demand.

iv Tourism industry (CBT Vietnam, 2014; Footprint Travel Guides, 2014; Footprint Vietnam Travel, 2014) – Can assist in on the marketing and promotion. Form partnerships with tour operators that have established networks with specialist tour operators.

b. Step 7: adopt an integrated approach

The tourism business is seasonal and volatile. Hence, an integration of the business to the overall development strategy and approach is critical. These integrations can be done through:

(i) Conservation, sustainable development and responsible tourism projects as seen in Misowalai (Mohd. Hasim Abd. Hamid, 2009), Ta Phin (Dang Xuan Son, 2009) and Lashihai Homestay (XinTuo, 2014) – This will provide spin-offs in the form of conservation, sustainable development and responsible tourism, and employment opportunities for locals.

(ii) Other economic sector as seen in Misowalai (Mohd. Hasim Abd. Hamid, 2009), Saung Angklung Udjo (Satria Yanuar Akbar, 2009), St. Jacobs County, Canada (Jenny Shantz, 2009; St. Jacobs, 2014) – This will provide a "training ground" for the local community to undertake non-tourism projects and provide stable and better paying jobs.

c. Step 8: identify market demand and develop marketing strategy

Effective marketing is critical for the sustainability of the CBT. The marketing strategy for CBT can be formulated based on the following six actions as practiced in some of the successful case studies:

i Action 1: Matching the product with the potential market segment (Lashihai Homestay, Lijiang, China) – CBT organization should determine the target market for their product based on its unique selling preposition (USP) (e.g. educational content will attract to students and adventure product will appeal to "hard ecotourists", and conservation/sustainable development elements of the project should attract the green tourists.

ii Action 2: Understanding the best channels of distribution (Lashihai Homestay, Lijiang, China; Ta Phin Village, Sapa, Vietnam) – CBT projects should leverage on the networking within the "green tourism" or "responsible tourism" circuit and not via mass promotion.

iii   Action 3: Embracing ICT as a promotion tool – Digital marketing through a website, portal, podcast, social media and travel blog are more effective as promotion tools for CBT projects. Thus, it is crucial for CBT organization to invest in hardware (computers and Internet connection) and software (training local youths) to manage the bookings and promotions.

iv   Action 4: Piggybacking on tour operators and ground handlers – As tour operators and ground handlers have excellent networking, riding on them will bring better visibility in terms of promotion of the CBT products while the CBT organization can focus on the overall management and product development. e only worry is that the distribution of profits may not be equitable, which in turn, may lead to accusations of exploitation etc.

v   Action 5: CBT organization to set up in-house travel agency (Whale Watch, Kaikoura, New Zealand; Lashihai Homestay, Lijiang, China) – As the CBT organization becomes more stable in terms of its capacity (in management, interpretation and communication skills), it may want to set up its own travel agency. In this phase of sustainable development, the local youths must be given an opportunity to move along a career pathway like setting up an in-house travel agency to nurture the spirit of entrepreneurship.

vi   Action 6: Leveraging on awards certification to shape the branding (Kaikoura (Kuku Yalanji Dreamtime Walk, Mossman, Australia) – Good certification (e.g. Green Globe/Green Globe Community, Responsible Tourism Award, etc.) will promote more effectively the commitment of the CBT to environmental protection and preservation of local heritage compared to advertising firms. Thus, improving the quality of product is essential to get these recognitions.

d. Step 9: implement and monitor performance

The success of any CBT projects can only be ascertained if their performance is monitored and measured as experienced in the case studies. The following two actions are vital:

i   Action 1: Construction of tourist facilities – getting the community involved in the implementation (Misowalai Homestay, Kinabatangan, Sabah, Malaysia). By getting the community involved in project implementation, the activity will empower them further. This approach will result in the community acquiring new skills or enhancing their existing skills.

ii   Action 2: Regular monitoring of performance (Saung Angklung Udjo, Bandung, Indonesia) – It is essential to build a monitoring mechanism into the whole planning and implementation process. Monitoring does not only measure the success and gaps in terms of monetary value but also include non-monetary gains such as pride in the local community, sense of ownership, and increase self-esteem. Examples of monitoring indicators that can be used for CBT projects are outlined in Table 2.3.

Table 2.3 Monitoring indicators for community-based tourism

Dimensions	Indicators
Effects of tourism on community	% of locals who believe that tourism has increased their:
	• Pride in local community • Sense of ownership • Self esteem • Social cohesion • Confidence level • Communication skills • Relationship with outsiders • General knowledge • Specialized skills
	% of locals who believe that tourism has positively changed their lifestyle/surrounding
Local community participation	% of goods and services supplied by local community Employment of local community in tourism operations (numbers/income level)
Product Quality Achieving equitable distribution of tourism funds/benefits across the community	% of tourists who are satisfied with the environmental/cultural experiences The amount of funding acquired by the community for:
	• General • Signage • Marketing • Infrastructure
	Number and type of development programmes given to the local community (education, training, health, natural resource management, conservation, etc.)
Professional and personal development	% of locals who are happy with their career path in tourism. Frequency of training programmes and level of participation.
Operation and support of community-based enterprises	Number of participants making use of incentives or programmes for SMEs Number of participants involved in tourism-related businesses (e.g. accommodation providers, catering, tour guiding, transportation, tour operation and etc.)
Environmental management systems and environment initiatives	Training of participants on environmental issues Application of environmentally friendly technologies and techniques (% of participants)
	• Water-saving techniques or devices • Energy • Recycling: glass, paper and plastic • Green purchasing

Source: Adapted from Nair et al. (2017) and APEC (2009)

Further, the following steps can be adopted in developing a monitoring plan for CBT organization:

i Determine monitoring objectives (specific goals to be achieved through the monitoring programme);

ii Determine boundaries of the area to be monitored (limits of the area to be monitored must be established);

iii Identify community attributes (consider the attributes/assets that make the community special or which conserve or protect);

iv Identify potential impacts (socio-cultural, economic and ecological or physical);

v Prioritize impacts (prioritize based on chance of occurring, potential degree or frequency of impact, and ease of monitoring);

vi Identify potential indicators (based on availability of existing data, easy to train local person in data collection methods, reliability, relates to community tourism vision/plans, ease of data collection, ease of analysis, easy to understand the results, and cost;

vii Collect data (appropriate methods of collecting the data – seasonal, annual or more often, longitudinal); and

viii Evaluate the data (based on the overall economic, environmental, political, social and cultural context of the community).

Conclusion

Over the years, CBT has evolved to become a pro-poor growth development tool in many developing countries across the globe. Today, there are a multitude of CBT networks across the Asia Pacific region such as the more popular Thailand Community Based Tourism Institute (CBT-i) and the Cambodia Community Based Ecotourism Network (CCBEN). Backed by international donor agencies, these CBT networks function as self-help and information/experience exchange bodies. Although tourism can be used as a tool for economic, social and psychological empowerment, many stakeholders have limited knowledge in guiding the local community to be successful in this industry. Hence, the availability of a structured toolkit to prepare, develop and sustain CBT projects based on transfer of knowledge from some of the best practice in Asia Pacific is certainly the way forward. The step-by-step approach and the actions for each step are not cast in stone. CBT projects can adopt and adapt these steps based on their needs and conditions which may vary. The toolkit acts merely as a checklist of essential tasks that may be considered in the development of CBT.

As seen in many case studies in this chapter, CBT is relatively easy to start but much more challenging to sustain. It is certainly not a panacea for poverty alleviation of the rural community. As discussed in Phase III of the chapter, sustaining CBT involves making the product competitive and thus scaling up becomes critical. The business model and the maximizing the spread of economic benefits are crucial for sustainability of CBT in the long term. The best practices in the case studies, have shown that a gestation period of five years should be sufficient for the CBT to be independent and should be weaned off direct support from donor and government agencies.

With scaling up, better leadership and management is required. The leadership in the community through the local champion will eventually be replaced by a broader management of the CBT organization which will comprise representatives from every section of the community especially women and youths. Scaling up also required the management of the CBT to be more systematic, transparent and accountable to ensure no individual or family will dominate for self-interest. With the expansion in the target market, the CBT can also move up the value chain. By this period, the CBT organization should be well experienced in terms of business savviness and managing smart partnerships with international and national tour operators.

In short, like any tourism product, CBT projects need careful planning and management. CBT projects needs product innovation, targeted marketing and regular monitoring. With the long gestation period to succeed in the CBT business, a community has to be resilient, persistent and dedicated to succeed. Only then can CBT projects become a catalyst to nurture thriving rural entrepreneurship in all economic sectors.

Acknowledgments

This publication was made possible via partial funding from the APEC Secretariat (2009) and the Ministry of Education's Long Term Research Grant Scheme (2011–2016), Reference No.: JPT.S(BPKI)2000/09/01/015Jld.4(67).

References

Angeles Gabinete (2009), Tourism Section Head, Provincial Economic Development Office, Province of Guimaras, The Philippines, Interviewed on 10 October 2009.

Ashley, C. and Garland, E. (1994), "Promoting community-based tourism development: why, what and how", *Directorate of Environmental Affairs, Ministry of Environment and Tourism Research Discussion Paper*, No. 4.

Asia Pacific Economic Cooperation (APEC) (2009). *Handbook on community based tourism: how to develop and sustain CBT.* APEC Publication, Singapore. APEC Tourism Working Group (TWG02/2008A).

Asia-Pacific Economic Cooperation (APEC) (2000), *2000 APEC tourism ministerial meeting: Seoul declaration on an APEC tourism Charter* [Online], available at: www. apec.org/Meeting-Papers/Ministerial-Statements/Tourism/2000_tourism.aspx (accessed 9 October 2014).

Association of Southeast Asian Nation (ASEAN) (2016), *ASEAN community based tourism standard.* The ASEAN Secretariat, Jakarta, Indonesia.

Bramwell, B. and Sharman, A. (1999), "Collaboration in local tourism policymaking", *Annals of Tourism Research*, Vol. 26, No. 2, pp. 392–415.

Canadian Universities Consortium (2000). *A manual for monitoring community tourism development.* Canadian Universities Consortium, Canada.

CBT Vietnam (2014), *Community based sustainable tourism training* [Online], available at: www.cbtvietnam.com/tours-in-sa-pa/ (accessed 3 October 2018).

Chebuskorn, S. (2003), *Recreation and ecotourism management.* Science of Management, Sukhothaithammathiraj, Nantaburi.

Dang Xuan Son (2009), Co-founder, operation and customer care of Footprint Travel, Hanoi, Vietnam, Interviewed on 8 February 2009.

Footprint Travel Guides (2014), *Footprint true value in travel* [Online], available at: www.footprintvietnam.com (accessed 3 October 2018).

Footprint Vietnam Travel (2014), *Taphin Sapa* [Online], available at: www.taphin-sapa. info (accessed 3 October 2018).

Hatton, M. J. (1999), *Community-based tourism in the Asia-Pacific.* School of Media Studies, Canada.

Hsiao-Yin Lin (2009), Coordinator, Shui-Li Snake Kiln Ceramics Cultural Park, Nantou County, Chinese Taipei, Interviewed on 11 Feb. 2009.

Jamal, T. B. and Getz, D. (1995), "Collaboration theory and community tourism planning", *Annals of Tourism Research*, Vol. 22, No. 1, pp. 186–204.

Jenny Shantz (2009), CEO, St. Jacob County, Ontario, Canada, Interviewed on 13 June 2009.

Jones, S. (2005), "Community-based ecotourism: the significance of social capital", *Annals of Tourism Research*, Vol. 32, No. 2, pp. 303–324.

Kang Ki Sook (2009), Chairperson of Seongeup Folk Village Preservation Committee, Seongeup Folk Village, Jeju Island, Seongeup Folk Village Management Office, Seogwipo City, South Korea, Interviewed on 19 March 2009.

Kiss, A. (2004), "Is community-based ecotourism a good use of biodiversity conservation funds?", *Trends in Ecology and Evolution*, Vol. 19, No. 5, pp. 232–237.

KOPEL (2014), *MESCOT sustainable tourism and conservation initiatives* [Online], available at: http://mescot.org/village_homestay_home.htm (accessed 11 February 2018).

Mitchell, R. E. and Reid, D. G. (2001), "Community integration island tourism in Peru", *Annals of Tourism Research*, Vol. 28, No. 1, pp. 113–139.

Mohd Hasim Abd Hamid (2009), Coordinator)/ Misowalai Homestay/ KOPEL, Batu Puteh Community Ecotourism Co-operative) Sandakan, Sabah, Malaysia, Interviewed on 6 March 2009.

Mountain Institute (2000), *Community based tourism for conservation and development. A resource kit.* The Mountain Institute, Kathmandu, Nepal.

Nair, V., Mohamad, B., Hamzah, A., Shuib, A., Jaafar, M. and Murugesan, R. K. (2017), *Multi-dimensional responsible rural tourism capacity framework for sustainable tourism.* Centre for Research & Innovation in Tourism Publication, Subang Jaya, Malaysia. ISBN: 978-967-0173-46-7.

Province of Guimaras (2009), *Discover Guimaras* [Online], available at: http://guimaras. gov.ph (accessed 18 June 2017).

Reed, M. G. (1997), "Power relations and community-based tourism planning", *Annals of Tourism Research*, Vol. 24, No. 3, pp. 556–591.

Responsible Travel (2000), *What is a community-based tourism?* available at: www. responsibletravel.com/copy/copy901197.htm (accessed 27 January 2017).

Satria Yanuar Akbar (2009), Operational Manager, Saung Angklung Udjo, Bandung, Indonesia, Interviewed on 13 June 2009.

Saung Angklung Udjo (2012), *Saung Angklung Udjo nature, culture in harmony* [Online], available at: www.angklung-udjo.co.id. (accessed 23 September 2018).

St Jacobs (2014), *St Jacobs County* [Online], available at: www.stjacobs.com (accessed 1 October 2014).

Thala Beach Nature Reserve (2014), *Kuku Yalanji* [Online], available at: www.thala beach.com.au/kuku-yalanji/ (accessed 23 August 2018).

Whale Watch Kaikoura (2014), *Whale watch Kaikoura, New Zealand's ultimate marine experience* [Online], available at: www.whalewatch.co.nz (accessed 9 June 2016).

World Tourism Organization (2008), *Why tourism?* [Online], available at: www.unwto. org/aboutwto/why/en/why.php?op=1 (accessed 25 September 2018).

XinTuo Ecotourism (2014), *Lijiang Xintuo ecotourism* [Online], http://ecotourism.com. cn/ (accessed 2 October 2018).

3 Systems approach to community-based tourism

Tadeja Jere Jakulin

Introduction

Tourism as a fast-evolving service industry plays an important role in local communities. It represents a base for new professions, culture sharing, and building local infrastructure. Tourism expands its benefits in common: as an accelerator of wellbeing and generator of new employment as well as a complex system. The concept of systems approach (thinking, systems modelling and simulation) in tourism helps the researcher and consequently the decision-makers as a tool for solving problems, decision-making and strategical (sustainable, systems) planning with all benefits and critical points of tourism. The benefits of well-planned community-based tourism (CBT) goes from alleviating poverty, developing local SME's, minimising environmental risks, and educating tourists about the community and its surroundings, to the assurance of high quality of experience for everyone involved in the tourism service. On the other hand, cases of over-tourism in communities all over the world show that decision-makers who planned tourism development of the community did not use a methodology that would enable them to anticipate the consequences of mass tourism. There are many methods of making a balanced, sustainable plan for CBT development (Tsung Hungh and Fen-Hauh, 2019; Okazaki, 2008). One of the methods belongs to the systems methodology, which researches problems from the point of view of a whole, with its tools systems thinking and systems modelling. Systems thinking became wider known with Peter Senge (Senge, 2006) and Donella Meadows (Meadows, 2008). Systems thinking approaches the community as a complex tourism system, which consists of many elements or subsystems (community members, decision-makers, companies, local tourism offer, tourists, community participation, infrastructure, environment, etc.). Systems thinking, holistic thinking and sustainable development are very much interrelated. "The Limits of Growth" (Meadows et al., 1972) and "Beyond the Limits" (Meadows et al., 1992) are milestones and focal points of this topic. Another important reference is "Urban Dynamics" by J. W. Forrester (1961).

As a description of what is going on within the community regarding tourism development, systems approach uses modelling in frame of systems dynamics. Models, which are essentially simple, serve as a graphic representation of reality. Qualitative models in systems methodology, which we develop in this chapter, are called causal loop diagrams. They show the dynamics between the parameters important for community-based tourism planning and development. The dynamics are explained with + and − signs which represent influence of one parameter to another.

Community as an open complex tourism system

Successful decision-making in the community-based tourism system is largely dependent on whether the planners truly understand the complexity of the system they are trying to manage. It is not surprising that the "intuitive" approach to policy design often falls short, or is counterproductive, to desired outcomes. Community-based tourism system is a complex system since it has a huge quantity of data to manipulate, low quality of information (e.g., uncertainty, measurement, errors), different spatial scales (e.g., from local to global), dynamic and stochastic behaviour and it is at the crossroad among many disciplines. Its structural properties are local interactions, non-linearity, feedback and openness; and its behaviour properties include emergency, self-organization and adaptiveness. Systems approach for community-based tourism planning searches for an optimal collaboration among people, tourism market, environment and their interactions and interdependency. Community leaders, decision-makers, tourism and tourism-connected companies, and inhabitants in cooperation can bring optimal answers whether to plan or not to plan tourism as a future generator of their community. An important base for community tourism planning is community members. As soon as companies are involved in tourism activities, scaffolding on their cultural heritage and natural attractions, one can talk about community-based tourism (Gursoy et al., 2002; Nelson, 2004; Okazaki, 2008). Another classical idea claims that community-based tourism is defined by a "ladder of citizen participation," the collaboration, power redistribution, and the creation of social capital (Arnstein, 1969: 218). Community involved in tourism benefits since the members of that community use their resources and provide either labour or indirect interactions with tourists and this arrangement allows communities to engage in mass tourism (Honggang et al., 2009: 3–4). To present these statements in frame of systems approach, one must know the systems theory. General systems theory is a "general science of wholeness", which can be applied to most diverse fields, such as thermodynamics, biological and medical experimentation, genetics, life insurance, statistics, (1968:37) and community-based tourism. Community-based tourism is an open system, since the flow of information circulates very fast from within the system to the environment and among its elements. Before the appearance of general system theory, conventional physics researched only closed systems; i.e., systems which are isolated from their environment. In his manifesto "General System Theory" Bertalanffy (1968: 39) states that every living organism is essentially an open system which maintains itself in a continuous inflow and outflow, a building up and breaking down of components, and that the laws that govern biological open systems can be applied to systems of any form. This

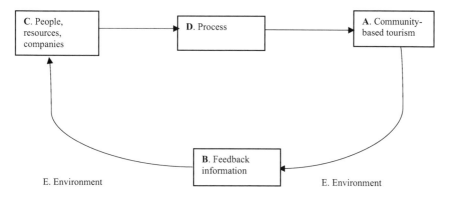

Figure 3.1 Feedback model of CBT as an open system
Source: Author

definition we present as a feedback model of community-based system as an open system. Interactions within the system's elements and with the environment are crucial for observing behaviour of a system and receiving constant feedback as presented in the Figure 3.1.

Figure 3.1 represents a circle and a communication between an open community-based tourism system and its environment. Their communication is constant, which is seen when the system receives feedback information. The community-based system is an output produced by the transformation process of the input (Checkland, 2004: 315). For example, to achieve an optimal community-based tourism system one must take into concern the feedback of that output and take control of the input (community members, resources, ideas, information, work), which will go to the process and receive the output (results) with consideration of the present and future environment. This simple model represents a natural cycle of a living community-based tourism system within the environment. The feedback loop (information) gives correct answers whether community decision-makers created an optimal or an average CBT plan. Many phenomena correspond to the feedback model. One is homeostasis or maintenance of balance (sustainability) in living organisms, e.g. thermoregulation, where cooling of the blood stimulates certain centres in the brain which "turn on" heat-producing mechanisms of the body, and the body temperature is monitored back to the centre so that temperature is maintained at a constant level (Bertalanffy, 1968: 47). Community-based tourism is a living system and feedback information shows the necessity for its balance because of environment preservation and crowding, which is presented with (−) signs in Figure 3.2.

Qualitative general model of community-based tourism

Modelling is a graphic representation of the observed object or real world. In tourism, model building seeks to understand a complex relationship and to aid

Figure 3.2 General model of CBT

Source: Author

the management of a place or process. For example, in econometric forecasting of tourism flows, the purpose is to help estimate future numbers of tourists to permit informed decisions (Jafari, 2000).

Business management simulation has been brought forward as a methodology of system dynamics, suggested by J. Forrester (Forrester, 1961). All discussions considering modelling lead to the same conclusions. There are few minor differences among graphic illustrations of elements and interactions among them. Forrester suggests that the System Dynamics (SD) method has some semantic advantages for users who have less experience with formal methods. In practice, some authors use causal loop diagrams or influential diagrams (Forrester, 1961). The methods are equivalent; the only difference lies in the fact that influential diagrams are like graphs of qualitative models. To illustrate the equivalency of modelling methods, one must present a causal loop diagram (CLD) of dependency among community attractiveness, tourists and community members participation and the tourism offer and education.

Following a definition of system equations one can define the basic elements of a system:

- Ei = environment, community attractiveness, number of tourists, community members participation, tourism offer, crowding and their interconnections.
- R = community environment, community attractiveness, number of tourists, which creates a simplified model.

For the explanation of systems methodology, we will present a simulation model in community tourism. Many equivalent illustrations of systems exist, all of which are appropriate for computer simulation.

The causal loop diagram in Figure 3.1 presents a general community tourism model, where a share of local tourism is visible regarding community members participation, tourism offer, and education. Causal loop circles and interactions of single branches are visible. Places described with variables represent elements of system state; arrows among them show trends of influence of single elements. A symbol at input or output of an element shows a trend of a change. A positive symbol means that if a value of the first variable grows, then the value of the second variable grows. A negative symbol means that if a value of the first variable grows, then the value of the second variable decreases. Understanding of a process is a base of R set connection. It can be described as follows: preserved environment (+) influences in the same direction as community attractiveness (+), attractiveness influences the number of tourists (+), the number of tourists influences the community members participation, tourism offer and education (+). On the other hand, it can be said that more tourists, crowding (+) causes environmental damage (−), which is a reason for a decrease of community attractiveness. From these qualitative descriptions one can see what must be taken into concern. If we connect the set of elements Ei on a base of their descriptions with a pointed arrow to the same direction and sign this with a symbol (+), opposite with a symbol (−), we get an influential diagram of a qualitative model of our simplified system, shown in Figure 3.2. From this model one can deduce that there is one basic circle (−) of causal loop, which means growth of the number of tourists and borders of growth, caused by tourism offer and environment damage. In a vision of community-based tourism development one must predict development as a whole to avoid limitations. If in the reinforcement circle, which consists of community members participation and environment preservation, only one element starts to fall (−); this means the fall of all other elements and the number of tourists decreases.

Mass tourism has a regulative function in systems approach to tourism. Usually it represents the crowding of tourists, which causes traffic standstills, detours, driver anxiety, accidents, anger and regrets about deciding to take a vacation in this area (−). To reduce regulative moments, the community decision-makers should include community members in the local tourism policy development. It is important that the community participates on the basis that the members of the community, minimise negative impacts and revitalise the economy (Hardy et al., cited in Sebele, 2010: 137). CBT has, according to Kiss (2004), been popular as a means of supporting biodiversity conservation, particularly in developing countries, and linking livelihoods with preserving biodiversity whilst reducing rural poverty and achieving both objectives sustainably.

The model in Figure 3.3 shows a system dynamics model depicting the interaction among dependence on community attractiveness, number of tourists and tourism offer and education. The model is based on a previously discussed causal loop diagram of tourism development. It tries to show the interactions between economy and community area, as well as their influence on tourism.

The data included are as follows: travelling (tourist arrivals), service quality (attractiveness), tourists' ecological awareness (community attractiveness),

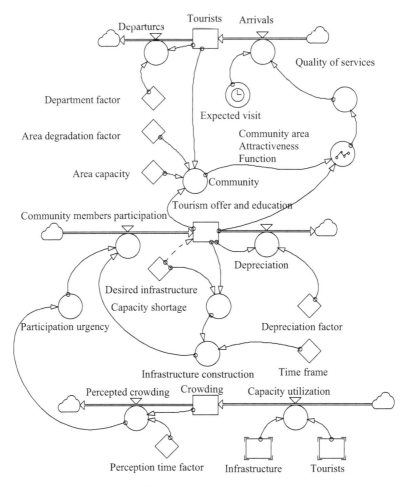

Figure 3.3 A simplified simulation model for the CBT development
Source: Author

infrastructure construction, and investment. The data were taken from the Statistical Yearbook of the Republic of Slovenia for 2018.

Challenges for qualitative modelling to community-based tourism

Modelling process and the involvement with modelling team is referred to as Group Model Building. Science explains a Group Model Building very well (Vennix, 1996). There are only few differences in the conceptual phase. Some modellers prefer to start with causal loop diagrams and other with simplified dynamics conceptual models. As it is shown on the causal loop diagram (Figures 3.2 and 3.3) systems dynamics modelling is a genuine transdisciplinary approach, as it integrates different disciplines and the stakeholders of the situation to be investigated (Fabjan et al., 2006).

Community-based tourism is becoming one of the most important branches of the economy, linking together numerous economic activities. Moreover, it is a major spur to regional development, raising the economic value of biodiversity, natural values and cultural heritage, and facilitating increased social prosperity. The activities of the local tourism organisations and supporters (companies, institutions) in tourism are aimed at creating the conditions for achieving the long-term competitiveness of the tourism sector and for increasing the current scope of tourism activities. There are some basic questions (Blackstock, 2005: 41–44) which occur as critical points of community-based tourism: is community co-opted or transformed by tourism, who speaks for the community, and which constraints to local control are present?

Community is not transformed but co-opted into tourism development with an illusion of power sharing, since it has no chance to speak for itself. Community is represented by local power structures (Blackstock, 2005: 41–44), with an intention to economically develop community through the interests of capital invested in tourism growth (de Kadt,1992; 47–75).

Figure 3.4 shows the causal loop diagram (CLD) with the elements for the case of capital investments to community-based tourism system, which can be explained as follows: local power structures have an increasing influence on choosing external tourism developers (+), which influence tourism products (+) and tourism product increases community attractiveness (+); community attractiveness causes the growth of capital investments (+) and the capital investments increase the number of mass tourism infrastructure (+). The infrastructure influences the local power structures (+), and local power structures increasingly influence community tourism office, which furthermore has positive influence (+) upon community tourism strategy. The tourism strategy influences the natural community attractiveness (+). This is the so-called reinforcement circle of a system. The regulation circle is visible through the dependency (relationship) between external developers of tourism, who cause the fall of local participation (−) and the tourism infrastructure, which causes decrease of the area attractiveness (−), when there is too much capital invested in it and hides natural environment. Positive causal loop circles mean development, yet it must be said that every aggravation is followed by a fall in growth. For example, if the community is ecologically poor, it influences negatively on the area's attractiveness, followed by a chain reaction resulting in a decreasing tourism investment reduction and financial decline.

Considering the preceding written descriptions, there are some challenges a modeller meet when recognising soft systems (people, organisations) features such as pressures, power issues, greed, etc. Systems thinking and modelling need an optimal decision-making team. According to Wyllie (1998) and Reed (1997: 567) the results of local decision-making depend on who is in power at

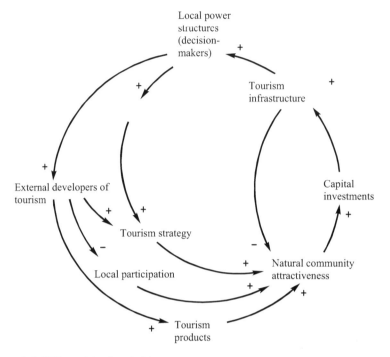

Figure 3.4 CLD model of capital investments
Source: Author

the local level and these power relations can change the results of collaborative efforts. This is a chain reaction to the finding that community cannot control big investors (Blackstock, 2005: 45) and that CBT paradigm is functional. It seeks the identification of potential problems and to overcome these before the tourism industry is damaged by adverse local reactions.

Qualitative causal loop diagrams are usually followed by quantitative simulation diagrams, sometimes remaining just the describers of real-life situations, to light the possibilities for overcoming the "black box" thinking of a "powerful individual" and transform it into "thinking out of the box" for the community and wider.

Conclusion and discussion

Central to a systems approach is recognising basic causes for problems and evaluating consequences caused by decision-making responses.

A simplified simulation model for the community-based open tourism system was developed using a systems methodology. This model was followed by two qualitative models in frame of systems dynamics, called also causal loop diagrams.

The first model presented a general causal loop diagram of community-based tourism with the interdependency of community-based tourism elements. As it is built in frame of systems dynamics, it wants to achieve systems development, protecting environmental quality and reducing the crowding effect of tourists that regulates community base. The protection and improvement of the environment require participation of community members and excellent tourism programs with education of people who will teach locals and tourists about environment protection. The simulation model was built according to the previous qualitative causal loop diagram. The available statistical data are most important to develop an optimal simulation model as well as the incorporation of qualitative "social and political" feedback mechanisms. The second model presented the invisible elements of a community-based tourism, which create the image of a community and its elements. This model was built upon the data on community-based tourism from the study "Critical look at community-based tourism," where the author (Blackstock, 2005) explains basic problems of hidden powers within and outside of the community, which drastically influence the tourism development and dynamics of the community. The elements on which this model comments are: local powers, capital investments, lack of community members participation and natural community attractiveness. It is essential to develop a system approach to environmental, economic, social and hidden factors in community-based tourism. The latter are crucial for thinking out of the box and finding optimal solutions for the community and the environment.

References

Arnstein, S. R. (1969). A ladder of citizen participation. *Journal of the American Institute of Planners*, 35(4), pp. 216–224.

Bertalanffy, L.v. (1968). *General System Theory.* New York: George Brazziler.

Blackstock, K. (2005). *Community Development Journal* Vol 40 No 1 Oxford University Press and *Community Development Journal* 2005; doi: 10.1093/cdj/bsi005.

Checkland, P. (2004). *Systems Thinking: Systems Practice.* Chichester: Wiley, 315.

De Kadt, E. (1992). Making the alternative sustainable: Lessons from development for tourism, in V. L. Smith and W. R. Eadington, eds, *Tourism Alternatives: Potentials and Problems in the Development of Tourism*, New York: John Wiley and Sons, 47–75.

Fabjan, I., Kljajić, M., Jere Jakulin, T. 2006. *Proceedings of Second International Conference on Tourism Economics.* Palma de Mallorca, University of Balearic Islands, Economics and Business Administration Faculty, 15.

Forrester, J. W. (1961). *Industrial Dynamics.* Cambridge, MA: MIT Press.

Gursoy, D., Jurowsky, C., Uysal, M. (2002). Resident attitudes: a structural modeling approach. *Annals of Tourism Research*, 29(1), 79–105.

Honggang, X. U., Sofield, T., Jigang, B. A. O. (2009). Community tourism in Asia: an introduction, in B. A. O. Jigang, eds, *Tourism and Community Development. Asian Practices*, Madrid: World Tourism Organization, 1–17.

Jafari, J. (2000). *Encyclopedia of Tourism.* New York: Routledge.

Kiss, A. (May 2004). Is community-based ecotourism a good use of biodiversity conservation funds. *Trends in Ecology and Evolution, 19*(5). doi: https://doi.org/10.1016/j.

tree.2004.03.010. Retrieved August 20, 2019, from https://www.cell.com/trends/ecology-evolution/fulltext/S0169-5347(04)00065-5?_returnURL=https%3A%2F%2Flinkinghub.elsevier.com%2Fretrieve%2Fpii%2FS0169534704000655%3Fshowall%3Dtrue

Meadows, D. H. (2008). *Thinking in Systems: A Primer.* Hartford, VT: Chelsea Green Publishing Sustainability Institute, White River Junction.

Meadows, D. H., et al. (1972). *The Limits to Growth: A Report for The Club of Rome's Project on the Predicament of Mankind.* New York: Universe Books.

Meadows, D. H., Meadows, D. L., Randers, J. (1992). *Beyond the Limits: Confronting Global Collapse, Envisioning a Sustainable Future.* Post Mills, VT: Chelsea Green.

Nelson, F. (2004). The evolution of community-based ecotourism in northern Tanzania (Paper No. 131). Arusha, Tanzania: International Institute of Environmental and Development Issue, Sand Country Foundation.

Okazaki, E. (2008). A community-based tourism model: its conception and use. *Journal of Sustainable Tourism*, 16(5), 511–529.

Reed, M. (1997). Power relations and community-based tourism planning. *Annals of Tourism Research*, 24(3), 566–591.

Sebele, L. S. (2010). Community-based tourism ventures, benefits and challenges: Khama Rhino Sanctuary Trust, Central District, Botswana. *Tourism Management*, 31(2), 136–146.

Senge, P. (October 2006). *The Fifth Discipline: The Art and Practice of the Learning Organization.* New York: Currency Doubleday.

Statistical Office of the Republic of Slovenia, available at www.stat.si/StatWeb/sl/Field/Index/24. (accessed 12 March 2019).

Tsung Hungh, L., Fen-Hauh, J. (2019). Can community-based tourism contribute to sustainable development? Evidence from residents' perceptions of the sustainability. *Tourism Management* 70, 368–380, available at https://doi.org/10.1016/j.tourman.2018.09.003 (accessed 14 March 2019).

Vennix, J. A. M. (1996). *Group Model Building: Facilitating Team Learning Using System Dynamics.* Chichester, West Sussex: John Wiley & Sons Ltd.

Wyllie, R. (1998). Not in our backyard: opposition to tourism development in a Hawaiian community. *Tourism Recreation Research*, 23(1), 55–64.

4   A responsible CBT approach

Lelokwane Lockie Mokgalo and Gwinyai
Mercy Musikavanhu (Manhotoma)

Introduction

Pressures on rural livelihoods are ever increasing, especially for peripheral areas adjacent to protected areas. To most of the communities, tourism is both a blessing and a curse. Tourism offers an avenue for employment, businesses and market opportunities; however, it also poses problems when protected animals damage crops and endanger lives, loss of access to veld foods and other resources as well as causing dependency on it in the communities. In Botswana, community-based natural resource management (CBNRM) is a community-based tourism approach used as a vehicle to improve both rural livelihoods and conservation of resources. However, according to Mbaiwa (2010), CBNRM in Botswana has caused changes from traditional livelihoods to a more cash economy mostly dependent on tourism. Furthermore, a blanket hunting ban imposed in Botswana in 2014 has adversely affected livelihoods in communities dependent on wildlife for sustenance and income through hunting safari concessions. On the other hand, tourism businesses in Botswana, especially around the Okavango, are mostly foreign owned, provide menial jobs to community members and weak linkages of tourism to other sectors, therefore providing few business opportunities (Mbaiwa, 2005, 2010). All these further compound livelihood problems within communities and calls to question the very viability and effectiveness of community-based tourism (CBT), a resource devolution approach meant to address both resource management and enhance livelihoods. Consequently, certain actions – or lack thereof – of various stakeholders go unnoticed and no responsibility is apportioned nor accepted when things do not go well. According to Ellis and Sheridan (2014) little consideration has been placed in the role of stakeholders in sustainable tourism practices. As a matter of fact, most of the blame is apportioned to communities' incapability or unsuitability without consideration of external stakeholders such as the industry, NGOs and public sector (Ellis and Sheridan, 2014).

The chapter considers an approach to CBT management through a responsible tourism management approach in Botswana in order for an envisioned good intention to be efficiently put to practice and to benefit the intended stakeholders: the community.

CBT, sustainable and responsible tourism nexus

The key to a harmonious relationship between tourism and sustainability is a significant and committed responsibility from stakeholders (Mitchell et al., 2013). Mathew and Sreejesh (2017: 84) further note that "destination sustainability induced by responsible tourism can have a multitude impact on the quality of life of people". This in essence is the point of departure in the link between the three concepts of community-based tourism, sustainability and responsible tourism.

Sustainable tourism started from the broader sustainable development concept which considers development that is cognisant of future generations to meet their own needs. Different literature credits the World Commission on Environment and Development's (WCED) Brundtland report as a forerunner and a catalyst of the debate on sustainable development (Mihalic, 2014; Mitchell et al., 2013; Leslie, 2012; Herman et al., 2011; Goodwin, 2009; WTO, 1999). The report was a precursor to the Earth Summit in Rio de Janeiro in 1992 which resulted in a Commission on Sustainable Development (Goodwin, 2009). Even though the summit and the commission that followed were about the sustainability of developments in broader terms, they had implications for tourism. This kickstarted the debate of the sustainability of the tourism industry and thus the concept has since dominated the tourism literature not only in terms of defining it but also operationalizing the concept. Central to defining and understanding sustainable tourism has been the consensus that economic, environmental and social impacts of tourism have to be addressed for the industry to be sustainable.

Sustainable tourism definition is complex, which is consistent with most concepts in the area of tourism in general. The concept of sustainability has not changed much from its early foundations in the 1987 Brundtland report. Therefore, at its basic form, sustainable tourism is defined as 'forms of tourism which meet the needs of tourists, the tourism industry and host communities today without compromising the ability of future generations to meet their own needs' (Swarbrooke, 1999: 13). The most recent of definitions of sustainable tourism by UNWTO is "Tourism that takes full account of its current and future economic, social and environmental impacts, addressing the needs of visitors, the industry, the environment and host communities" (UNEP & UNWTO, 2005).

Breaking down the UNEP and UNWTO definition highlights the fundamental role of the three elements of economic, social and environmental impacts also known as the 'triple bottom line'. These pillars are what underpin sustainability in that the negative impacts have to be minimised and the positive maximised to achieve an optimum sustainable development growth. Secondly, the definition also highlights the stakeholders whose needs have to be addressed, namely; visitors, the industry, the environment and host communities. These are the main stakeholders in the provision of tourism products and services save for the public sector who, one can argue, represent all the stakeholders.

As part of the evolution towards sustainability, there were so-called alternative forms of tourism that were advanced. Sustainable tourism was seen as a concept riddled with its own flaws and inadequacies prompting criticism from the academic discourse. Wheeler (1993 in Mihalic, 2014) argued that sustainable tourism lacks practicality and it has been turned into a public relations tool which is similar to Goodwin's (2009) observation that it is difficult to operationalize. Leslie (2012) highlights Butcher's (1997) critique that sustainable tourism has little to offer the tourist and fails to consider the local community's interests. However, notwithstanding this critique, Leslie also asserts that the concept is being advanced by major businesses to manage destinations for the enjoyment of tourists over other opportunities for development. Therefore, names such as; 'alternative, soft, quality, eco, responsible, minimum impact tourism, green and ethical tourism' were mentioned, all advocating for the move away from what is termed 'mass-tourism' which had increasingly become intolerable and jeopardized the very existence of tourism in many areas (Mihalic, 2014: 1). However, most of the 'alternative' concepts represented a niche market; though not competing with sustainable tourism, they maligned other forms of tourism and put the sustainability of tourism in danger again (Goodwin, 2009). Blackstock et al. (2008) argued that in 1989 World Tourism Organisation (WTO) which was later came to be known as United Nations World Tourism Organisation (UNWTO) adopted the term 'responsible tourism' in an effort to differentiate mass tourism from what was known as 'alternative' forms of tourism. Such a focus was from the notion that there was need for accountability and an ethical approach to tourism consumption. Blackstock et al. (2008) assert that responsible tourism draws attention to the link between actions by tourists, tourism businesses and their impact on host communities. Goodwin (2002, 2009: 89) emphasises that responsible tourism is not a niche product but that 'all forms of tourism can be engaged in and organised in a responsible manner' including mass tourism. The tourism literature draws similarity in responsible and sustainable tourism. Mihalic (2014) argues that responsible tourism is based on the concept of sustainable tourism and likewise Blackstock et al. (2008: 276) contend that 'responsibility is a central facet of sustainability'. Herman et al. (2011) argue that although the two concepts are similar, what differentiates them is that responsible tourism focuses on the short-term practice of triple bottom line which in turn addresses the long-term focus of sustainable tourism.

According to Goodwin (2002: 37) responsible tourism "emphasizes the importance of consumers, operators and people in destinations taking responsibility to make a better form of tourism". In other words, to address the needs of those concerned, tourism players need to take responsibility in sustaining tourism for the benefit of themselves and others. As such, the same stakeholders whose needs have to be addressed are the ones responsible for addressing those needs themselves.

Nonetheless, the two concepts appear similar in that they advocate for the same kind of principles. However, responsible tourism advocates for all concerned in the development, provision and management of tourism to individually take responsibility for its sustenance (Harrison and Husbands, 1996; ICRT, 2002). Therefore, responsibility is viewed as a process towards sustainability.

Mihalic (2014) considers sustainability as a theoretical concept and responsibility a practice, and views these terms as different yet not competing, with responsible tourism based on the concept of sustainable tourism. Therefore, while both are grounded in the same principles, responsible tourism is viewed as a more practical approach. As highlighted previously, one of the criticisms of sustainable tourism is its difficulty in being put into practice. Therefore, responsible tourism is seen as an avenue or a process towards sustainability which addresses the operational issue. Mihalic (2014) states that sustainable tourism is considered at destination level rather than the micro-firm level of responsible tourism. The author opines that the relationship between the two concepts is one of a 'discourse between a concept and its practical application' (Mihalic, 2014: 3). As such for most destinations, the desire to pursue a sustainable tourism agenda is often evident; however, the challenge has been how to operationalize such aspirations. Further to that what is fundamental to responsible tourism is that "all forms of tourism can be engaged in and organised in an increasingly responsible manner" (Goodwin, 2002). The author further contends that responsible tourism practice should be localised. In this case practitioners should consider what is relevant to their destination in as far as what is feasible and not resort to a copy and paste approach.

Van Niekerk (2014) argues that destination management directs stakeholders towards a common goal and the success of a destination hinges on the understanding of roles by the stakeholders. Although it is often complex to define and clarify who a stakeholder is especially in tourism which is characterised by complexity, Freeman's 1984 (in Freeman, 2010) definition is the most cited and referenced definition. Van Niekerk (2014: 703) notes that Freeman defines 'stakeholders as any group or individual who can affect, or who is affected by, the achievement of the destination's objectives'. Moreover, Carroll (1993) states that "stakeholders are individuals or groups that may influence or be influenced by the actions, decisions, policies, practices or goals of an organisation". Though the definitions are from two distinct disciplines, there is similarity and a common theme in the definitions. Both acknowledge that stakeholders can either be groups or individuals and they either influence and influenced or affect and affected by organisations or destinations which means their actions or lack thereof are affected or affect the said entities. Stakeholders also have varied interests which often are incongruent. Therefore, the actions of one stakeholder have implications on the performance of the other. As such tourism literature has employed the stakeholder theory to identify and model the relationships between stakeholders (Van Niekerk, 2014; Saftic et al., 2011; Bryd, 2007). D'Angella and Go (2009) note the use of the theory in performance assessment of the relationship between DMOs and other stakeholders. The theory therefore helps in clarifying that organisations, in this context destinations, are accountable to all stakeholders and management has to balance the interests of these stakeholders for sustainability to be achieved (Sternberg, 1997). However, the author is critical of the theory in that it excludes organisations that aim at anything other than 'balancing stakeholder's benefits' (4). The theory also, the author continues, is flawed in assuming that 'balancing stakeholder benefits' is always possible as the list of these stakeholders is infinite. Steinburg argues for the numbers of affected groups or individuals to be limited. However, practicality of limited affected groups is questionable as there is no clarity as to who has the authority over who is affected. In the context of destination management, Morrison (2013) categorised the stakeholders into five groups; tourists, tourism organisations, community, the environment, and government. World Tourism Organisation (WTO) categorises the stakeholders in to three divisions; the tourism industry, environmental support and the local community/government (Anuar et al., 2012). However, regardless of the categorization, the stakeholders in tourism remain the same even within the outlined categories. As observed by Van Niekerk (2014), there is no clarity of relationships between these stakeholders though and that lack of clarity is more profound were roles are not defined.

The Oxford Dictionary (2019) defines a role as a 'the function assumed, or part played by a person or thing in a particular situation'. In the same token the same dictionary also defines responsibility as 'the state or fact of being accountable or to blame for something'. The definitions show that there is a clear distinction between the two terms in that while 'role' is about function, responsibility is more about the accountability that comes with that particular function. However, responsibility comes with a role. Which means there can never be expectations of responsibility where a role is not assigned or implied. Blackstock et al. (2008: 278) argues that responsibility has both a collective and behavioural dimension as well as an individual and ethical dimension which implies that "social actors are answerable to others". Therefore, there is need to consider roles of various stakeholders and their responsibility if we are to achieve sustainability in tourism. As noted by Goodwin and Wherrit (2005 cited in Blackstock et al., 2008) responsible tourism draws our attention to how shared social norms and ethical principles influence our individual actions.

Community-based tourism (CBT) is management that favours a community-centric approach by incentivizing conservation of resources through accrual of benefits to the concerned community. This has become critical where different pressures on resources are escalating, most of which coming from the communities themselves as they are in close proximity. The concept itself is derived from the "alternative development paradigm" which was a departure from the laisse fare approach of the more econo-centric approaches. CBT has variations in its definition, with The Thailand CBT Institute (2013: 3) defining it as "Tourism that takes environmental, social and cultural sustainability into account. It is owned and managed by the community, for the community with the purpose of enabling visitors to increase their awareness and learn about the community and the locals' way of life". Goodwin and Santilli (2009: 12) offer a more simplified version as *"Tourism owned and/or managed by communities and intended to deliver wider community benefits"*. Therefore, from the preceding definitions, there is elements of the convergence in ideology with sustainability. In fact, Dangi and Jamal (2016: 5) note the idea of espousing *"host communities, equity and cultural recognition"* among others as principles shared by the two concepts. Nonetheless, while CBT is by design a community-centric approach, Sustainable tourism is viewed as more business-centric. However, such an emphasis on business considerations is not viewed negatively as it is at the centre of sustenance. Therefore, the nexus between CBT, sustainable and responsible tourism is solidified as CBT "applies the objectives of sustainable tourism" (Dangi and Jamal, 2016: 10) while responsible tourism operationalises and holds stakeholders accountable for communities to draw maximum benefit from resources which in turn sustains the industry.

Community-based tourism in Botswana

CBT in Botswana, just as in most parts of Africa, is founded and driven by the community-based natural resources management (CBNRM) concept (Centre for Applied Research (CAR), 2016; Mbaiwa, 2015; Lenao, 2014). The basic tenet of the concept is to use tourism development to benefit communities by devolving management of natural resources in their proximity. The CBNRM approach *"seeks to improve natural resource conservation, improve rural livelihoods and reduce human wildlife conflicts as well as poverty"* (CAR, 2016: 8). The dual role of management and conservation of resources is believed to be achievable once communities derive benefits from the resources which will incentivize sustainable resource use.

To date, CBNRM has existed in Botswana for 25 years (CAR, 2016). From its inception in 1992, CBNRM was mostly driven by wildlife utilisation by communities but has since included historical sites, landscapes, veld products and cultural heritage. According to (CAR, 2016) tourism is the main driver of CBNRM in Botswana especially using wildlife managements areas and cultural heritage tourism. This has been facilitated using financial aid from the various stakeholders such as government and international cooperating partners (ICPs). The approach required communities to have a legal entity or a Representative Accountable Legal Entity (RALE) in the form of a trust or otherwise known as Community-Based Organisation (CBO). Since CBOs were formulated on the grounds that there will be collective ownership of resources, devolution of management and conservation of the natural resources as well as deriving economic benefits (Mbaiwa, 2015; CAR, 2016), it was required that they produce a land use management plan (LUMP). The LUMP would help articulate the way land will be managed to ensure sustainability of resources. After satisfaction of this requirement, CBOs were allocated a Wildlife Management Area (WMA) or a concession of land for a lease period of 15 years by the local land board (a government land management entity) (Government of Botswana, 2007). The formulation of LUMP would also allow the Department of Wildlife and National Parks to allocate hunting quotas to CBOs who resolve to have hunting as part of their planned land use. By 2007 the CBNRM policy was brought into effect through an enactment by parliament to formalize the approach and address some anomalies noted since inception. According to CAR (2016) by 2016 there were 94 registered CBNRM projects with 53 of them believed to be operational. The author notes that many of the projects were community-based tourism-related ventures operating activities such events, canoe trips, culture shows, ecotourism, camping, handicraft sales, and photographic drives. The number of active CBO projects were low due to lack of diversification opportunities once the ban on hunting tourism was instituted in 2014.

The CBNRM policy of 2007 provided a framework that the prevailing CBOs could use in their operations which included procedures that would allow the CBOs to benefit from the income the projects made. Prior to the 2007 CBNRM Policy, the CBNRM approach in Botswana was rooted in the Botswana Wildlife Conservation Policy of 1986. Under this Wildlife Conservation Policy of 1986 vast communal land was changed into wildlife management areas (Chipfuva and Saarinen, 2011). However, this policy has since been superseded by the Wildlife Conservation Policy (Government of Botswana, 2013) which focuses more on resources and development issues. The Wildlife Policy of 2013 was also set up in order to work hand in hand with the CBNRM Policy of 2007. The Wildlife Policy of 2013 addresses CBNRM, co-management of wildlife resources, stakeholders and privatization. The emphasis being the appropriation of advantages, costs and challenges of the wildlife sector amongst the various stakeholders. In addition, the Wildlife Policy of 1986 advocated for the involvement of communities in protected areas management using 'stakeholder management committees' (Wildlife Conservation Policy, Government of Botswana, 2013: 14). An analysis of the policy shows initiatives towards responsible tourism as the community was needed to plough back into the environment initiatives on fire control and management, research and monitoring along with problem animal control. To what extent this was implemented, it is uncertain as it appears that this initiative was not really put into practice.

Despite the initiatives discussed here, the government of Botswana introduced a hunting ban in 2014 as discussed earlier, which had detrimental effects on CBOs' revenues as they lost their hunting rights (CAR, 2016). This is something that the government needs to relook at. The question of sustainability comes into effect here as the economic well-being of the communities involved in CBOs through hunting is compromised and there lies the probability of having unsustainable numbers of animals e.g. elephants. To date CBOs are now represented by an organisation named BOCOBONET which depends on the government, NGOs and ICPs for funding and technical support.

Gaps in CBNRM policy and its implementation

The 2007 CBNRM policy acknowledges the need for guidance of the approach through policy. Nonetheless, in its introduction, the policy makes a case for its necessity: the need to fight poverty and sustain livelihoods, the advocacy for natural resources to benefit society, the realisation of conservation goals once communities 'earn tangible benefits' from the resources and the need to guide communities in prudent financial management to curb any misuse of returns. The policy also seeks to ensure beneficial partnerships between CBOs and private joint venture partners in the process facilitating for communities to assume more responsibilities in managing both resources and business partner-ships. However, gaps exist both due to weaknesses in the policy itself or its implementation.

Limited skills transfer

The policy notes with concern the need for mutually beneficial partnerships due to the fact that "*in most cases the private sector partner purchases a com-munity's wildlife quota without actively involving the community in the manage-ment of the business*" (Government of Botswana, 2007: 2). While the intention was for the communities to move from passive participants to playing a mean-ingful role in business operations in their concessions, the status quo remains. Mbaiwa (2015) observed that CBOs generally sub-lease their concession areas along with the resources therein to private tourism operators and thereby delegate their land use and management rights. This shows weakness in the implementation of the policy as the Technical Advisory Committee (TAC) charged by the policy as CBNRM implementer at local level clearly failed to play its advisory role. Therefore, an anomaly clearly highlighted by the policy remains unresolved which ultimately affects skills transfer to commu-nities due to their passive engagement. One of the noted issues challenging CBT projects is lack of market access (Lenao, 2015; Zapata et al., 2011; Goodwin and Santilli, 2009). At the centre of the noted market access challenge is the lack of tourism marketing skills within communities as well as practitioners advising CBT projects (Ashley and Goodwin, 2007 in Stone and Stone, 2011). However, private tourism operators have knowledge in accessing markets, yet the communities are failing to tap into such knowledge. The crux of the problem rests with both communities and public institutions. Communities choose the easy way out in sub-leasing land and delegating resource manage-ment to private partners in return for financial benefits in the form of fees, in the process forgoing the much more meaningful skills capacitation benefits. The public sector through the TAC fail to adequately play their advisory role due in part to incapacitation themselves. Furthermore, it can be argued that the exclusion of local structures such as village and district development com-mittees weaken communities' involvement in planning and management of CBNRM programmes (Chipfuva and Saarinen, 2011). This approach therefore questions the intention to devolve power to communities, a point which is dis-cussed next.

No devolution of power

The core of the CBNRM programme as a driver of CBT projects is to devolve powers to local communities. In fact, section 2.4 of the Botswana CBNRM policy highlights this aspect as it states in page 4;

The approach embraces democracy and good governance as it involves devolution of authority and the development of accountable and representative decision-making institutions at community level.

At the centre of this well-intended section is the implied engagement, participation and empowerment of communities to make decisions on the different aspects of resource management entrusted to them. However, as alluded previously such aspects are weakened in communities. Lenao (2015) notes the authoritativeness of the TAC in overruling community trust decisions in the Lekhubu project development in central Botswana. Likewise, Stone and Stone (2011) observed that 95% of residents in a community trust running Khama Rhino Sanctuary are not aware the project is owned by their communities. This issue was attributed to the dominance of the elites, lack of participation by communities and lack of transparency which disempowered communities. Okazaki (2008) attributes such problems to lack of actions that are practical to implement local participation, engagement and consequently power devolution to communities. The author maintains that the major difficulty is not lack of will by those in power but rather how to cascade such power down to communities. The end product then remains a top-down approach within a bottom-up framework. Chipfuva and Saarinen (2011: 152) concurs that in practice public institutions "have kept their central role instead of devolving power to the locals".

Inadequate resource benefits

Prior to the ban on hunting in 2014, community benefits from CBT projects were mainly in the form of financial benefits as well as other non-cash benefits like game meat and reduction in human-wildlife conflict (CAR, 2016). From inception, the few CBNRM projects in operation at the time had unfettered access to all financial benefits that accrued to them from resource utilisation. However, with the advent of the CBNRM policy in 2007, a new revenue sharing model was devised through section 10.3 of the policy which prescribed a 35% earnings retention by communities while the remaining 65% went into a National Environment Fund. This was necessitated by the noted misuse and mismanagement of community trust funds by those entrusted (Mbaiwa, 2004). The government also wanted to finance environmental management and ecotourism projects countrywide. The policy approach meant that the 35% retained earnings by CBOs was inadequate for communities who bear the burden of resource custodianship (CAR, 2016). Even before the policy stance in 2007, Swatuk (2005) noted that at the third and fourth annual CBNRM conferences there was a reiterated message that no CBO had broken even in Botswana and that they will collapse if left to run on their own. This then begs the question: if CBOs could not run sustainably when they retained 100% of their earnings, how can they survive on 65% less? This therefore led Chipfuva and Saarinen (2011) to argue that the policy distribution model is counterproductive as it negates the idea of incentivising conservation and management by communities. The irony is that the policy elevates the idea of resource management through incentives by noting that for communities to actively participate in conservation, "the benefits from such resources must exceed the costs of conservation" (Government of Botswana, 2007:1). Therefore, this clause stands against the very ethos of the CBNRM concept.

Choice of private partners

As noted earlier in the discussions on 'limited skills transfer', the idea to turn communities from passive to active participants remains a pipe dream. However, the status quo is propagated by the contradiction in the policy itself. While there is mention of consultation of the community in choice of private partner, section 9.3 goes on to state that "the decision to award the tender to a particular joint venture partner will however rest with the TAC" (Government of Botswana, 2007:13). This then nullifies the intention to create a platform "in which communities assume responsibilities for business cooperation and adequately manage such partnerships for the benefit of all community members" which is ingrained in section 1.5 of the same policy. Indeed, the current practice relegates a community's role in business partnerships to the periphery and at the same time gives overarching powers to the TAC which was only meant to advise. The expressed pursuit by the policy to have communities manage the partnership is of no value as communities might be hamstrung in managing a co-operation, they were not party to. Consequently, the role of communities in business operations will ultimately be passive.

Other gaps in CBT approach in Botswana

There are other noted gaps in the management of CBT which compound the already precarious situation especially from the community's perspective. Following is an analysis of these gaps and how they impact on the CBT process.

Legislation across different departments

It should be noted that while all CBT projects are pursued through a CBNRM approach, it is not all CBNRM initiatives that are tourism related. Nonetheless, due to most CBT projects' dependence on natural resources, the laws that govern resource use are numerous and straddle across different departments. According to Rozemeijer (2001) the following legislations informed the CBNRM policy draft and individually are instruments used to manage tourism's interaction with natural resources: National Conservation Strategy (Government of Botswana, 1990a), Tourism Act (Government of Botswana, 1992), Tourism Policy (Government of Botswana, 1990b), Wildlife Conservation and National Parks Act (1992), WMA Regulations (Government of Botswana, 1998) and the Wildlife Conservation Policy (Government of Botswana, 2013). While mostly these legislative instruments are within one ministry, their coordination presents a challenge. Chipfuva and Saarinen (2011) also reiterate the difficulty in coordination which presents gaps in implementation. Such an anomaly causes a sustainability challenge as any gaps in enforcement of the instruments will have environmental repercussions. Furthermore, some of the departments are only accessible in urban centres, making communities detached from their services.

Over- dependence on hunting

The hunting ban was initiated in 2014 and there have been arguments for and against it when it was mooted and ever since it was introduced. However, what it is notable is that hunting tourism was the bedrock of most CBOs. In some cases, it was the only source of revenue, so much that in those CBOs (Mmadinare trust, Mekgatshi trust, Koinaphu trust) the ban led to their collapse (CAR, 2016). CAR (2016) notes that others still struggle. Mbaiwa (2018) also remarks that CBOs in the Ngamiland district alone lost revenue amounting to P7 million (about $700,000) and over 200 jobs due to the hunting ban. As CAR (2016) observed, Mbaiwa (2018) also argues that the gravity of the effects was felt by those communities that were wholly dependent on hunting due to unsuitability of photographic tourism in their areas. Diversification efforts have been hampered by lack of financial donor support due to Botswana being classified as a middle-income nation; therefore few CBOs have invested in other sources of income (CAR, 2016). This dependence by communities and to some extent complacency during the height of increased hunting revenue has come back to haunt them. Lack of foresight to diversify in other income-generating ventures has therefore threatened sustainability of resources and community livelihoods.

Clarity on BTO'S role

The Botswana Tourism Organisation (BTO) is the closest entity to what resembles a destination management organisation (DMO) in Botswana. The organisation was created by an act of parliament in 2009 from its predecessor, Botswana Tourism Board (Botswana Tourism, 2019). According to the organisation's website, their mandate covers marketing and promotion strategies for the country, advising government on policy issues, grading facilities, and conducting and disseminating research as well as developing and improving existing opportunities. However, in the area of CBT, their mandate is ambiguous. According to CAR (2016) BTO seems to have taken over responsibilities of TAC or at least they are seen to be performing parallel duties. BTO is noted to have taken the identification and appointment of joint venture partners for communities. This is even more confusing given that the organisation's role is not clearly stated in the CBNRM policy. Therefore, for communities who have been grappling with effects of usurped powers by TAC, the situation couldn't get any worse. Communities cannot rationalise who among the two entities is responsible for what, a situation which doesn't help the already weakened position of local communities.

A responsible community-based tourism approach

A stakeholder approach (government, local communities and private sector) is recommended in order to mitigate the gaps in the policies and other issues regarding CBNRM discussed previously. An understanding by stakeholders of the synergies between themselves is critical. At the centre of this approach is understanding that each stakeholder has a role to play and is accountable and imperative in the whole scheme for the benefit of all. While responsible tourism is not the "be-all and end-all", it strives to minimise the negative impacts while maximising the positives (Goodwin and Santilli, 2009; Spenceley et al., 2002). Following is the approach which centres around roles and responsibilities that each stakeholder can perform to improve the sustainability of CBT. The list is not exhaustive and can be added to when the need arises.

As a policy formulator and implementor, government through various agencies sets the stage for tourism development. Thus, even in CBT, government role remains unchanged from facilitator but rather their accountability needs to be taken seriously as all tourism development pivots on the tasked agencies playing their responsibilities well as illustrated in Table 4.2.

The private sector is critical in the CBT approach. However, more often the focus in terms of management of CBT is primed on communities and the public sector. This could be that interaction between the latter two stakeholders is often heightened. Nonetheless, the private sector are the drivers and commercial experts in natural resource utilisation which makes their role critical. Therefore, they remain an important ally to both public and community stakeholders because of the value they bring to both. Table 4.3 best illustrates the role this stakeholder plays what they are responsible for.

Table 4.1 Local communities' role and responsibilities

Roles	Responsibilities
Planning	• Participate in the planning process of CBT initiatives along with other interested stakeholders
Management	• Be actively involved in management of resources in their area • Gain skills and capacitate themselves to play an active role in business operations. • Avail and share their indigenous knowledge for the benefit of resource management • Through community and trust leaders, create awareness of CBT and their role in the CBNRM approach • Seek other income-generating activities to lessen dependence on one income source
Decision-making	• Hold the public sector responsible where powers are taken from communities • Make and contribute to policy formulation and revision

Source: From authors' literature review

Table 4.2 Government's role and responsibilities

Roles	Responsibilities
Planning	• Create an enabling environment for other stakeholders to participate in CBT planning • Avail channels of communication on policy formulation by other stakeholders • Constantly review policies to accommodate contemporary issues arising
Management	• Be actively involved in management of resources through monitoring efforts • Include local community structures in management of CBNRM projects • Accommodate indigenous knowledge in management programmes for the benefit of resource management • Ensure TAC does not usurp community powers and their role in the CBNRM approach remain advisory • Revise the revenue distribution model for the benefit of community livelihoods and resource management • Rationalise departments responsible for CBT management to minimise bureaucracy and eliminate ambiguity
Decision-making	• Hold the private sector and communities accountable • Take deliberate steps to ensure benefits accrue to communities
Marketing	• Through BTO, market CBT projects to appeal to responsible travellers • Help community/trust members in marketing skills to ensure they take control in accessing external markets

Source: From authors' literature review

Table 4.3 Private sector's role and responsibilities

Roles	Responsibilities
Planning	• Participate in the planning process of CBT projects
Management	• Be actively involved in management of resources in collaboration with both communities and government agencies • Be partners in business operations with local communities to ensure skills transfer • Accommodate indigenous knowledge in management programmes and interpretation • Advice communities and community members in available opportunities arising in their business operations • Train and upskill local employees from communities • Create avenues for tourists to have access to communities to learn and consume additional products
Decision-making	• Hold the public sector and communities accountable • Take deliberate steps to ensure benefits accrue to communities • Include communities in issues regarding management of tourism within their area
Marketing	• Help community/trust members in marketing skills to ensure they take control in accessing external markets

Source: From authors' literature review

Conclusion

The chapter set out to introduce the state of community-based tourism in Botswana. What can be concluded is that CBNRM and natural resource utilisation are at the core of CBT in the country. The formulation of the CBNRM policy in 2007 was a welcome development after the industry yearned for one for quite some time. However, the policy proved to be not without faults which added to an already increasing array of issues found to be negative with CBT by varied literature sources as outlined. Furthermore, while hunting tourism played a role in creating an avenue for communities to supplement the sources of their livelihoods, the imposition of the hunting ban left some CBT projects in varied financial positions. The chapter introduces the concept of responsible tourism approach in consideration of CBT management as a practical avenue towards sustainability. At the centre of the approach is the identification of stakeholders critical to CBT and how their roles and responsibilities could be aligned for the benefit of CBT and be accountable to each other. The rationale is responsibility comes with accountability for effectiveness of one's role to be realised.

References

Anuar, A., Ahmad, H., Jusoh, H., & Hussain, M. (2012). Understanding the role of stakeholders in the formation of tourist friendly destination concept. *Journal of Management and Sustainability* Vol. 2 (2), 69–74.

Ashley, C., & Goodwin, H. (2007). *Pro Poor Tourism: What's Gone Right and What's Gone Wrong?* London: Overseas Development Institute.

Blackstock, K., White, V., McCrum, G., Scott, A., & Hunter, C. (2008). Measuring responsibility: An appraisal of a Scottish National Park's sustainable tourism indicators. *Journal of Sustainable Tourism* Vol. 16 (3), 276–297.

Botswana Tourism. (2019). *Botswana Tourism Organisation; About Us*. Retrieved from Botswana Tourism: www.botswanatourism.co.bw/bto/.

Bryd, E. (2007). Stakeholders in sustainable tourism development and their roles: Applying stakeholder theory to sustainable tourism development. *Tourism Review* Vol. 62 (2), 6–13.

Butcher, J. (1997). Sustainable development or development? In M. Stabler, *Tourism and Sustainability: Principles to Practice* (pp. 27–39). Wallingford: CABI.

Carroll, A. (1993). *Business and Society: Ethics and Stakeholder Management*. Cincinnati: SouthWestern.

Centre for Applied Research. (2016). *2016 Review of Community Based Natural Resources Management in Botswana*. Gaborone: USAID Southern Africa.

Chipfuva, T., & Saarinen, J. (2011). Community-based natural resource management, tourism and local participation: Institutions, stakeholders and management issues in Northern Botswana. In R. Van der Dium, D. Meyer, J. Saarinen, & K. Zellmer, *New Alliances for Tourism, Conservation and Development in Eastern and Southern Africa* (pp. 147–164). Wageningen: ACP-EDULINK.

D'Angella, F., & Go, F. (2009). Tale of two cities'collaborative tourism marketing: Towards a theory of destination stakeholders assessment. *Tourism Mangement* Vol. 30 (3), 429–440.

Dangi, T., & Jamal, T. (2016). An integrated approach to "sustainable community-based tourism". *Sustainability* Vol. 8, 1–32.

Ellis, S., & Sheridan, L. (2014). A critical reflection on the role of stakeholders in sustainable tourism development in least-developed countries. *Tourism Planning & Development* Vol. 11 (4), 467–471.

Freeman, R. E. (1984). *Strategic Planning: A Stakeholder Approach*. New York. Pitman Publishing.

Freeman, R. E. (2010). *Strategic Management: A Stakeholder Approach*. Cambridge: Cambridge University Press.

Goodwin, H. (2002). The case for responsible tourism. In T. Jenkins, *Ethical Tourism: Who Benefits?* (pp. 35–46). London: Hodder & Stoughton.

Goodwin, H. (2009). *Responsible Tourism Theory and Practice – MSc Responsible Tourism Management Handbook*. Leeds: International Centre for Responsible Tourism.

Goodwin, H., & Santilli, R. (2009). *Community-Based Tourism: A Success? ICRT Occasional Paper 11*. Greenwich: GTZ, University of Greenwich.

Goodwin, H., & Wherrit, S. (2005, June). Interview with Harold Goodwin. *Geographical*, p. 91.

Government of Botswana. (1990a). *National Conservation Strategy – National Policy on Natural Resources Conservation and Development. Botswana Paper No.1 of 1990*. Gaborone: Government Printers.

Government of Botswana. (1990b). *Tourism Policy, Government Paper No.2 of 1990*. Gaborone: Government Printers.

Government of Botswana. (1992). *Tourism Act. Act No.22 of 1992*. Gaborone: Government Printers.

Government of Botswana. (1998). *WMA Regulations. Government Paper No.1 of 1998*. Gaborone: Government Printers.

Government of Botswana. (2007). *Community-Based Natural Resources Management Policy: Government Paper No.2*. Gaborone: Botswana Government Printer.

Government of Botswana. (2013). *Wildlife Conservation Policy: Government Paper No.1*. Gaborone: Botswana Government Printer.

Harrison, L., & Husbands, W. (1996). *Practicing Responsible Tourism*. London: Wiley.

Herman, U., Geldenhuys, S., & Coetzee, W. (2011). Are responsible tourism indicators in the event sector applicabe? The case of Gauteng Province, South Africa. *African Journal of Business Management* Vol. 5 (22), 9616–9622.

ICRT. (2002). *Capetown Declaration on Responsible Tourism*. Retrieved from International Centre for Responsible Tourism: www.icrtourism.org/capetown.html

Lenao, M. (2014). *Rural Tourism Development and Economic Diversification for Local Communities in Botswana: The Case of Lekhubu Island; A Doctoral Thesis*. Oulu: Nordia Geographical Publications.

Lenao, M. (2015). Bringing heritage management and tourism in Botswana under the spot light: Notes from Lekhubu Island. *Botswana Journal of Business* Vol. 7 (1), 30–42.

Leslie, D. (2012). Responsible tourism debate. In D. Leslie, *Responsible Tourism: Theory, Concepts and Practice* (pp. 17–42). Wallingford: CABI.

Mathew, P. V., & Sreejesh, S. (2017). Impact of responsible tourism on destination sustainability and quality of life of community in tourism destinations. *Journal of Hospitality and Tourism Management* Vol. 31, 83–89.

Mbaiwa, J. (2005). Enclave tourism and its socio-economic impacts in the Okavango Delta, Botswana. *Tourism Management* Vol. 26, 157–172.

Mbaiwa, J. E. (2004). The socio-economic benefits and challenges of a community-based safari hunting tourism in the Okavango Delta, Botswana. *Journal of Tourism Studies* Vol. 15 (2), 37–50.

Mbaiwa, J. E. (2010). *Tourism, Livelihoods and Conservation: The Case of the Okavango Delta, Botswana.* Saarbrucken: Lambert Academic Publishers.

Mbaiwa, J. E. (2015). Community-based natural resource management in Botswana. In R. Van der Duim, N. Lamers, & J. v. Wijk, *Institutional Arrangements for Conservation, Development and Tourism in Eastern and Southern Africa* (pp. 59–80). Amsterdam: Springer Science+Business Media Dordrecht.

Mbaiwa, J. E. (2018). Effects of the safari hunting tourism ban on rural livelihoods and wildlife conservation in Northern Botswana. *South African Geographical Journal* Vol. 100 (1), 41–61.

Mihalic, T. (2014). Sustainable-responsible tourism discourse: Towards 'responsible' tourism. *Journal of Cleaner Production*, 1–10.

Mitchell, R., Wooliscroft, B., & Higham, J. (2013). Applying sustainability in national park management: Balancing public and privatte interests using a sustainable market orientation model. *Journal of Sustainable Tourism* Vol. 21 (5), 695–715.

Morrison, A. (2013). *Marketing and Managing Tourism Destinations.* London: Routledge.

Okazaki, E. (2008). A community-based tourism model: Its conception and use. *Journal of Sustainable Tourism* 16 (5), 511–529.

Oxford Dictionaries. (2019). *Definition of Role in English.* Retrieved from English Oxford living Dictionaries: https://en.oxforddictionaries.com/definition/role

Rozemeijer, N. (2001). *Community-based Tourism in Botswana: The SNV Experience in Three Community-tourism Projects.* Gaborone: SNV/IUCN CBNRM Support Programme, otswana.

Saftic, D., Tezak, A., & Luk, N. (2011). Stakeholder approach in tourism management: Implication in Croatian tourism. In *30th International Conference on Organisational Science Development* (pp. 1–8). Portoroz, Slovenia: Future Organisation.

Spenceley, A., Relly, P., Keyser, H., Warmeant, P., McKenzie, M., & Mataboge, A. (2002). *Responsible Tourism Manual for South Africa.* Pretoria: Department for Environmental Affairs and Tourism.

Sternberg, E. (1997). The deffects of stakeholder theory. *Scholarly Research and Theory Papers* Vol. 5 (1), 3–10.

Stone, S., & Stone, M. (2011). Community-based tourism enterprises: Challenges and prospects for community participation; Khama Rhino Sanctuary Trust, Botswana. *Journal of Sustainable Tourism* Vol. 19(1), 97–114.

Swarbrooke, J. (1999). *Sustainable Tourism Management.* Wallingford: CABI.

Swatuk, L. (2005). From "project to context": Community based natural resource management in Botswana. *Global Environmental Politics* Vol. 5 (3), 95–124.

Thailand CBT Institute. (2013, May 3). *Community Based Tourism Institute.* Retrieved from CBT-I: http:www.cbt-i.org

UNEP and UNWTO. (2005). *Making Tourism more Sustainable – A Guide for Policy Makers.* New York: United Nations.

Van Niekerk, M. (2014). The role of the Public sector in Tourism destination management from a network relationship. *Tourism Analysis* Vol. 19, 701–718.

Wheeler, B. (1993). Sustaining the ego. *Journal of Sustainable Tourism* Vol. 1 (2), 121–129.

WTO. (1999). *Global Code of Ethics*. Madrid: World Tourism Organisation.

Zapata, M., Hall, M., Lindo, P., & Vanderschaeghe, M. (2011). Can community-based tourism contribute to development and poverty alleviation? Lessons from Nicaragua. *Cultural Issues in Tourism* Vol. 14 (8), 725–749.

5 Community-based festivals in the context of community-based tourism

Allan Jepson and Alan Clarke

The focus of this chapter and indeed our work over the last ten years is not just on festivals but specifically on community festivals. We want to explore the connections between communities and their festivals and between festivals and their communities. We do not see this as a static relationship but rather a dynamic one of interconnections, reinforcements and contradictions. We see community festivals as being at the core of societies and cultures and, for this reason we celebrate the ways that they create and innovate within and around those histories that generate community values and particular types of behaviour (Jepson & Clarke 2015:1). Community festivals have been recognised as a significant global phenomenon (Chacko and Schaffer, 1993; Derrett, 2003; Gabr, 2004; Getz, 1997). We came across evidence of over four hundred active festivals in Europe alone (Maurin, 2003: 5) but this number will be far greater today. What was characterised as an emergent, growing and vibrant sector of the tourism and leisure industries (Arcodia and Whitford, 2006) is now well established.

Festivals research has developed in many ways but often adopts a positivistic paradigm focussed on benefits and impact research. This chapter presents an inclusive definition of community festivals, firmly grounded in the local communities themselves. Our research explores the literature surrounding festivals, in the context of community development and CBT.

Towards a definition of community festivals

Dugas and Schweitzer (1997) argued that to develop a sense of community is hard work, long term, especially where support levels, connectedness and belonging were being targeted. We believe that the nexus of cultures and communities should be seen as inseparable as they constantly revolve together. Therefore any definition of a community festival must reference local cultures, including popular cultures and ethnic cultures. Inclusive cultural definitions provide a greater opportunity for the festival or event to include and recognise all ethnic groups within its boundaries. Festivals are multi-faceted both as a result of the culture contained within them and also because of the multitude of relationships within local community groups (Quinn, 2006). The other and most crucial aspect is that if a community festival is to represent the 'way of life' of its communities then it needs to have community inclusivity within the planning and decision-making process, otherwise there is an inherent danger that the festival will not accurately represent the local community.

We have defined a community festival as a:

> themed and inclusive community event or series of events which have been created as the result of an inclusive community planning process to celebrate the particular way of life of people and groups in the local community with emphasis on particular space and time.
>
> (Jepson and Clarke, 2014: 15)

This definition is one which promotes all stakeholders equally through the planning process and also helps to bring attention to preserving sensitive natural, cultural, social environments and in particular community values.

Successful community events can be seen as being largely based on local traditions which are held to be significant and on the need to be connected with other people sharing that sense of significance, creating and sustaining the sense of belonging to a community or a place. The festivals and events may have other features attached to them which allow them to boost tourism and in this way become something of an economic resource for the host community (Jepson & Clarke 2015: 5). In the recent years, we have observed that many of the community festivals being reported to or experienced by ourselves or our colleagues have changed rapidly and become an important and integral part of the tourism product and the joyful celebrations of the locals turned out to be cash machines (Jepson & Clarke, 2015: 7). Therefore we have to recognise that community festivals have become outward looking as well as internally grounded. As we shall see this has consequences for the planning and organisation of these festivals and also on the range of stakeholders involved with them.

The word 'festivity' is used to describe a festive activity, or a series of events that are undertaken to celebrate something. Festivity and celebration have always been part of the social life of humanity since the very early days. We note that these festivities evolved slowly over time, through several phases such as the purely organic festivals, then the purposeful organic festivals, the organised, and subsequently the commercially organised. The first festivities were an organic part of the social life of the times. However, ever since this time the enthusiasm of communities for their own interests and entertainment has given them cause to organise a colourful range of events on almost every subject. Since the dawn of time societies have always found a reason to mark important events in their lives: the changing of seasons, unification of lovers or the arrival of a new life (Allen et al. 2002: 5). For instance, the earliest *Homo sapiens* recorded spending a night by the fire where the tribe gathered to apparently sing and feast. These gatherings were considered a festivity and they did not require any organisation or a special time and place to happen as they were spontaneous, natural and obvious to all those involved. These types of festivities were considered organic (Biaett 2015: 21). These organic festivities slowly evolved and became more organised through time. With the onset and maturation of orga-nised farming, it becomes possible to observe the increased codification of the range of those festivities as they became more seasonal and their purpose was to celebrate a special event or day in a year. Other calendars were also introduced and used festivities to mark the important dates of stages in the years, often bor-rowing from the previous events but changing the significance of the events.

By 800 BC the ideas of mythology started to decline. At this time the organic festivity was replaced with the organised festivity and the small group celebra-tions evolved into community festivals (Biaett 2015: 23). Then by 1600 AD the organised festivals became an important part of society bringing together indi-viduals as well as various distinct groups within the societies. These community festivals strengthened the sense of belonging and offered an opportunity to bond with friends and family (Biaett 2015: 24).

In the 20th century the community festival fell victim to the ideas of capitalism. It rooted from Europe and America where the logic of civilization followed the capitalist philosophy. The increasing industrialization and consumption lead to the reduction of holidays and the new discipline required workers to relocate to metropolises and they had to leave behind their rural lifestyle (Biaett 2015, p. 24).

After World War II festivals became manufactured to generate publicity and consumption. This tendency started in America and slowly evolved to the global level. For example Christmas became a shopping event and the harvest festivals became the commercialized Halloween (Biaett 2015, p. 25).

Getz argues that the term "festival" is overused and in a wrong way. He states that some festivals are no more than commercial promotions. The meaning of fes-tival has been reduced to a public entertainment programme, or a special time for activities, rather than celebration (Getz, 2007: 32)). Festivals are created to reflect the local and ethnic culture, and by this become a part of cultural tourism. However, since many festivals are created solely for tourists, it raises the question of their authenticity and appropriateness (Getz, 2007: 33)).

The definition of culture defined by Schultz and Lavenda (cited in Getz, 2007: 51) is the following: "sets of learned behaviour and ideas that human beings acquire as members of society." Culture has to be learned and passed on to the next generations; it reflects the belief systems, symbols, and ritualistic behav-iour of a particular community.

Festivals can be seen as prime manifestations of the experience economy (Pine and Gilmore, 1999) as they entertain, educate, hold aesthetic value and provide the platform for escapism. This means that they contain certain unique elements which are not replicated or mass produced in other sectors of the economy.

Falassi (1987: 2) saw festivals as 'a sacred or profane time of celebration marked by special observances' maintaining that the social functions of a festival are closely related to community values. Farber (1983) investigated festivals and public celebrations and concluded that much could be learned about a commu-nity's symbolic, economic, political and social life. Falassi (1987) then added to Farber's notions of symbolism by commenting that both the social and sym-bolic meanings were closely linked to a series of overt values that the local community sees as essential to their ideology, worldview, social identity, history, and its physical survival, all of which the festivals celebrate. It is these very elements that constitute local culture and give each festival its uniqueness, which it is suggested is ultimately what visitors desire.

Within the mainstream definitions of festivals, there is an agreement that the local community is an integral part of the success of any festival. Goldblatt (1997) for example observed that a festival's key characteristic is the sense of a community which can be created. Within this, festivals are seen to perform many roles for communities including providing a forum for developing local cultural values and traditions, and promoting a shared purpose (Dunstan, 1994). Getz (1997) goes further suggesting that festivals provide a unique opportunity for community cultural development (Getz, 1997). Dunstan (1994), Frisby et al. (1989) and Getz (1991, 1997) highlight that festivals:

- Can be used as building blocks for communities,
- Promote ethnic understanding within society
- Preserve and celebrate local traditions, history and culture,
- Be used as a strategy to extend a destinations lifecycle (Chacko and Schaffer, 1993).

We include the final point here because it brings together CBT and community-based festivals.

A review of literature surrounding community festivals

The festivals have to be located within the local community to ensure that any creation or reinforcement of cultural identity is built on solid cultural foundations, which will in turn ensure that the events have full community representation and support. Community festivals are susceptible to a system of cultural production which aims to make the festival product as widely appealing as possible and in doing so can change it to a more homogenous or commodified product which then disconnects from the local communities it set out to serve (Saleh and Ryan, 1993). This was explored further by Ferris (1996) and Robinson (2004) who gave the term 'placeless festivals ' to ones which had fallen victim to a globalised marketplace and had become detached from place, space and cultural identity.

Community identity and even a sense of community is a facet of local culture, and that culture is thought to be the blood that flows through society. Wheatley and Kellner-Rogers (1998) for example see festivals as providing the heart of a community as their celebratory nature enables residents to experience freedom, and the ability to connect to the cultural values and indeed the society in which they live rather than seeing the fixed structures and rules surrounding the community. Festivals also have the potential to enhance or improve a destination's development, and economic regeneration through maximising event marketing to both existing and prospective tourists (Getz, 1991), but with this potential there are problems. Getz's perspectives are also carried forward by academics who identify regional and central government involvement in festivals as a way of attracting both tourists and possibly new residents to economically neglected regions, to improve the economic and social life of the area.

It can also be noted that research in community festivals has been slow to examine how festivals can have an impact on society and social change, and also have a real impact on the quality of life (Liburd and Derkzen, 2009) of those who live, work, learn and represent the local community of a place.

Researchers have explored how festivals are constructed and much of the research agenda has focused on the festival and its numerous and often complicated stakeholder interactions and relationships (Larson, 2000, 2002; Larson and Wikstrom, 2001). This has led to an identification of stakeholder roles and responsibilities (Reid and Arcodia, 2002; Getz et al., 2007), and also to an analysis of management (Andersson and Getz, 2007) and more profoundly why festivals could actually fail to deliver on their overarching aims, objectives, or promises to the local community (Getz, 2002). Clarke and Jepson (2011) took this one stage further by exploring the festival planning process through relationships of power and hegemonic control which manipulated the decisions of key stakeholders within a community festival.

This festival further highlighted Church and Coles (2007) position that power does not exist but must be created, and it demonstrated that one of the major factors within this was the location and space where power was being defined, which may be more important if it is within a politically charged site such as the city council chambers. It also reinforces that once established power within the creation of community events, a defined group of people will obey a chain of command, especially if power is linked to authority (Weber, 1978).

Power was also achieved by organisers through restricting knowledge or 'Disciplinary Power' (Foucault, 1978) about the festival and its events. For example, English language-only invitations were sent out to local communities in to attend a one-off meeting about the festival and its proposed programme of events, followed by not inviting local community groups to planning forums. In terms of the impact in the community, this accelerated the distrust for the city government and led to almost all of the local community cultural groups ignoring the invitation to meet and discuss the proposed festival. The organisers failed to understand the diversity of the local populations within the city and concentrated instead on the 87% white population and the culture they were thought to enjoy. What this tells us is that the organisers also failed to understand and use a definition of inclusive culture, preferring instead to view culture as a process of intellectual development. The four decision makers in the Derby Jubilee festival therefore achieved hegemony over all stakeholders involved within the festival by:

• Restricting their knowledge, both in terms of the organisations who contributed financially and the local communities themselves,

- Retaining discipline and governance (helped in addition by the spatial dimensions of power held by the political venue of the forums),
- Limited the opportunity for any resistance to power.

As a result of this hegemony exerted by the four festival planners very little community resistance was possible, leading to all the decisions being taken with no input from any of the local communities within the city. This power over decision making and hegemonic control produced as a result:

- A non-inclusive community festival,
- Community unable to challenge the established order of the planning process on decisions affecting the festival which meant that community opinion was not demonstrated (Marston, 1989; Rinaldo, 2002),
- Local cultural identity was defined by the dominant social group (Saleh and Ryan, 1993),
- Little democracy existed within the festival planning process because the four organisers were consistently in charge of making festival planning and construction decisions which meant other stakeholders were unable to hold any influence or have an effect on the decision-making processes.

Community values and valuing the community

There is a great need for policy makers, politicians and the local public sector to understand the community values associated with wards in their community. Over the last decade festival planners, whether full time or occasional, have tended to adopt a generic approach to understanding the communities for whom they will stage festivals. And in doing so have created community events which do not live up to local expectations in favour of following a political agenda linked to tourism marketing or urban regeneration. There is then a need to understand, measure, and create a framework to categorise community values in order to understand the types of events which should become a feature of a community festival or event. In addition to this, studies have yet to show the value of a community and its cultures to its locality, region or national identity.

Community cultural preservation

Festivals, although cultural and 'living' products, are still susceptible to the production process, as well as pressures of globalization, which can make events more prone to being copied and mass produced which is leading to more events becoming homogenous with very little recognisable culture as documented in the review of literature in earlier sections of the chapter. The public sector has a duty to preserve and protect local cultural traditions and sustain them for future generations. There are large gaps within event research as to how local cultural traditions are presented within a structured programme of events or festivals, and if local traditions are presented, how these cultures engage with a more modern and globalised world to ensure they are preserved and passed down through the local community. Community culture and its representation has not yet been fully explored within academic studies; it could for example be examined at all stages of a festival planning process to explore its evolution or how it may change or become commodified to ensure it fits within the festival theme or programme of events.

Creating inclusive cultural festivals

Another future research direction is the need to explore much deeper the development of practical guidelines for monitoring best practices and community inclusion within the festival planning process. Researching practical guidelines for organisers to implement to monitor the planning processes surrounding local cultural events should ensure that equality and democracy become end products of the planning process along with the inclusion of community voice.

The ideology of the 'community' within local cultural events should also form an area of research enquiry especially within the current climate of immigration and transitionary economies.

The perspective of the 'community' as a research direction can be realised through researching motivational dimensions which became a prominent part of this research context to allow comparisons between organisers and visitors and elaborate on organisers' cultural motivations in light of creating a local community festival. This research has established that there is a clear need to research and understand multi-cultural or ethnic minority cultural motivations if local cultural events are to realise the potential they have to become fully inclusive. Further research should centre on the idea of 'community' and how they are best included within planning processes that produce events for them. The creation of inclusive festivals should be the main priority of those involved in the creation of community events and many are falling short in what they can achieve within society where they deny a voice throughout the festivals' key development stages. Without the creation of inclusive festivals cultural diversity will not be a positive feature of the festival, and communities will be denied positive opportunities.

It is often the case that the cultural relationships within community festivals manipulate and shape decisions within the planning process, which is why the active inclusion of the local community is so important.

This leads to the dilemma between the command economy of top-down approaches with a more community-focussed bottom-up approach (see Table 5.1)

Community festivals can serve as the tools to explore and contextualise local traditions. They can be the catalyst for tourism, and also they can help to create a sense of identity for the very community that they are giving expression to (Jepson & Clarke, 2015: 3). Therefore it can be assumed that festivals would not live on if their communities were to abandon them. Several case studies show that when festival visitors were asked how an event can be ruined the key element in their answers was the absence of residents and the lack of

Table 5.1 Top-down versus bottom-up organisation

Top Down	Bottom Up
The foundations of the community and men's, women's and youth organisations are fragmented and unorganised	The community is already well organised and cohesive
Decision making is purely the domain of powerful individuals (usually males), and the benefits are not equitably distributed	When community members, women, men and youth are, widely involved in decision making processes, and financial management around the CBF
Land and resource disputes are rife and recurrent	Land ownership and other 'resource' issues are clear and well defined
Little marketing or misplaced marketing	The activity is supported by good marketing mechanisms
When people think they can invite tourists then sit back and 'the money will roll in' and there is a lack of future planning (to the detriment of the community and the natural landscape)	A strong plan for expansion, and/or to limit visitor numbers in balance with the carrying capacity of the community and environment to avoid adverse effects on both
'Top down' centralised decision making and management structures where CBF is 'placed' on a community by an outsider particularly if this is from international sources and there is a local perception that the motivations are purely financial	'Bottom up desire', in the community reflected in the facility design, decision making and management structures
There is no real local decision making or it is based on limited information and no consideration of options	Decisions for CBF are made by the community based on informed choice of impact, options, risk, and outcomes
Participation wanes during implementation of the CBF programmes	High participation levels
Drivers are solely financial	Drivers are not purely income generation but also cultural and natural heritage conservation and intercultural learning
Established through external funding mechanisms	Strong partnership with local NGOs, relevant government bodies and other supporters
The CBF venture is seen as a 'one size fits all'	Approaches are contextually and locally appropriate and not just 'imported' from other contexts
CBF is seen as a quick fix 'way up and out' of a poverty cycle	CBF is part of a broader/wider community development strategy
No attempt to inform visitors of the specific nature of local natural and cultural heritage so there is no sense of the uniqueness of 'place'	Linked to visitor education on the value of culture and resources present. Clear zoning of visitor and non-visitors areas
OR Infrastructure is inadequate and there is no potential for investment	There is good existing infrastructure to access the product

Source: Authors' own construction from various CBT texts

local characteristics of the community. The locals are the key feature that gives the events their authenticity and this is what makes the festivals memorable as well (Jepson & Clarke, 2015: 4).

Participants of community festivals

The participants of the community festivals can be placed into two groups: the locals and the non-locals. When organising a community festival the needs of these two groups can be taken into consideration. By taking advantage of the local characteristics a community festival can differentiate itself from other festivities that may have the same attributes. During the organisational phase the question can be asked which of the two groups are more important. The simplest would be that none of them are more important than the other but in reality this statement would not stand. Studies show that the locals are a little bit more important than non-locals, e specially in cases of smaller community festivals, as the locals are those who attract the non-locals. At these festivals the non-locals are almost always the relatives or friends of the locals. Without the local base non-locals would probably not hear about the event and the marketing power of word-of-mouth could be considered as significant as any other organised marketing campaign. Also if we take the local community out of a local community festival then we do not have a festival to begin with. Visitors come to see and experience the life of the local community and that is impossible to manage without the contributions of the locals.

This also stands in the case of historical community festivals since it is the history of the locals; they are the ones who guard the traditions and show them to the outside world in the course of the festival.

In empathy-based stories describing an imaginary failure of the community festival, the local people and the local characteristics of the community were absent (Kiunnen & Haahti 2015, p. 49).

The sense of community

It is assumed that the purpose of a festival event is that it aims to be a community-building activity. As Robert Lavenda describes it "people celebrating themselves and their community in an 'authentic' and traditional way, or at least emerging spontaneously from their homes for a communitywide expression of fellowship" (Duffy & Mair 2015, p. 54).

By initializing events that have the atmosphere of old traditions, the sense of shared identity and belonging is a successful way to create community. These community events tend to support ideas and place-based identities so that participants come to feel connected and united (Duffy & Mair 2015, p. 55).

Hosting a community festival gives the possibility for the locals to get involved by volunteering or taking on temporary jobs. It gives a chance to the local people to mix with others on a wide range of backgrounds and interests (Duffy & Mair 2015, p. 57).

Beside the benefits there are significant negative effects of the festivals on the community that have to be taken into consideration. For example one can be when the event excludes certain groups or individuals not allowing them to contribute to the festival. A research illustrates this in case of the "Up Helly Aa" festival hosted in Lerwick, Shetland where the men are allowed to take part in the procession while the women are restricted to cooking for the festival. Some of the women said that they are happy with this division, because it is according to the tradition, but this kind of negative discrimination shows no progress and may not be sustainable on the long run (Duffy & Mair 2015, p. 57). Those festivals which fail to adapt to the changes of the community which they were created for will, over time, lose their relevance to the locals (Duffy & Mair 2015, p. 58).

Community festivals and tourism

Tradition is usually the base on which community events are built. There is an obvious relationship between tourism and events. Events play a key role in inducing tourism and have an impact on all the services that are closely linked to the event as well as on other ancillary services. This has an impact on both demand and supply. On the demand side are the visitors who come for the event, but the impact not only affects the event itself but the whole image of the destination. On the supply side are the locals whose interest is to keep a positive destination image. This attracts more tourists which causes a positive cashflow and may help to renovate the urban and tourist infrastructure (Pedrana 2015, p. 67).

Not only can the event attract tourists but in some cases the local community itself is the attracting factor (Pedrana 2015, p. 69). The reactions of the locals to tourists coming to their community event is not always welcoming. There are various aspects that influence the reaction of the community. Fredline and Faulkner's (cited in Pedrana 2015, p. 70) studies have shown that these aspects are the geographical proximity to activity, and the concentration and involvement in tourism. Those who are involved in tourism are more likely to accept the visitors positively since they gain benefits from both the tourism and events industries.

The event cannot preference the tourists over the locals. The community has to be involved and given some benefits for the event to be sustainable for the local people (Pedrana 2015, p. 75). Events must aim for authenticity and for the expression of the unique characteristics of the host community. Visitors wants to experience what the locals do on an everyday basis and what they can enjoy at the destination (Allen et al. 2002, p. 35). Despite the goal to be authentic, destinations produce festivals exclusively for tourists without any value to their own communities. This results in inauthentic and shallow, meaningless events (Allen et al. 2002. p. 36). In the rapidly globalizing world local cultures already face a great threat of losing their uniqueness and identity due to fast homogenisation. The organisers must be aware of these trends and must learn to operate in the global environment (Allen et al. 2002. p. 55).

The range of positive and negative impacts has to be taken into consideration by the event managers and organisers and they need to balance them to reach the best possible outcome for all parties (Allen et al. 2002. p. 25).

Social and cultural impacts

Every event has a direct social and cultural impact on those who take part in it. And in various cases it even affects its wider host community. The impact can be as simple as shared experience but it can also result in increased pride, which results from some community events (Allen et al. 2002. p. 26.). Sometimes it can change the base of the host community, as happened in Sydney and Melbourne in 1997 after the Grand Australian Sumo Tournament. The event introduced the Japanese Sumo tradition with its religious and cultural associations, to the Australians. It formed a relationship between Japan and Australia and created a genuine Japanese-Australian cultural exchange (Allen et al. 2002. p. 27.). Getz defines cultural festivals as events that have cultural meaning (Getz, 2007: 31). The cultural celebrations are those events that strive for knowledge, to teach and show something new, so that visitors as well as locals appreciate the different aspects of culture. Cultural authenticity is the cultural meaning attached to an event (Getz, 2007: 200).

There are three types of authenticity according to Wang (cited in Getz, 2007: 201):

- Object-related authenticity, in this context the elements of the event have to be a genuine reflection of the culture being displayed,
- Constructive authenticity is projected onto the event in terms of images, expectations and beliefs. In this case the event might not be a true cultural expression it only strives to entertain visitors,
- Existential authenticity occurs whatever the nature of the event because event visitors might have their own experience which they interpret as authentic.

An example of negative social impact is the 1985 Australian Formula One Grand Prix in Adelaide. After the event the number of road accidents casualties increased by 34 percent compared to the same time of year in previous years. Fifteen percent of the casualties were left unexplained but it was suggested that they happened due to off-track emulation of Grand Prix race driving (Allen et al. 2002. p. 27).

Events and the economy

Various studies by Janiskee on rural festivals showed the importance of events on social life and tourism. Rural communities are quiet, vulnerable to the social impacts caused by tourism and the large influxes of new residents seeking amenities, although events and tourism can help by boosting the community development. Events are the type of tourism product that can be produced by even the smallest of communities without large capital (Getz, 2007: 60–61). However in the recent decades the economic significance of planned events has dramatically grown. This started the process of 'corporization' of the events, which resulted in loss of authenticity and growing standardistaion of the planned events. The economic significance does not have only negative effects on events because it resulted that events have more access to resources which are used to help them develop and flourish (Getz, 2007: 110).

References

Allen, J., McDonnell, I., O'Toole, W., Harris, R. (2002) *Festival and special event management*. Milton, QLD: Wiley Australia tourism series.

Arcodia, C. and Robb, A. (2000) A Taxonomy of Event Management Terms. In: J. Allen, R. Harris, L. K. Jago, and A. J. Veal (Eds.), *Events Beyond 2000: Setting the Agenda: Proceedings of Conference on Event Evaluation*, Research and Education. Sydney.

Arcodia, C. and Whitford, M. (2006) Festival Attendance and the Development of Social Capital. *Journal of Convention and Event Tourism*, 8(2).

Biaett, V. (2015) Organic Festivity: a missing element of community festival In Jepson, A. and Clarke, A. (eds), (2015) *Exploring community festivals and events*, London, Routledge.

Chacko, H. and Schaffer, J. (1993) The Evolution of a Festival: Creole Christmas in New Orleans. *Tourism Management*, 14(4): 475–482.

Church, A. and Coles, T. (2007) *Tourism, Power and Space*. London: Routledge.

Clarke, A. and Jepson, A. (2011) Power, Hegemony, and relationships in the festival planning and construction process. *International Journal of Festival and Event Management*, 2(1): 7–19.

Derrett, R. (2003) Making Sense of How Festivals Demonstrate a Community's Sense of Place. *Event Management*, 8: 49–58 (53).

Duffy, M. and Mair, J. (2015) Festivals and sense of community in places of transition: The Yakkerboo Festival, an Australian case study, in Jepson, A. and Clarke, A. (eds), *Exploring community festivals and events*, London, Routledge. pp. 54–65.

Dugas, K. J. and Schweitzer, J. H. (1997) cited in: Derrett, R. (2003) Making Sense of How Festivals Demonstrate a Community's Sense of Place. *Event Management*, 8: 49–58.

Dunstan, G. (1994) cited in: Derrett, R. (2003) Making Sense of How Festivals Demonstrate a Community's Sense of Place. *Event Management*, 8: 49–58.

Falassi, A. (1987) *Time Out of Time: Essays on the Festival*. Albuquerque: University of New Mexico.

Farber, C. (1983) cited in: Getz, D. (1991) *Festivals, Special Events, and Tourism*. New York: Van Nostrand Reinhold: 56.

Ferris, W. R. (1996) In Derrett, R. (2003) Making Sense of How Festivals Demonstrate a Community's Sense of Place. *Event Management*, 8: 49–58 (53).

Foucault, M. (1978, 1981, 1982) cited in: Church, A. and Coles, T. (2007) *Tourism, Power and Space*. London: Routledge.

Frisby, W. and Getz, D. (1989) Festival Management: A Case Study Perspective. *Journal of Travel Research*, 28(1, summer): 7–11.

Gabr, H. S. (2004) Attitudes of Residents and Tourists towards the Use of Urban Historic Sites for Festival Events. *Event Management*, 8: 231–242.

Getz, D. (1991) *Festivals, Special Events, and Tourism*. New York: Van Nostrand Reinhold.

Getz, D. (1997) *Event Management and Event Tourism*. New York: Cognizant Communication Corp.

Getz, D. (2002) *Why Festivals Fail. Event Management*, 7. New York: Cognizant Communication Corp: 209–219.

Getz, D., T. Andersson, and M. Larson (2007) "Festival Stakeholder Roles: Concepts and Case Studies". *Event Management*, 10(2/3): 103–122.

Goldblatt, J. (1997) *Special Events: Best Practices in Modern Events Management*. New York: Van Nostrand Reinhold.

Jepson, A. S. (2009) Investigating Cultural Relationships within the Festival Planning and Construction Process in a Local Community Festival Context. unpublished PhD Thesis University of Derby.

Jepson, A. and Clarke, A. (eds) (2014) *Exploring Community Festivals and Events*. London Routledge.

Jepson, A. and Clarke, A. (eds) (2015) *Exploring Community Festivals and Events*. (Routledge Advances in Events Management Series). London, Routledge.

Jepson, A. and Clarke, A. (eds) (2016) *Managing and Developing Communities. Festivals and Events*. London: Palgrave.

Jepson, A. and Clarke, A. (eds) (2017) *Power, Construction, and Meaning in Festivals*. London: Routledge.

Kiunnen M. and Haahti, F. (2015) Visitor Discourses on Experiences: reasons for festival success and failure. *International Journal of Festival and Event Management*, 6(3): 251–268.

Larson, M. (2000) Interaction in the Political Market Square: Organising Marketing of Events. In Larson, M. (2002) A Political Approach to Relationship Marketing: Case Study of the Storsjoyran Festival. *International Journal of Tourism Research*, 4(2): 119–143.

Larson, M. and Wikstrom, E. (2001) Organizing Events: Managing Conflict and Consensus in Apolitical Market Square. *Event Management*, 7(1), 51–65.

Liburd, J. J. and Derkzen, P. (2009) Emic Perspectives on Quality of Life: The Case of the Danish Wadden Sea Festival. *Tourism and Hospitality Research*, 9(2), 132–146.

Marston, S. (1989) cited in: Jeong, S. and Santos, C. A. (2004) Cultural Politics and Contested Place Identity. *Annals of Tourism Research*, 31(3): 640–656.

Maurin, F. (2003) Festivals. *Contemporary Theatre Review*, 13(4). London and New York: Routledge (2001: 5).

Pedrana, M. (2015) New and Old Tourist Traditions In Jepson, A. and Clarke, A. (eds), *Exploring community festivals and events*, London, Routledge.

Pine, B. J. and Gilmore, J. H. (1999) *The Experience Economy: Work Is Theatre and Every Business Is a Stage*. Cambridge, MA: Harvard Business School Press.

Quinn, B. (2006) Problematising 'Festival Tourism': Arts Festivals and Sustainable Development in Ireland. *Journal of Sustainable Tourism*, 14(3): 288–306.

Reid, S. and Arcodia, C. (2002) In: Getz, D. and Andersson, T. (2008) Stakeholder Management Strategies of Festivals. *Journal of Convention and Event Tourism*, 9(3).

Rinaldo, R (2002) cited in: Jeong, S. and Santos, C. A. (2004) Cultural Politics and Contested Place Identity. *Annals of Tourism Research*, 31(3): 640–656.

Robinson, M., Picard, D. and Long, P. (2004) Festival Tourism: Producing, Translating, and Consuming Expressions of Culture. *Event Management*, 8: 187–789.

Saleh, F. and Ryan, C. (1993) Jazz and Knitwear; Factors That Attract Tourists to Festivals. *Tourism Management*, August: 289–297.

Try Weber, M. (1978) The distribution of power within the political community Economy and Society 2: 926–940.

Wheatley, M. and Kellner-Rogers, M. (1998) The Paradox and Promise of community In Hesselbein, F., Goldsmith, R., Beckhard, R. and Schubert, R. (eds) The Community of the future San Francisco, Jossey-Bass.

6 Rethinking tourism in Belarus

The opening of a rural economy

Susan L. Slocum and Valeria Klitsounova

Introduction

The rise in ecotourism, community-based tourism, and agritourism is a result of new types of production and consumption, where independent travellers help to create alternative and beneficial types of responsible tourism (Mowforth and Munt, 2015). While many theorists question whether responsible travel actually empowers local communities (Lee et al., 2015; Spenceley, 2012), there is evidence that small-scale tourism can reduce economic leakages, promote cultural sustainability, and lead to a more inclusive decision-making process at the local level (Slocum & Curtis, 2018). Belarus has recently engaged tourism as an economic development tool for the rural regions that depend on agriculture for job creation and business development. Agro-ecotourism is a mix of activities that provide food-related products and leisure activities on productive agriculture properties and has recently been recognized as a path to sustainable development by incorporating natural landscapes with food traditions as the basis for the tourism product. Through partnerships with nongovernmental organizations (NGOs), specifically Country Escapes, the federal government has addressed many of the challenges facing rural tourism enterprises, including reductions in visa entry requirements to support tourism growth and a reassessment of tax challenges facing small farms engaged in tourism.

The natural and cultural resources of Belarus have recently been acknowledged as a viable development path into tourism. The main potential of tourism in Belarus lies in the beauty and diversity of its nature, its unique historic cultural heritage, and the people themselves – a very hospitable, diligent and tolerant people. Since the late 2000s, the government of Belarus has decided to treat tourism as a primary economic sector in order to increase profits from the tourist industry. According to a report by the World Travel and Tourism Council (2017), the tourism sector has had a positive impact on the Belarusian economy and will continue its progress in the future. The direct contribution of travel and tourism to the gross domestic product was $900 million and the total contribution to the economy was $2.8 billion in 2016. According to the Ministry of Sport and Tourism, the main types of tourism in Belarus include: ecotourism, religious tourism, agro-ecotourism, battlefield and historical tours, business tourism and medical tourism (The Republic of Belarus, 2016).

Homestays on working farms are a rising phenomenon in Belarus, growing from 34 homestays in 2006 to 2,319 in 2017 (National Statistical Committee of the Republic of Belarus, 2018). Much of this growth is attributed to the work of Country Escapes, a Belarussian non-governmental organisation (NGO), through their interaction with the Ministry of Sport and Tourism. Using unique bottom-up approach processes, which has led to extensive national and international partnerships, Belarus provides examples of clusters and creative tourism products contributing to the success of agro-ecotourism. Belarus has become a learning arena for tourists in culture, folk, crafts, culinary, and traditional agriculture. The result has been a unique form of sustainable tourism at the onset of tourism development for a newly emerging economy where enhancements in social capital have had a direct influence in the political process and governance of tourism.

Governance can be described as the tool that helps societies adapt to change, and good governance implies collective action in negotiating this change (Baggio et al., 2010). Bramwell (2011) argues that governance is more than just the formal institutions of the state, it should also include an assessment of how governmental and non-governmental agencies work together. He writes, "Attention is directed to how policy decisions are made and how power is distributed because the state cannot be understood in isolation as it is dependent on its relationships with society, including societal groups seeking to influence its policies" (p. 460). In the World Travel and Tourism Council's (2003) Blueprint for New Tourism, sustainable tourism is noted to require strong alliances that match the needs of economies with the needs of local authorities, communities, and businesses throughout the development process. For an emerging tourism economy, such as Belarus, the role of Country Escapes in helping the government negotiate neoliberal changes in the political economy cannot be understated. Therefore, an understanding of the unique partnership that has formed between the Belarussian government and Country Escapes is at the forefront of this chapter.

Understanding the political economy

The study of the political economy stems from modernization and dependency theories and has traditionally focused on tourism as an economic development strategy or the unequal power distributions within the tourism system. Rostow (1960) highlights the evolutionary path that societies take in the progression from traditional to modern economies. In traditional economies, production is based on ethnicities, customs, and beliefs, which influence the type of goods and services produced, as well as the direction of their distribution. As countries develop modern structures, certain industries encourage greater investment and growth. This evolution involves increased international investment, which in turn enhances infrastructure and brings support industries, creating new jobs and new opportunities. As these political-economic relationships become more global in nature, industrialized nations become more influential resulting in unequal power distributions that exploit weaker nations (Nash, 1981). Mosedale

(2015) recognizes that "human societies tend to be organised according to hierarchical territorial containers in which social, political and economic life takes place (local, regional, national, international, transnational, supranational, etc.) with related power struggles between different scales (e.g. the politics of scale)" (p. 507). Therefore, political inequalities that lead to power struggles can happen between countries and international agencies, or within countries between urban power centres and rural communities. In tourism, not only are poorer regions dependent on international investment, national policy decisions, and local resources, but communities may become dependent on cultures where tourism planning reflects western value systems (Erisman, 1983) and where lucrative tourism markets exist.

The political economy is concerned with the political nature of decision-making and how politics affects choices in a society. It is intricately involved in the influence of capitalism on societies, and much literature on the political economy emphasizes the role of neoliberalism as an influencing factor (Duffy, 2013). Neoliberalism is the political and social perspective that human well-being can be enhanced through policies that promote entrepreneurial freedoms within an institutional framework characterized by strong private property rights, free markets, and free trade (Harvey, 2005). Neoliberalism provides avenues to privatize tourism resources as a means to reduce the economic burden of the state (Slocum, 2017). Neoliberalism has transformed the way tourism is developed, specifically the ways in which state governments view natural resources, communities, and the tourism product (Kline and Slocum, 2015). Even in 1995, Leheny recognized the potential impact of tourism on the political economy when he wrote, "the industry continues to do more to shape the roles and identities of its producers and consumers, or hosts and tourists, than does perhaps any other" (p. 367). The political economy offers insightful ways to analyze tourism development (Bramwell, 2011), especially in emerging economies such as Belarus.

Belarus, once known as White Russia, was formerly part of the Soviet Union until its independence in July 1990. As the first president of Belarus, Lukashenko promoted a market socialism agenda that allowed the state to maintain tight controls over prices and currency exchange rates within its well-developed industrial economy. After the global recession in 2011, Belarus still faces severe economic challenges related to a devalued currency. In the five-month period from December 2010 to May 2011, salaries in Belarus dropped from an average wage of $550 to $330 (Infographics, 2013). While there is little economic data available, the World Bank (2017) estimates that the current real unemployment rate is seven times higher than the official rate of 6.1%. Agriculture remains a major industry, along with manufacturing and petrochemicals.

Eastern European countries have taken one of two paths to establish market privation after the fall of communism. Countries like Hungary, Poland, and the Baltic states have embraced western values and sought alliance with the European Union. Other countries, such as Belarus, have maintain strong ties with Russia. In 2004, The European Union imposed sanctions against Belarus for human rights violations. These sanctions were discontinued in 2016, opening the door to new trade negotiations with western European countries and allowing Belarus to become a member of the European Neighbourhood Policy (Rankin, 2016). However, Russia still accounts for almost 50% of Belarus's foreign trade and significant investment in tourism infrastructure. It is estimated that approximately 80% of foreign visitors come from Russia and the Commonwealth of Independent States (National Statistical Committee of the Republic of Belarus, 2017). Recognition of the dependency on the Russian economy and Russian visitation has resulted in avenues to open Belarus to the international market. New tourism policies, in turn, are helping to reduce this dependency in order to increase economic returns and provide a diversified political economy.

As Belarus has negotiated the transition from a communist economy to a modern economy, tourism partnerships have strengthened institutional environments and aligned policies with the needs of the state, the needs of the society, and the needs of the international tourism industry. Hamm et al. (2012) argue that a successful transition from communism to capitalism has depended on three factors: (1) successful countries rapidly implemented neoliberal policies; (2) failures were not due to policies but to poor institutional environments; and (3) policies were counterproductive because they damaged the state. Belarus has recently acknowledged the advantages of neoliberalism, in part through tourism development and the appeal of international visitation. In turn, advancing tourism within Belarus is moving the country towards a more open economy as a means to reduce dependence on former soviet partners. The goal is to align policies with institutional capacities to ensure successful development as described by Hamm et al. (2012).

The national tourism policy of the Republic of Belarus is formulated in the context of the social development ideology of the country and takes into account the transfer of the national economy towards a path of innovative development. At the national level, socio-economic development is promoted through the current Social and Economic Development Programme (for the years 2016–2020) and the National Strategy for Sustainable Development, which will be in effect until 2030. The National Strategy for Sustainable Development uses a neoliberal approach to recognize tourism as a powerful lever to support the development of innovation and infrastructure, create jobs, and increase export earnings. The strategic goal is to move its development of the tourism industry to a new level and to maximize the socio-economic benefits of tourism activities as suggested by Duffy (2013). From 2016–2020, the development of tourism will be aimed at increasing the competitiveness of tourist services and the formation of high-yield sectors, whereas in the period 2021–2030, the tourism industry should become one of the highly export-oriented sectors of the economy, which will create new jobs and ensure the development of small and medium-sized businesses. This neoliberal opening of the tourism market will be used to structure tourism around innovation, creativity, and entrepreneurship as prescribed by Harvey (2005).

As one of the potential policies for economic development, sustainable tourism is seen as an economic impetus for Belarus in several development documents of national importance. One of the popular types of tourism, and an incentive for sustainable tourism, is agro-ecotourism, which utilizes the capacity of rural regions, such as local historical and cultural heritage. Thus, rural tourism is a relatively new type of tourism for Belarus, although the country has already made significant progress in its development.

Agro-ecotourism as sustainable development in Belarus

The nature of rural areas has changed with the increasing reliance on global food chains and international food transportation. Export agricultural policies have left small-scale farms increasingly dependent on the international food industry as a diversification strategy, resulting in higher barriers of entry, increased input costs, lower prices for agricultural commodities, and unequal power distributions towards developed nations with stronger buying power (Bolwig et al., 2010). Reduced profits have led to the reduction of small-scale agriculture on a global level, changing rural land use, reducing open space access, and weakening the economic opportunities of rural regions. The result has been outward migration as young people move to urban areas where employment opportunities are greatest, leaving behind an aging population (Tregear, 2003). Moreover, as rural governments realize a reduction in the earning potential of farms, resulting from lower tax revenue, there is a lack of investment in infrastructure, heath care, and education. Rural areas may have limited opportunities to participate in tourism (due to a lack of "traditional" tourist attractions), yet agro-ecotourism provides the primary draw to tourists who are seeking open space, idyllic communities, unique recreational activities, and exposure to traditional livelihoods (Slocum and Curtis, 2018).

According to the World Fact Book, agricultural (47%) and forestry (43%) constitute the majority of land usage in Belarus, showing the rural nature still prevalent in the country (Central Intelligence Agency, 2018). The majority of farmland is state owned, and the modernization of agriculture has been state funded. This policy has resulted in a low level of capital inflows to Belarus, with agriculture only accounting for about 1.7% of foreign direct investment in 2013 (Wengle, 2017). Moreover, agricultural wages are estimated at 70% of the average wage rates in Belarus, resulting in rural to urban migration at a rate of approximately 30% (Bobrova et al., 2012). While urban areas constitute 77% of the total population in Belarus, the rate of urbanization is on the decline.

Sustainable development has the potential to become an organizing force that can shape the political economy and support a broader social agenda, especially in rural areas. In 1997, O'Riordan and Voisey claimed that sustainable development has the capacity to enhance social and political movements that support empowerment through "a common evaluative yardstick, coalitions of supportive interests, and a machinery of execution that co-ordinates a host of governmental and non-governmental actors" (p. 15). Yet, they acknowledged that this is not happening in an efficient manner because the agencies with the responsibility of sustainability (environment ministries) do not wield the administrative power held by the economic ministries. Moreover, urban policies may take priority over rural needs. This implies that the governance structures, often influenced by the election process, are reliant on short-term accomplishments rather than the institutional innovations required in sustainable development. Moreover, policy often spans multiple disciplines, resulting in conflicting strategies from different branches of the governing agencies (Bramwell, 2011).

As one of the potential policies for economic development, sustainable tourism is seen as an economic impetus for Belarus in several development documents of national importance. In 2004, a special Committee on Sustainable Development in Belarus was established under supervision of the Vice Prime Ministry. This committee was inefficient because it did not have its own office or secretary and the agency was disbanded in 2009 (Klitsounova, 2014). Recently, a new institute was launched called the National Coordinator on Implementation of the Sustainable Development Goals. In Belarus, several state ministries are responsible for sustainability policy, such as the Ministry of the Environment, the Ministry of Economy, and the Ministry of International Affairs (Bramwell, 2011). Belarus has signed (and ratified) Agenda 21 (Agenda for Sustainable Development), the main international agreement in sustainable development, as well as the 2030 Sustainable Development Goals. The Republic of Belarus now has obligations to report the steps taken to achieve these goals. Some regions have developed and adopted a strategy of sustainable tourism development, however the Ministry of Sport and Tourism is not involved in sustainable development directly (Klitsounova, 2014).

In partnership with the United Nations Development Programme (UNDP), Belarus has launched a number of special projects, such as Support to the National Coordinator on Implementation of Sustainable Development Goals and Strengthening the Role of the Parliament in the Implementation of Sustainable Development Goals. These projects have assisted the country in moving forward with a sustainability agenda. There are also a number of international projects, which have been realized in Belarus, specifically aligning components of sustainable development with rural tourism. These include: Local Entrepreneurship and Economic Development (2012–2014), Support to Sustainable Tourism Development in Belarus (2015–2018), and Supporting the Transition to a Green Economy in the Republic of Belarus (2014–2017). Moreover, there are many projects for sustainable tourism development at the local level.

Since O'Riordan and Voisey's (1997) study, emphasis has been placed on the local ownership of tourism resources (and businesses) which has shown to encourage a more inclusive type of development. Poon (1993) argues that new innovations, specifically within indigenous communities, have reduced dependency on multinational corporations in favour of a more sustainable form of tourism development. In turn, local ownership of tourism resources has the potential to instil pride in local culture, build networks between local entrepreneurs, and develop social capital within and between communities (Everett and Slocum, 2013). Ownership may be in the form of independently run businesses, or it may be in the local management of natural areas. Moreover, through local ownership, the descriptive narratives are crafted that communicate sense of place to the visiting public.

Social capital is a key component of sustainability and is vital in developing agro-ecotourism (Everett and Slocum, 2013). Social capital is defined as "networks together with shared norms, values and understandings that facilitate co-operation within or among groups" (Cote and Healy, 2001, p. 41). Slocum (2018) writes, "A high level of social capital can facilitate the flow of information, bring collective access to resources, and lower transaction costs, all important elements of agricultural-based tourism product development" (p. 86). Strong social capital has the potential to support civic engagement and social connectedness, leading to a better functioning government and good governance partnerships (Alonso and Bressan, 2013). Social capital involves information sharing, coordination of activities, and collective decision-making and requires cultivation as levels of tourism change and grow (McGehee et al., 2010).

The role of non-governmental organizations

Another emerging aspect of the political economy is the role of NGOs in empowering communities and individuals as a means to support or reject neoliberal changes in government ideologies. NGOs provide needed assistance through community involvement of tourism product development and specific expertise through marketing and networking with tour operators (Jänis, 2014). Moreover, NGOs provide avenues for tourism investment through donor funding and/or grant aid as a means to send scarce funds to areas and activities with the greatest economic and social needs (McAffee, 2012). As powerful funding allies, NGOs are actively supported by the United Nations World Tourism Organisation and other multinational agencies. In turn, the global governance system has used these fiscal transfer agencies to help shape the way tourism is represented and valued (Kline and Slocum, 2015). NGOs are often the voice of the disenfranchised and have the potential to change the way governments view environments, communities, and tourism as a development tool.

Country Escape is national non-profit NGO created in November 2002. Its members comprise more than 600 people, which are mostly Belarusian countrymen who are willing to master a new profession and provide bed & breakfast services for tourists in their rural communities. The association has aggregated significant experience and implemented many successful tourism innovative initiatives including

- Tourist product development – designing products based on Belarusian intangible heritage, greenways, eco-museums, thematic farmsteads, festivals, and excursion;
- Local development – initiating the establishment of tourism clusters;
- Management – establishing public councils on agro-ecotourism development at the national, regional, and local level.

Table 6.1 Country Escape's grant-funded initiatives

Grant	Funding Agency	Amount	Timeline
Volozhin without barriers: increasing local capacities for provision of social and recreational services for people with disabilities	EU	€1,000,000	2015–2018
Supporting the transition to a green economy in the Republic of Belarus: ecotourism in Berezinsky Biosphere Reserve, innovative approaches, partnership models, and "green" consciousness	EU/UNDP	$119,854	2016–2017
Support to local development in the Republic of Belarus: Volozinslky District, the territory of creative economy	EU/UNDP	$18,000	2016
Local entrepreneurship and economic development: information and awareness campaign in the sphere of agro- and ecotourism	USAID/UNDP	$50,000	2013–2014
Sustainable development of Dribin regional community on the basis of cultural heritage	U.S. Embassy	$23,764	2013–2014
Leveraging partnerships for sustainable development in rural Belarus	EU and Eurasia Foundation	€1,615,777	2011–2012
Community-based tourism for conservation, partnership and development of rural territories	U.S. Embassy	$23,740	2011–2012
Reviving culinary traditions: creating a common tourist product	Eurasia Foundation	$5,000	2010
AGORA 2.0 heritage tourism for increased BSR identity (9 countries, 24 partners)	Baltic Sea Region Programme	€115,000	2009–2012
Sustainable development of the Belarusian Polesie	U.S. Embassy	$24,000	2009
European quality for rural tourism	Eurasia Foundation	$25,879	2005–2006
Development of rural tourism in Belarus	Eurasia Foundation	$15,075	2004

Table 6.1 shows a detailed picture of their grant-funded projects.

Opening rural Belarus to tourism

One of the main challenges in the Belarussian tourism sector is that it has remained underdeveloped in terms of regional and local competences and capacities. This is closely related to two major problems in the system of territorial organization of tourism: poor efficiency of complex tourist territorial administration and low territorial status of recreational resources (Klitsounova, 2014). Public ownership of land dominates in Belarus, and administrative methods of management and the development of, and communication within, the tourist industry are of great importance. Thus, the implementation of strategies and action plans requires greater attention (Everett and Slocum, 2013). Moreover, better communication and decision-making between different administrative levels, such as national, regional, and local authorities, is needed in order to circumvent the inherent power struggles recognized by Nash (1981).

The process of rural tourism development started as a bottom-up approach in Belarus. In 2002, the regional NGO Agro- and Ecotourism was created, which brought the rural tourism stakeholders together. The association was transformed into the National Association of Agro- and Ecotourism, commonly known as Country Escape, in 2003. From the beginning, members showed enthusiasm and believed in the success of this project. Using a popular tourism attraction in Belarus, the Museum of Rural Culture "Dudutky", helped to show stakeholders the potential demand for tourism products based on rural traditions, culture, food, and agricultural technology. Dudutky became a perfect model for rural dwellers who started to develop tourism in their regions. Through their grant partnerships and accumulated expertise in tourism, Country Escapes has built social capital around agro-ecotourism development in Belarus and changed the political economy of Belarus, resulting in the opening of the rural tourism economy.

Rural tourism is an industry with a human face, and the host is the key attribute for its success (Mowforth and Munt, 2015). From the beginning, Country Escape focused attention on education and capacity building for people working in rural tourism. They developed special programs for training, such as classes for new entrants, advanced education, and specific themes (organic agriculture, traditional cooking, green technology, creative economy, etc.). Country Escapes organized the Branch of International Tourism Department of Belarusian State University and involved students in real projects, bringing a new wave of innovation to rural tourism. Country Escape has managed to build a strong team around agro-ecotourism in Belarus and develop social capital. This network of a few thousand people who share certain values, norms, and standards has been effective in lobbying for the interests of the whole group (Baggio et al., 2010) and effecting change in the country.

Increased social capital has provided an avenue to create innovative local tourism products based on a partnership network approach. Villages within a region work together to develop clusters, or groups of businesses that complement each other provide a variety of experiences for the tourists (Porter, 1998). Examples include greenways, thematic tourism clusters, and festivals. One case in point is the greenway Volozhinskiye hascincy, created in 2008. At the time, there were only eight farmsteads in Volozhin district, however because of the greenway the growth in tourism has increased the number of farmsteads to 40. Each farmstead has its own specialization: music, honey, ecology, flowers, and water touring, which supports interesting and unique programs on the greenway that attracts tourists. In turn, the number of tourists is also growing steadily. In 2011, the region was visited by 10,191; 13,500 in 2015; and 15,000 agritourists in 2016 (National Statistical Committee of the Republic of Belarus, 2018). The district also hosts a number of annual festivals including the music festival Volnae Pavetra, the festival of traditional cultures, Rakovski Fest, and the festival of ceramics masters, Glinyany zvon. As Kline and Slocum (2015) identify, liberalizing the greenway has increased entrepreneurial activities and transformed the way tourism is developed in the region.

Country Escapes has provided new avenues to promote tourism, specifically in rural areas where marketing skills and website promotion is difficult to initiate. Their website is free for all rural tourism business (www.ruralbelarus.by) and now there are more than 10 special websites for the promotion of rural tourism farmsteads and products. Country Escapes has also encouraged the use of www.booking.com and www.airbnb.com as a means to increase reach to international travellers. Working in partnership with local tour operators, farmstead owners have developed innovative tourism programs that bring tourism to rural areas. To date, more than 50 press-tours and hundreds of events (festivals, presentations of ecomuseums and farmsteads, new trails opening) have been organized along with numerous TV programmes, articles, and radio programmes promoting agro-ecotourism. In line with Jänis (2014), Country Escapes has provided the expertise needed to develop effective marketing partnerships.

The long process of building partnerships and facilitating the flow of information has changed the political environment related to rural tourism in Belarus. The development of social capital has resulted in a new lobbying effort around the interests of rural tourism providers as a means to ensure good governance (Alonso and Bressan, 2013). Media was used to demonstrate how a rural tourism initiative could be mutually beneficial for all through developing the rural economy, creating new jobs, reviving traditions, encouraging environmentally friendly behaviour, promoting Belarusian identity, and setting up links between urban and rural tourism stakeholders. The result was a liberal decree by the president supporting rural tourism, which was signed in 2006 (No. 372) followed by a more liberal updated policy (No. 365) signed in 2017. Simultaneously, Country Escapes developed a new partnership by creating public councils for rural tourism development at the local and district level. The public councils are informal institutions which unite local authorities, community leaders, rural tourism providers, local media, local businesses, and industry experts. By providing grounds for negotiation, rural tourism stakeholders have the opportunity to influence the decision-making process (McGehee et al., 2010). The primary factor for success is in consensus building because most participants of the public councils are local citizens who want prosperity in their small motherland (Klitsounova, 2014).

The same approach has been used to create public councils in the higher hierarchical territorial containers, such as the regional and national level. As a result, a partnership scheme in the field of rural tourism has united Country Escape representatives, rural tourism providers, local business, local authorities, and experts to provide good governance with stakeholders' participation. There are more than 20 public councils for rural tourism development at different administrative levels in Belarus. One key success is the newly formed presidential council for entrepreneur development, which has decreed that the participation of professional NGOs in any decision-making process is now mandatory.

President Decree No 372 demonstrates how political decision-making can stimulate economic development on the basis of neoliberalism (Leheny, 1995). The decree gives entrepreneurial freedom to rural dwellers through tourism development. People can now use their personal houses as tourism accommodations and provide meals, guided tours, and a number of onsite events such as weddings, seminars, and sporting events. Rural farmsteads no longer need special licenses (the size of business is considered too small) and do not have to pay any taxes on tourism revenue. This legislation has led to a burst of rural tourism development, new investments, and creative tourism product initiatives. Moreover, people can use local resources (natural and cultural, tangible and intangible) for free to create interesting tourism products.

Country Escape has organized 10 international conferences (2003, 2009–2017) to ensure communication channels between the federal authorities and the farmsteads remains productive. Invited speakers from Italy, Russia, Lithuania, Poland, and the United States have used this forum to share best practices and common challenges in rural tourism development with the Belarussian tourism community. As a primary sponsor of these conferences, the bank Belagroprombank has remained a strong supporter of ago-ecotourism and provides preferential loans to individuals and farm households for agro-ecotourism ventures and finances agro-ecotourism projects. By bringing together national political entities, regional governance bodies, entrepreneurs, and tourism stakeholders (tour operators, hotels), these conferences have maintained high levels of social capital and encouraged the open flow of information within the tourism sector of Belarus.

Conclusion

This chapter has highlighted the emerging tourism economy in Belarus, specifically the opening of rural tourism and agro-ecotourism development. The formation of the national NGO, Country Escapes, was vital in the neoliberal process and helped provide a comprehensive modernization strategy to support entrepreneurship, mediate grant investment, and build social capital in the tourism economy (McAffee, 2012). As Belarus negotiates dependence on its former soviet partners by promoting a more global tourism economy, Country Escapes is ensuring that the balance of power within the hierarchical territorial containers provides an inclusive form of tourism development (Mosedale, 2015). It is believed that neoliberalism can deliver the political and social opportunity to support human well-being through the support of entrepreneurial freedoms within an effective institutional framework (Harvey, 2005). Neoliberalism has transformed the ways in which the Republic of Belarus has engaged natural resources, communities, and the tourism product (Kline and Slocum, 2015).

However, Belarus has only just started on the path towards an open economy. Rather than using the rapid approach to neoliberalism employed by other Eastern European countries (Hamm et al., 2012), Belarus is aligning policies with institutional capacities as it negotiates a tradition of socialism and a mistrust of outsiders. For example, capacity building is still necessary in terms of building tourism clusters (especially rural tourism clusters), which could then compete for market share across Europe through innovative tourism product development (O'Riordan and Voisey, 1997). Improvements are still needed in transit and cross-border tourism as part of the programme on good neighbourliness and twin-town relations between the neighbouring countries of Russia and the European Union. More effort needs to be put into the development of international tourist routes including cross-border educational, sport, recreational, medical, and environmental tourism, as well as agro-ecotourism. In general, the Republic of Belarus and its government need to increase the attractiveness of the country for tourists through the creation of modern international tourist centres and complexes based on new technologies and international investment projects and programmes. Moreover, a lack of international identity is a challenge when competing for tourists at the international level. As Belarus negotiates the east-west divide, opening tourism to western markets and using sustainable development practices is seen as a lucrative investment strategy that can support job creation and business development. Therefore, international tourism is well aligned to open the Belarussian economy.

References

Alonso A. D., & Bressan, A. (2013). Small rural family wineries as contributors to social capital and socioeconomic development, *Community Development*, 44(4), 503–519.

Baggio, R., Scott, N., & Cooper, C. (2010). Improving tourism destination governance: A complexity science approach. *Tourism Review*, 65(4), 51–60.

Bobrova, A., Shakhotska, L., & Shymanovich, G. (2012). Social impact of emigration and rural-urban migration in Central and Eastern Europe: Final country report, Belarus. European Commission Directorate General Employment, Social Affairs and Inclusion.

Bolwig, S., Ponte, S., du Toit, A., Riisgaard, L., & Halberg, N. (2010). Integrating poverty and environmental concerns into value-chain analysis: A conceptual framework. *Development Policy Review*, 28(2), 173–194.

Bramwell, B. (2011). Governance, the state and sustainable tourism: A political economy approach. *Journal of Sustainable Tourism*, 19(4–5), 459–477.

Central Intelligence Agency (2018). World Fact Book. Retrieved from www.cia.gov/library/publications/the-world-factbook/geos/bo.html.

Cote, S., & Healy, T. (2001). *The Well being of Nations. The Role of Human and Social Capital*. Paris: Organisation for Economic Co-operation and Development.

Duffy R. (2013) The international political economy of tourism and the neoliberalisation of nature: Challenges posed by selling close interactions with animals. *Review of International Political Economy*, 20(3), 605–626.

Erisman, H. M. (1983). Tourism and cultural dependency in the West Indies. *Annals of Tourism Research*, 10(3), 337–361.

Everett, S., & Slocum, S. L. (2013). Food and tourism: An effective partnership? A UK-based review. *Journal of Sustainable Tourism*, 21(6), 789–809.

Hamm, P., King, L. P., & Stuckler, D. (2012). Mass privatization, state capacity, and economic growth in postcommunist countries. *American Sociological Review*, 77(2), 295–324.

Harvey, D. (2005). *A Brief History of Neoliberalism*. Oxford: Oxford University Press.

Infographics (2013–06–26). За май реальная зарплата в Беларуси выросла на 7,7%. NAVINY.BY – БЕЛОРУССКИЕ НОВОСТИ (in Russian). Retrieved March 3, 2018.

Jänis J. (2014) Political economy of the Namibian tourism sector: Addressing post-apartheid inequality through increasing indigenous ownership, *Review of African Political Economy*, 41(140), 185–200.

Kline, C., & Slocum, S. L. (2015). Neoliberalism in ecotourism? The new development paradigm of multinational projects in Africa. *Journal of Ecotourism*, 14(2–3), 99–112.

Klitsounova, V. (2014). *Agro-ecotourism: Teaching Aid*. Minsk: RIPO.

Lee, D., Hampton, M., & Jeyacheya, J. (2015). The political economy of precarious work in the tourism industry in small island developing states. *Review of International Political Economy*, 22(1), 194–223.

Leheny, D. (1995). A political economy of Asian sex tourism. *Annals of Tourism Research*, 22(2), 367–384.

McAffee, K. (2012). The contradictory logic of global ecosystem services markets. *Development and Change*, 43(1), 105–131.

McGehee, N., Lee, S., O'Bannon, T. L., & Perdue, R. R. (2010). Tourism-related social capital and its relationship with other forms of capital: An exploratory study. *Journal of Travel Research*, 49(4), 486–500.

Mosedale, J. (2015). Critical engagements with nature: Tourism, political economy of nature and political ecology. *Tourism Geographies*, 17(4), 505–510.

Mowforth, M., & Munt, I. (2015). *Tourism and Sustainability: Development, Globalisation and New Tourism in the Third World*. London: Routledge.

Nash, D. (1981). Tourism as an anthropological subject. *Current Anthropology*, 22(5), 461–481.

National Statistical Committee of the Republic of Belarus (2017). Tourism in the Republic of Belarus. Retrieved from www.belstat.gov.by/en/ofitsialnaya-statistika/social-sector/naselenie/turizm/operativnye-dannye_16/tourism-in-the-republic-of-belarus.

National Statistical Committee of the Republic of Belarus (2018). The development of tourism, the activities of tourism organizations, collective accommodation facilities of the Republic of Belarus for 2017. Retrieved from www.belstat.gov.by/ofitsialnaya-statistika/solialnaya-sfera/turizm/publikatsii_9/index_8622/.

O'Riordan, T., & Voisey, H. (1997). The political economy of sustainable development. *Environmental Politics*, 6(1), 1–23.

Poon, A. (1993). *Tourism, Technology and Competitive Strategies*. Boston, MA: CAB International.

Porter, M. (1998). Clusters and the new economics of competition. *Harvard Business Review*, 76(6), 77–90.

Rankin, J. (2016). EU lifts most sanctions against Belarus despite human rights concerns. *The Guardian*, February 15, 2016. Retrieved from https://www.theguardian.com/world/2016/feb/15/eu-lifts-most-sanctions-against-belarus-despite-human-rights-concerns

Republic of Belarus (2016). Belarus' social and economic development program for 2016–2020 enacted. Retrieved from www.belarus.by/en/government/documents/belarus-social-and-economic-development-program-for-2016-2020-enacted_i_0000050329.html.

Rostow, W. W. (1960). *The Stages of Economic Growth: A Non-communist Manifesto*. Cambridge: Cambridge University Press.

Slocum, S. L. (2017). Operationalising both sustainability and neo-liberalism in protected areas: Implications from the USA's National Park Service's evolving experiences and challenges. *Journal of Sustainable Tourism*, 25(12), 1848–1864.

Slocum, S. L. (2018). Developing social capital in craft beer tourism markets. In Slocum, S. L., Kline, C., & Cavaliere, C. T. (Eds.), *Craft Beverages and Tourism Volume 2: Environmental, Social and Marking Implications* (pp. 83–100), Switzerland: Palgrave Macmillan.

Slocum, S. L., & Curtis, K. R. (2018). *Food and Agricultural Tourism: Theory and Best Practice*. London: Routledge.

Spenceley, A. (2012). *Responsible Tourism: Critical Issues for Conservation and Development*. London: Routledge.

Tregear, A. (2003). From Stilton to Vimto: Using Food History to Re-think Typical Products in Rural Development. *Sociologia Ruralis*, 43(2), 91–107.

Wengle, S. (2017). *Plentiful Harvests in Eurasia: Why Some Farms in Russia, Ukraine, Belarus, and Armenia Are Thriving Despite Institutional Challenges*. PONARS Policy Memo No. 490.

World Bank (2017). Belarus Country Brief 2017. Retrieved from https://en.wikipedia.org/wiki/Economy_of_Belarus#cite_note-42.

World Travel and Tourism Council (2003). *Blueprint for New Tourism*. Oxford: WTCC.

World Travel and Tourism Council (2017). *Travel & Tourism Economic Impact 2017, Belarus*. Oxford: WTCC.

7 The importance of information and communication technology for dissemination, commercialization and local protagonism in community-based tourism initiatives

A case study of CBT in Castelhanos, Ilhabela, Brazil

Daniella S. Marcondes

Introduction

Cultural diversity and the natural beauty found in developing countries are factors that promote tourism in these destinations. In 2017, this amounted to approximately US$470 billion (UNWTO, 2018). Yet, despite the continued growth in revenues from tourism, its contribution to the development of the social aspects in these places is widely discussed (Inversini and Riga, 2016). Globally, in Asia, Africa and Latin America, most of these countries, as opposed to developed countries, are characterized by natural areas historically inhabited by marginalized populations with little political power (Diegues, 1993).

Similar to many destinations, tourism in the Brazilian coastal zone, internationally known for the sun and the beach, had the pillars of management planning focused on the economic and private property perspectives that triggered a series of negative impacts and consequent socio-environmental conflicts. These can be seen as based on the struggle of the local populations, in disagreement with the inequalities of development, by the control of the management of the services and resources of common use necessary for the maintenance of the associated traditional activities, that is to say, subsistence (Alier, 2017; Coriolano, 2006, 2012).

In this scenario, community-based tourism (CBT) presents itself as a management model with a coherent proposal to the principles of sustainable tourism. It stands out for differentiating its products, transforming them into experiences, reinforcing the characteristics of participation, conservation, social and cultural rescue (Bartholo, 2009). It is sustained by social, environmental and economic aspects that enhance traditional livelihoods, protect natural resources and generate income through low-impact experiences linked to the primary activities of the communities involved. Given this, CBT can be complementary to participative management based on community empowerment, where the actors become the protagonists of the decisions, promoting local engagement and resistance, influencing the formulation of public policies for the promotion of social and territorial development.

On the other hand, the growth of tourism with a more responsible premise and an increase in consumer awareness for engaging in actions related to environmental and social causes is notable worldwide (Bursztyn, 2014). In a recent survey commissioned by tourism agency Exodus Travels, 78% of respondents felt they are more aware than in the past decade and 91% said they consume trips where stakeholders are committed to ethical values.

Technological innovation involves socio-economic transformations that directly reflect the provision of services and productive processes in the most diverse segments. The United Nations (2004) developed an area of study (Information, Communication, Technology for Development – ICT4D) with the objective of analyzing how technology can contribute to the development of society and stimulate the use of ICT. In this perspective, meeting the current concerns of sustainability through the use of ICTs as a tool to reduce the gaps in social and territorial development in countries such as Brazil. This study has as a general objective to discuss how ICTs contribute to the process of promotion, commercialization and local protagonism at Castelhanos CBT, Ilhabela/SP – Brazil.

The main results on the discussion about the importance of ICT for CBT refer to a) the possibility of empowerment and protagonism of the local population; b) the strengthening and opportunity for success of CBT initiatives, and c) the reflexes it provides for the social and territorial development of the communities involved.

The specific objectives for this chapter are:

- To map the potential for the implementation of the E-Commerce systems within Castelhanos CBT;
- To identify the challenges of using ICTs in promoting and marketing the communitarian initiative.

Methodology

This study is based on the descriptive approach, using the case study method (Veal, 2011). The community initiative is located on the North Coast of the State of São Paulo and since 2017 has organized to develop more responsible tourism.

Literature review

The studies on CBT are recent, but they are gaining strength worldwide. For some authors, CBT is configured as a tourism modality, for others, a tourism segment or a territorial development model and also, for some even a management model. In this way, it can be said that there is a lack of consensus leading to the belief that the concept of CBT is still under construction and can be presented, depending on the segment, by using different terms (community-based tourism, community tourism, rural tourism), objectives and criteria (Fabrino, 2013; Maldonado, 2009).

In discussing the diversity of concepts and assumptions about CBT, Fabrino (2013) systematized terminologies and definitions presented by CBT stakeholders in Latin America – nongovernmental organizations, local initiatives, networks, government, associations and academia. Through this research, the author identified some components that permeate most of the concepts and premises discussed, such as aspects related to community organization, control and management, community participation, benefit generation and distribution, valuing the way of life and local culture, solidarity economy, incorporation of the environmental dimension, economic integration and interculturality.

In this study, we chose to present some concepts of CBT used in Brazil and with which we corroborate. Thus, from the point of view of tourism networks, the definition of Turisol Network mentions that CBT is presented as:

> Any form of business organization based on ownership of the territory and self-management of community and private resources with democratic practices and solidarity in the work and distribution of benefits generated through the provision of services aimed at cultural encounter with visitors.
>
> (REDE TURISOL apud CNPQ, 2012, p. 20)

Among many definitions in the literature, Maldonado (2009) presented a concept that includes the components mapped by Fabrino (2013) and, like Coriolano (2006), presents the concept with an approach that values the importance of the economic aspect and ownership of commonly used resources. For Maldonado (2009), community tourism is understood as:

> any form of business organization based on ownership and sustainable self-management of community assets, in accordance with practices of cooperation and equity in the work and distribution of the benefits generated by the provision of tourist services. The distinctive feature of community tourism is its human and cultural dimension, that is to say, anthropological, in order to encourage dialogue between equals and quality intercultural encounters with our visitors, with a view to knowing and learning with their respective ways of life.
>
> (Maldonado, 2009: 31)

According to Coriolano (2006), community tourism presents itself as: "a strategy of survival, and entry of those with the lowest economic conditions in the tourism production chain. A form of tourism that thinks of the place, the environmental conservation and the cultural resignificance "(Coriolano, 2006: 374). The author also identifies as a principle of CBT the need for communities to be organized in an associative way, having effective control of land and economic activities associated with tourism (Coriolano, 2009).

These definitions present a number of key elements and/or components that should be recognized in the CBT experiences, understanding that the role of the community is a fundamental element for the development of local initiatives regardless of their specific characteristics. With regard to the development of CBT, Bursztyn et al. (2009) comment on the need for public institutions to respond to the aspirations of society and add that it is a fundamental role of these to support local initiatives and monitor them. The authors also point out that CBT, as a tool that promotes authentic and participative experience, works towards the transformation of spaces through a situated economy, linking tourism to the continuum of traditional activities, social inclusion and territorial protection, and this reason requires the lower density of infrastructure and services in place of the valorization of the environments in which they are installed.

On the other hand, according to Maldonado (2009):

The globalization of tourism creates an important stimulus for communities, but also exerts strong pressure, particularly difficult to deal with by small businesses operating in isolation. Several studies have highlighted the severe restrictions that most communities face in the market, as they remain excluded from government institutions and discriminated against access to production resources, markets, business services and other incentives offered to the business strata. In particular, the deficit in education, vocational training, basic health services and road infrastructure is notorious. All this leads to a great instability and weak competitiveness of the community business.

(Maldonado, 2009, p. 31)

Among the shortcomings of the CBT offer systematized by Maldonado (2009), the main aspects are related to management, professionalism, deficiencies in communication mechanisms, information, commercial organization, uncertain positioning and poorly publicized image in markets and dynamic segments, and finally, the deficit of public services, which include communications and tourism signaling (Maldonado, 2009).

The challenges, mainly related to the communication and commercialization of the experiences of CBT, have been thoroughly discussed in forums dedicated to the theme and in the community tourism networks because they present themselves as fragilities and fundamental for economic viability and for the autonomy of the communities involved, as well as being among the causes of the mortality of CBT initiatives (Bursztyn and Bartholo, 2012).

In this case, the initiatives are located in rural areas, and as with most of the communities that organize for the CBT, the difficulty of obtaining access to the Internet network is a limiting factor, considering the importance of the availability of information for the development of tourism. Therefore, the facilitating role of the Internet and social media in the sale, promotion and marketing of tourism products is widely recognized. In this case, the lack of information can cause tourists to be unaware of the existence of many initiatives and/or do not feel safe to visit the destination.

It is through this context that many CBT initiatives begin to develop ICT–supported strategies to try to overcome such an obstacle, as investigated by Marcondes and Corrêa (2016) on the use of ICTs by local productive arrangements in the traditional Caiçara communities of Bonete and Castelhanos in Ilhabela, Brazil; by Cabanilla and Gentili (2015), who examined the Internet pages related to the provision of community tourism services in the American countries – Ecuador, Peru, South America, Guatemala, Costa Rica, Central America, Brazil, Canada, the United States, Nicaragua and Panama. Recently, Coutinho et al. (2015) analyzed 23 websites of Brazilian destinations that offer experiences of community tourism in order to evaluate their presence in the virtual space.

Case study – Castelhanos community-based tourism

In view of this, we intend to present a case study and discuss how ICTs contribute to the process of promotion, commercialization and local protagonism in Castelhanos Community-Based Tourism, Ilhabela/SP – Brazil.

Study area

The Ilhabela archipelago is located on the north coast of the State of São Paulo, with 34,750 ha of land, of which 27,025 ha are part of an Integral Protection Conservation Unit, Ilhabela State Park – PEIb, created in 1977. Most of the archipelago remains unoccupied, resulting in a rather low total population density of only 0.92 inhab/ha.

Of the 12 islands that make up the archipelago, only the islands of São Sebastião, Búzios and Vitória are inhabited. The Búzios and Vitória islands are part of the Caiçaras Traditional Communities. The island of São Sebastião is the largest of the archipelago and it houses, in its continental portion, the seat of the municipality – Ilhabela.

In the oceanic portion of the archipelago, there are 17 traditional Caiçaras communities and five are located inside the State Park of Ilhabela. Located to the east of São Sebastião Island, the Bay of Castelhanos houses the traditional communities, approximately 75 families, located on the beaches of Castelhanos, Mansa, Vermelha, Figueira and Saco do Sombrio. Saco do Sombrio and Figueira Beach are inserted in the territory protected by Ilhabela State Park.

Castelhanos Beach is the largest of all in the bay and the only one with access by the Castelhanos Park Road, which runs 18 kilometers along a dirt track inside the Conservation Unit. The other beaches and communities of the bay can be accessed by footpath or by sea, from Castelhanos Beach or the urban part of the island. Approximately two kilometers long, despite changes caused by colonial agricultural production, it has preserved characteristics, typical coastal plain vegetation and slopes covered with Atlantic Forest. It is formed by the segments: south, north and central and it houses a population of 124 inhabitants in 47 families, divided in the two Caiçaras villages – the Canto da Lagoa Community and Canto do Ribeirão, both located respectively in the south and north segments of the beach.

Map 7.1 Location of the Ilhabela archipelago

Source: Alain Briatte Mantchev, 2017

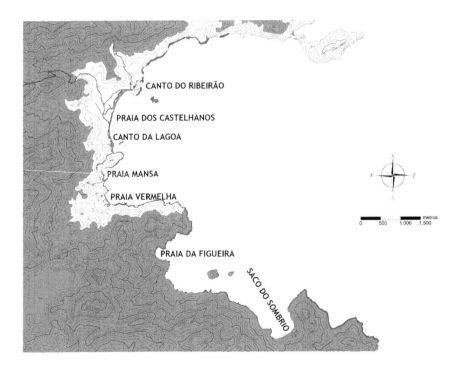

Map 7.2 Location of Castelhanos Beach in the bay of the same name

Source: Alain Briatte Mantchev, 2018

Like the other coastal Caiçaras villages, the traditional communities of Canto da Lagoa and Canto do Ribeirão were formed during the periods of retraction of agricultural production for export and resisted the partial isolation imposed by the distances and difficulties of displacement. The Caiçaras adapted their way of life to the resources of the forest and the sea, removing from the nature the sustenance of the family and the necessary utensils for reproduction of their culture.

Tourism in the Castelhanos Beach

It was in the mid-1950s and early 1960s, with the installation of the ferry and the construction of the Rio-Santos Highway, that tourism began to emerge as an economic alternative. Since the 1970s, Ilhabela has established itself as a tourism and residential tourism destination and is currently known worldwide for its scenic beauty and its beaches. In the last decade, with the facility offered with ICTs for the promotion and commercialization of the destination, the urban area of the island has been experiencing problems related to this centralized activity in the segment of sun and beach that has been strengthened over the decades, without much planning and control. A series of negative social impacts are seen as, for example, population growth, disorderly occupation, marginalization of the natives, the promotion of informal and precarious work, the multiplication of residential tourism that has generated high costs for the municipality for demanding the urban infrastructure that remains idle for most of the year, increasing deforestation and urban expansion works, the launch of illegal sewage, irregular occupations, mass tourism, unorganized visitation and the advance of large connected enterprises in the gas and oil chain (Ilhabela, 2015; Instituto Pólis, 2013).

In recent years, in the search to reduce the economic impacts that these developments have on businesses, tourism service providers have been creating new itineraries, in addition to those traditionally marketed, to include attractions in places with little anthropization, as in the case of the traditional communities of Caiçaras that are located in the rural area of the archipelago, in territories of little transformation and with a low supply of infrastructure.

On the other hand, the natural fragility of these areas where the traditional Caiçaras communities are inserted, together with their historical and cultural richness, bring to the fore the concern for sustainable development in order to avoid repetition of the decharacterization process applied on the oceanic face of the Island of São Sebastião, caused by the advance of the disordered tourism that left as inheritance the natural damages and the exclusion of the communities of its territories and the process of the tourism.

The traditional Caiçaras communities, located near the State Park of Ilhabela, are inserted in the so-called traditional territories that, due to the difficulty of access, have remained until a short time ago in isolation relative to the pressures of real estate speculation, and consequently, forgotten by the government. They are formed for Caiçaras villages that, for the most part, have as their main source of income fishing, family farming and handicrafts, but, more recently, tourism for some of these communities has begun to occupy a prominent place in the local economy.

Traditional dwellers, known as Caiçaras, have a peculiar way of life. Typical elements such as the canoe of vogue, which plays a fundamental role in the transport and flow of fish and the architecture of mudflats, typology of the housing culture that follows the centuries-old tradition of building with clay, constitute, alongside other aspects, the cultural landscape of the traditional Caiçaras communities of Ilhabela, the so-called traditional Caiçaras territories. The PNPCT (Política Nacional dos Povos e Comunidades Tradicionais) understands as traditional territories in Article 3 §1 "the spaces necessary for the cultural, social and economic reproduction of traditional peoples and communities, whether they are used permanently or temporarily" (Brazil, 2007).

The term Caiçara, of Tupi-Guarani origin, is used to identify the inhabitants of coastal communities in the states of Paraná, São Paulo and Rio de Janeiro (Adams, 2000). However, the main factor that characterizes these populations as Caiçaras is the way of life based on the organization of the system of production formed by the itinerant agricultural activities, subsistence fishing, the extractivism and handicraft, occupying some coastal areas of the Brazilian coast (Diegues and Arruda, 2000)

However, considering the pressure vectors presented earlier in this study, these traditional territories present themselves as potential "products" for commercial and real estate exploration of the private sector, and the hope of success for many tourism companies. It is in this context of management focused on the economistic view that the tourism activity in Castelhanos Beach increases exponentially, year by year, and jeopardizes the socio-environmental and cultural quality of the local population.

According to the Ilhabela Strategic Tourism Marketing Plan (2017), Castelhanos Beach occupies the sixth place in the ranking of visits in relation to the other attractions offered to tourists and consists of the second most visited beach in Ilhabela, receiving 17% of the interviewees (Ilhabela, 2017). The tourists, who come from national and international destinations, visit the beach all year round. However, it is during the summer season of the Southern Hemisphere that the activity appears in the local economy, generating more jobs in the beach restaurants, as well as warming the fishing market and the local handicraft.

Since the 1990s, studies (São Paulo, 1992; Pirró, 2002, 2004, 2008, 2010; Noffs, 2007) have pointed to tourism and residential tourism as potential economic activities in Castelhanos Beach. They recorded the incipient flow of the first tourists of the 1970s and 1980s – adventurers who enjoyed the adventure along the dirt road and the deserted beach, and who spent the day and/or camped in the backyards of Caiçaras. By this time, most of the properties had been sold and the Caiçaras worked as landlords of lands that no longer belonged to them. Thus, tourism in Castelhanos Beach, as in the rest of the coast, followed the "vocation" of conventional sun and beach tourism, and in the 1990s, the jeep visit to the Castelhanos became mandatory.

The same studies registered the arrival of exogenous actors who saw in the absence of food infrastructure an opportunity and increased the script with the installation of beach kiosks. In this way, in a short time, tourism activity – initially aimed in meeting a small demand – with the growth of demand and the consequent increase of 4×4 tourism operators that was strengthened in the 2000s, involving other actors and becoming an economic activity of relevance to the municipality. In a decade, in-home and restaurant service jobs have increased. To the space that was previously disputed by Caiçaras, squatters and speculators were added new stakeholders, such as jipeiros, hoteliers, receptive agencies and owners of local trades. With no experience and infrastructure to work directly with tourism, Caiçaras adapted to the new economic activity offering their camping grounds and fresh fish in small beach restaurants (Noffs, 2007).

As of 2010, there has been an increase in the pressure on tourism activity due to improvements in the access route, the increase in the supply of tourism operators and the advertising by operators, tourists and municipal public authorities, which has completely changed the tourism in Castelhanos Beach. Currently, there are 97 jeeps (2017/2018 season) registered to operate on the Castelhanos State Park Road. According to data collected by Ilhabela State Park, Castelhanos Beach receives, on average, 80,000 tourists/year. From 2013, restaurants owned by exogenous actors expanded the service structure to absorb the growing flow of tourism that arrives via State Park Road and, more recently, by sea (Marcondes, 2018).

The model day trip that was developed is based on the number of visitors and started to generate a series of conflicts related to the socio-environmental transformations and way of life of the Caiçara community. The growth of conventional tourism has proved ineffective in the financial empowerment of local Caiçaras. Trade remains concentrated in the hands of the same outsider protagonists of the previous decades and to the local residents the benefits are reduced, characterizing the exogenous and excluding character of the practiced tourism.

In Castelhanos, the tourist operation follows the same criteria of mass tourism that creates standard models. The absence of integrated planning for the commercial exploitation of local attractions, a factor that polarizes segregation and marginalizes the community, jeopardizes the local environment, and is incapable of generating improvements and quality of life for local actors.

In general, tourism has not generated positive impacts on social and territorial development, with deficiencies such as lack of investments in basic infrastructure, education, health, access, communication, professional qualification and development of public policies based on the definition of guidelines and actions aimed at an agenda for participatory and inclusive tourism development that values traditional knowledge associated with the empowerment of local actors (Marcondes, 2018).

For Oliveira (2009), there are many challenges for tourism in traditional communities, and due to the absence of regulatory instruments of public power tourism is, on the one hand, an opportunity for income for these populations and, on the other hand, it presents itself as a threat to their way of life (Oliveira, 2009).

This scenario of concentrating the provision of tourism services primarily in the hands of exogenous groups and the consequences reflected in the reduction of land and sea areas fundamental to the exercise of traditional activities linked to fishing, increased pollution of natural resources and the emergence of social problems force, once again, the social and economic reorganization of the Caiçaras directly affected with conventional tourism and its exclusive benefits.

Despite the rapid development of tourism, especially since the beginning of the 2000s, as explained previously, the traditional communities of the Bay of Castelhanos still preserve much of the culture and way of life at its roots. In this context, in 2017, provoked by external agents, these Caiçara communities organized themselves to participate in the Community Based Tourism Project in the Castelhanos: strengthening and sustainable development. Idealized by a multidisciplinary group of volunteer technicians, the objective was to bring the concepts and practices of CBT to the communities and to identify the local potentialities, to promote the appreciation of the associated traditional knowledge for the generation of income, to spread sustainable tourism, to promote and commercialize the CBT and, last but not least, to stimulate the leading role in the local development process.

Castelhanos community-based tourism and information and communication technologies (ICTs) in the local scene

After almost 10 years of the beginning of the discussions on the relevance of the strengthening of the traditional Caiçaras communities of Ilhabela for local development, through the valorization of initiatives of CBT, the theme was contemplated in public policies in the local scope.

The project was formed by several professionals who work on initiatives linked to sustainable tourism in Ilhabela and at national level and, through the partnership between these liberal professionals, the Association Amor Castelhanos and Castelhanos Vive and Ilhabela Convention & Visitors Bureau under my coordination.

However, in spite of this stimulating scenario, little was done regarding the planning of strategies and actions at the real implementation of these programs aimed at the inclusion and participation of Caiçara communities in the decision-making process in their territories, as in the case presented in this study, regarding the discussion of alternatives to tourism practiced in Castelhanos Beach.

In this scenario, in order to initiate a movement that would demonstrate to local managers the need for greater community participation in the tourism processes in traditional territories, to involve and develop together with the Caiçaras aspects foreseen in public policies, I coordinated a proposal to discuss with the community of Castelhanos Beach the principles of CBT, highlighting the importance of the protagonist role of Caiçaras for territorial development – the Castelhanos Community-Based Tourism Project: strengthening the local development.

There were approximately five months of weekly meetings planned in thematic modules. The main topics covered were: concepts and principles of CBT, exchange of experiences with Quilombo do Campinho, participatory construction of the desired tourism proposal, identification of attractions and services with elaboration of the respective descriptions, safety and tourism activities in natural areas, pricing of experiences and services, mapping of community actors, procedure of management and operationalization, dissemination and commercialization of CBT, preparation of manual of good conducts for community and tourists and the creation of the Center of Community Based Tourism and its Internal Regulation that determines, between other aspects, the administration of the Tourism Fund, the logistics and the general operation.

During these meetings, the potentialities, weaknesses and challenges for the management, commercialization and operationalization of CBT were also mapped in the extremely crowded territory by mass tourism managed by exogenous actors and external investors. In the community context, the Caiçaras were involved in conflicts arising from the increase in tourism visitation, the strengthening of outsourced enterprises, the increase in the number of 4×4 operators, the difficulties of regularization and implementation of a parking area, conflicts arising from land regularization process of the marine areas (Term of Authorization for Sustainable Use), as well as the absence of the State in what concerns the provision of basic rights.

The communities of Castelhanos Bay, three nearby beaches, the Ribeirão, Lagoa and Mansa villages, totaling 15 people, involved in the construction of the proposals, participated in these meetings. With regard to the technicians, all volunteers, they formed a multidisciplinary team with professionals from the areas of Law, Designer, Journalism, Tourism, Business Administration, Architecture, Forestry Engineering and Geography.

As a product of this first stage, scripts were developed focusing on the socioeconomic and cultural experience of the community. Among the experiences they have offered are a conversation with the elders, fishing net workshops and the production of bamboo balloons, boat trips and observation of traditional activities such as visit to the fishnet enclosures, besides the services such as lodging and food options.

The result of any process, built by the community in a participatory and horizontal way, was systematized and transformed into the Castelhanos community-based tourism website (www.castelhanos.org) and, also as part of this initial phase, through the website the initiative was invited to participate in trade fairs and tourism events to share the challenges and successes faced so far.

With regard to the contribution of ICTs to the process of strengthening CBT in Castelhanos, one can identify that the website and social media play an important role in increasing community participation.

During the year 2018, the dissemination of Castelhanos CBT was based on the spontaneous media on the Internet and on the website and social media resources. The use of images and videos on Instagram and Facebook was appreciated by the followers and widely shared, helping more people to know the initiative. A volunteer consultancy specialist in communication and marketing in sustainable tourism (Viajar Verde) produced press releases and campaigns on social media, a factor that promoted the initiative and undoubtedly stimulated the spontaneous media. The website contributed to generate spontaneous media with approximately 40 articles published in newspapers, blogs and magazines disseminating the experiences.

The website played a fundamental role in the provision of information and supported the sale of the experiences, both in terms of guaranteeing the security that tourists value and also by giving credibility to the service offered by presenting the Castelhanos CBT proposals, as well as who are the main actors. It was verified in that period that the website played a relevant role in the dissemination of the scripts and brought the consumers closer to the Caiçara community, eliminating the need for "middlemen".

At that time, the commercialization of the experiences and services was done through the technical team, via e-mail and bank deposit. This dynamic was due to the difficulty of access to the Internet and telecommunications network on the Castelhanos Bay and, as a consequence of the low community training, a condition that reinforced the need to qualify a community to exercise the management of the initiative.

The start of operation of the first roadmaps confirmed the requirement for continuous adjustments on several fronts, including on the website. The first challenges came with the need to train local actors to take over the management, dissemination and commercialization of CBT, and not least, to find alternatives to boost sales.

During the operation and with the accumulation of the experience of the sales dynamics, it was verified that some technological resources could be implemented in the website aiming to offer autonomy and protagonism to the community. In this way, the use of ICTs with the development of e-commerce facilitated the commercialization procedure and, at the beginning of 2019, the management of the CBT was officially assumed by a community that became responsible for the logistics of the operation, commercialization and financial management of the Castelhanos CBT.

The new website is made up of information that helps tourists to format their own itineraries. It has options for activities, including lodging and meals. With the e-commerce tool, the dynamics of the sale will be as follows: the tourist should choose the experiences and services and make the online payment by the platform itself. The management of Castelhanos CBT will receive a message of confirmation request and, through the cellular device, may release the sale. This tool cauterizes the problem of the low supply of Internet, because it does not require the dynamics of the pre-sale and places the Caiçara as protagonist of the process.

It is believed that, with e-commerce and the dissemination of complete information in the English and Portuguese languages, the Caiçara community will have the autonomy to market its product to tour operators and independent tourists in the national and international market.

The benefits of e-commerce are also related to the maintenance of the proposal of sustainable tourism and conservation of natural resources by establishing the limited supply in the experiences and respecting the capacity of support in each activity.

Because it was an initiative developed without any type of financial resources, it is clear that its success rests exclusively on community organization and autonomy, and on the capacity to commercialize the services and experiences offered.

Therefore, the implementation of e-commerce increases the potential for competitiveness and enables the increase of sales. Thus, the use of ICTs in the promotion and commercialization of the community initiative has contributed to address weaknesses related to the educational training gap.

Among the challenges faced is restricted access to the Internet in most rural communities, as seen on the beach of Castelhanos. The lack of government investment in setting up networks supports the exclusion of market-based CBT initiatives.

Thus, in an attempt to alleviate these shortcomings, an alternative is the use of ICTs, such as the implementation of e-commerce, which, on the other hand, regrettably eliminates the pre-sale of CBT initiatives, an aspect that should be valued.

Financial resources and communication specialists are substantial elements in the production of information and content for dissemination and marketing. The absence of these entails the misuse of the Internet and social media and may lead to negative consequences in the commercialization of the initiative. In the case of Castelhanos CBT the technical support to feed networks and to elaborate content in the initial phase was valuable, however the discontinuity in the actions can be perceived with the sales decline.

In this way, it can be observed that the possibilities of including ICTs for such initiatives, despite obstacles such as access to the Internet and low educational training, strengthen a range of other aspects related to the community's local management and territorial development.

Results

CBT is interlinked with other elements such as education, health and the environment. In this sense, the initiatives, as presented in this study, are not exclusively dedicated to tourism, but rather to the strengthening of aspects related to the valorization of culture and way of life, representing a proposal for territorial development.

In this way, ICTs can contribute as tools to facilitate the development of cases such as the Castelhanos CBT that aims at the convergence between valuing the way of life, the balance of economic, social and environmental dimensions, empowerment, community organization and protagonism.

This differentiation in the type of experience and service offered makes it profitable because it attributes more value to the commercialized product, while at the same time it compares with conditioning factors of the behavior of the postmodern tourist. However, the most significant contributions can be demonstrated through strengthening and social organization, participation in decision-making processes, inclusion in the benefits of tourism and, finally, in the traditional territory.

The CBT aims for the organizational strengthening of the Caiçaras and, therefore, faces the consequences of the insertion of these territories in the capitalist modes of production. The process of implementation of Castelhanos CBT has sought to be the answer to the beginning of the transition from conventional tourism to the local associative development that guarantees permanence in the lands and the valuation of the associated traditional knowledge (Marcondes, 2018).

The results of the last year were the involvement of approximately 20 community members, the achievement of the management and operation of a parking area with the purpose of restricting the entry of vehicles on the beach, a greater articulation of power for the formulation of public policies, the establishment of partnerships with tourism operators to meet CBT demands such as translators, and the appreciation of the culture and importance of Caiçara and its role in local development.

ICTs, in turn, offer the possibility for this political and social movement to be known and recognized. It is a catalyst in the capacity to engage people – tourists, partners, governments, community – and, because they present themselves as instruments of promotion and commercialization, they offer possibilities for community protagonism in territorial development, given the limited options historically available to rural communities.

References

Adams, Cristina. As populações e o mito do bom selvagem: a necessidade de uma nova abordagem interdisciplinar. *Revista de Antropologia*, São Paulo: USP, vol. 43, n. 1, 2000a. p. 145–182.

Alier, J. M. O ecologismo dos pobres: conflitos ambientais e linguagens de valoração. 2ª ed., São Paulo: Contexto, 2017.

Bartholo, R. Sobre o sentido da proximidade: implicações sobre um turismo situado de base comunitária. In: Bartholo, R.; Sansolo, D. G.; Bursztyn, I. (Org.). *Turismo de base comunitária: diversidade de olhares e experiências brasileiras*. Rio de Janeiro: Letra e Imagem, 2009. pp. 45–54.

Brasil, Decreto 6.040 de 7 de fevereiro de 2007. Institui a Política Nacional de Desenvolvimento Sustentável dos Povos e Comunidades Tradicionais.

Brasil, Lei nº 13.123 de 20 de maio de 2015. Regulamenta o inciso II do § 1º e § 4º do art. 225 da Constituição Federal, o Artigo 1º, a alínea j do Artigo 8º, a alínea c do Artigo 10º, o Artigo 15º e os §§ 3º e 4º do Artigo 16º da Convenção sobre Diversidade Biológica, promulgada pelo Decreto nº 2.519, de 16 de março de 1998; dispõe sobre o acesso ao patrimônio genético, sobre a proteção e o acesso ao conhecimento tradicional associado e sobre a repartição de benefícios para conservação e uso sustentável da biodiversidade; revoga a Medida Provisória nº 2.186–16, de 23 de agosto de 2001; e dá outras providências. 2015.

Bursztyn, I.; Bartholo. O processo de comercialização do turismo de base comunitária no Brasil: desafios, potencialidades e perspectivas. *Sustentabilidade em Debate*, v. 3, n. 1, pp. 97–116, 2012.

Bursztyn, I. Comercialização no turismo de base comunitária: inovar é preciso! In: Costa Novo, C. Barroncas; Cruz, Jocilene (Org.). *Turismo comunitário: reflexões no contexto amazônico.* Manaus: Edua, 2014. pp. 41–77.

Bursztyn, I.; Bartholo, R.; Delamaro, M. Turismo para quem? Sobre caminhos de desenvolvimento e alternativas para o Brasil. In: Bartholo, R.; Sansolo, D. G.; Bursztyn, I. (Org.). *Turismo de base comunitária: diversidade de olhares e experiências brasileiras.* Rio de Janeiro: Letra e Imagem, 2009. pp. 76–91.

Cabanilla, E. A.; Gentili, J. O. Características de las páginas de la Internet de turismo comunitario en países de América. *PASOS. Revista de Turismo y Património Cultural,* v. 13, n. 1, pp. 157–174, 2015.

CNPQ – Conselho Nacional de Desenvolvimento Científico. Relatório Técnico: Turismo de base comunitária no Brasil: consolidação de instrumento de análise e avaliação na perspectiva da sustentabilidade. Edital chamada MCTI/CNPq/MEC/CAPES n 18, 2012.

Coriolano, Luzia N. M. T. A contribuição do turismo ao desenvolvimento local. In: Portuguez, A. P.; Seabra, G.; Queiroz, O. T. M. M. (Org.). *Turismo, espaço e estratégias de desenvolvimento local.* João Pessoa: UFPB, 2012. pp. 61–70.

Coriolano, Luzia N. M. T. Turismo: prática social de apropriação e de dominaçãode territórios. In: Lemos, A. I. G. de; Arroyo, M.; Silveira, M. L. *América Latina: cidade, campo e turismo.* Consejo Latinoamericano de Ciencias Sociales – CLACSO. São Paulo, 2006.

Coriolano, Luzia N. M. T. et al. *Arranjos produtivos locais do turismo comunitário: atores e cenários em mudança.* Fortaleza: Ed. UECE, 2009. 312 p.

Costa Novo, Cristiane M. B. *Turismo comunitário: um olhar sobre a região metropolita de Manaus.* Manaus: UEA Edições, 2015.

Coutinho, G. C. T. P.; Thomaz, G. M.; Sampaio, C. A. C. Turismo comunitário e internet: análise dos sites das experiências no Brasil. *Caderno Virtual de Turismo.* Rio de Janeiro, v. 15, n. 1, pp. 35–51, 2015.

Diegues, A. C. *Populações tradicionais em unidades de conservação: o mito moderno da natureza intocada.* n. 1. São Paulo: NUPAUB – USP, 1993. (Série documentos e relatórios de pesquisa).

Diegues, A. C.; Arruda, R. S. V. (Org.). *Saberes tradicionais e biodiversidade no Brasil.* São Paulo: NUPAUB – USP: MMA, 2000.

Fabrino, Nathália H. *Turismo de base comunitária: dos conceitos às práticas e das práticas aos conceitos.* 2013. Dissertação (Mestrado em Desenvolvimento Sustentável). Centro de Desenvolvimento Sustentável. Universidade de Brasília.

Ilhabela. Lei Municipal nº 421 de 2006. Dispõe sobre a instituição do plano diretor de desenvolvimento socioambiental do município de Ilhabela e dá outras providências.

Ilhabela. Secretaria de Desenvolvimento Econômico e do Turismo. *Plano Gestor de Turismo de Ilhabela,* 2015.

Ilhabela. Secretaria de Desenvolvimento Econômico e do Turismo. *Plano de Marketing Turístico Estratégico de Ilhabela,* 2017.

Ilhabela. Secretaria Municipal de Meio Ambiente. Conselho Municipal de Meio Ambiente. *Plano Municipal de Conservação e Recuperação da Mata Atlântica,* 2015.

Instituto Pólis. Litoral Sustentável: desenvolvimento com inclusão social. Diagnóstico urbano socioambiental: município de Ilhabela. Relatório n. 6, fev. 2013.

Instituto Socioambiental Guapuruvu. *Relatório técnico-científico sobre a comunidade tradicional caiçara residente na Baía dos Castelhanos.* Ilhabela, 2014.

Inversini, A.; Riga, I. E-Tourism for socio-economic development. *Symphonya Emerging Issues in Management,* n. 1, pp. 75–82, 2016.

Inversini, A.; Riga, I.; Pereira, I.; Bartholo, R. The rising for e-Tourism for development. In: Tussyadiah, I.; Inversini, A. (eds.). *Information and Communication Technologies in Tourism*. Switzerland: Springer International Publishing, 2015.

LTDS, Laboratório de Tecnologia e Desenvolvimento Social. *Relatório Técnico: Marco Referencial Teórico para o Turismo de Base Comunitária*. Rio de Janeiro: PEP/ COPPE/ UFRJ, 2011.

Maldonado, C. O turismo rural comunitário na América Latina: gênesis, características e políticas. In: Bartholo, R.; Sansolo, D. G.; Bursztyn, I. (Orgs.). *Turismo de base comunitária: Diversidade de olhares e experiências brasileiras*. Rio de Janeiro: Letra e Imagem, 2009. pp. 25–44.

Marcondes, D.; Corrêa, C. H. W. Tecnologias da Informação e Comunicação na promoção de empreendimentos locais nas comunidades tradicionais caiçaras de Ilhabela. *Caderno Virtual de Turismo*. Rio de Janeiro, v. 16, n. 2, p. 168–182, ago. 2016.

Marcondes, Daniella S. Os conflitos decorrentes do veraneio e do turismo sobre o território tradicional caiçara na Praia de Castelhanos a partir da década de 1950. 2018. Dissertação (Mestrado em Ciências). Programa de Pós-Graduação em Turismo. Escola de Artes, Ciências e Humanidades, Universidade de São Paulo – EACH/USP.

Noffs, Paulo da Silva. *A disputa pela hegemonia do espaço na Baía dos Castelhanos*. Tese (Doutorado). FFLCH – USP, 2007.

Oliveira, A. C. Turismo e população dos destinos turísticos: um estudo de casodo planejamento turístico da Vila de Trindade – Paraty/RJ. In: Bartholo, R.; Sansolo, D. G.; Bursztyn, I. (Org.). *Turismo de base comunitária: diversidade de olhares e experiências brasileiras*. Rio de Janeiro: Letra e Imagem, 2009. pp. 319–333.

Pirró, M. S. A. *A Baía dos Castelhanos e seus lugares: um olhar para o lugar*. 2004. 190 p. Trabalho de Graduação Individual – Departamento Di Geografia, FFLCH – USP, 2004.

Pirró, M. S. A. *Práticas de pesquisa de campo com comunidades tradicionais: contribuições para a gestão participativa no arquipélago de Ilhabela*. 2010. Dissertação (Mestrado em Geografia). Universidade de São Paulo, São Paulo.

Pirró, M. S. A. *Relatório Socioambiental das Comunidades Tradicionais Caiçaras do Arquipélago de Ilhabela (SP): impactos do de saneamento ambiental nas comunidades contempladas*. Ilhabela: Projeto Bela Ilha, 2008.

Pirró, M. S. A & Mattos, M. F. *Ilhabela: Diagnóstico Sócio-Econômico e Ambiental das Comunidades Isoladas*. São Paulo. Trabalho de Iniciação a Pesquisa. Departamento de Geografia, FFLCH – USP, 2002.

São Paulo (Estado). *Secretaria do Meio Ambiente. Coordenadoria de Planejamento Ambiental Estratégico e Educação Ambiental. Zoneamento Ecológico-Econômico: litoral norte de São Paulo*. São Paulo: SMA/CPLEA, 2005b. 56 p.

São Paulo (Estado). *Secretaria do Meio Ambiente. Fundação para Conservação e a Produção Florestal do Estado de São Paulo*. Plano de Manejo do Parque Estadual de Ilhabela, 2015.

São Paulo (Estado). *Secretaria do Meio Ambiente. Instituto Florestal*. Diagnóstico Socioeconômico e Ambiental de Ilhabela, 1992.

United Nations. Partnership for Development: Information and Knowledge for Development in United Nations Conference on Trade and Development, São Paulo, 13–18 June, 2004.

Veal, A. J. *Metodologia de pesquisa em lazer e turismo*. São Paulo: Aleph, 2011. Série Turismo.

Sítios eletrônicos

IBGE (Instituto Brasileiro de Geografia e Estatística). 2018. Disponível em: <http://cidades.ibge.gov.br>. Acesso em: 16 fev. 2018.

UNWTO (World Tourism Organization). 2019. Disponível em: <www.e-unwto.org>. Acesso em: 04 fev. 2019. Tourism Highlights 2018 Edition.

8 Community-based tourism

Planning processes and outcomes in the developing world

Adenike Adebayo, Peter Robinson and Ade Oriade

Introduction

The growth of tourism in many developing countries necessitates more than ever before that the local community that host tourists benefits from such development. Tourism development has been criticised for causing negative environmental, social impacts, as well as economic leakage in host communities in the developing world (Novelli and Gebhardt, 2007). This sometimes happens when government agencies or international organisations manage tourism development projects in local communities without residents' involvement. A call to allow local community involvement in tourism development has led to the adoption of a community-based approach to tourism development, which was pioneered by Murphy (1985). Such an approach can ensure that tourism development is sustainable because the host community can play a vital role in the planning processes (Murphy, 1985; Bramwell, 2004).

It has been discussed that local communities often lack the material, human and financial resources to help themselves in tourism development which accounts for why the state is involved in the first instance (Sofield, 2003). For community participation to be successful it is essential that they get the necessary support from other stakeholders in the tourism industry.

This chapter discusses community-based tourism (CBT), planning processes and outcomes in the developing world. It begins with the description of CBT, followed by a discussion of four distinct but connected topics. The chapter starts by exploring community participation and empowerment, which is crucial to CBT processes. The chapter then turns to the tourism resource base, often used in CBT projects. The way resources can be managed in a sustainable way, as one of the outcomes of CBT, is also emphasised. The need for CBT projects to be supported by stakeholders is then highlighted. The chapter closes with the case study of Zambia to discuss the practicality of CBT processes and outcomes.

Community-based tourism (CBT)

Community-based tourism (CBT) emerged as an alternative to conventional mass tourism. This has been adopted in tourism scholarship, especially in rural tourism development. This is due to the increasing awareness of the way tourism affects the wider community negatively without delivering benefit to them, which has led to a growth in participatory, community-oriented approaches to tourism planning (Mair and Reid, 2007; Hübner et al., 2014). CBT aims to promote community development by combining income generation, social inclusion, gender equity, and environmental sustainability (Burgos and Mertens, 2017). It is recognised as an appropriate approach to community development, as it can promote community empowerment as well as social and environmental sustainability (Okazaki, 2008). Development agencies increasingly use CBT as a strategy to diversify product for community development, particularly in rural areas characterised by limited alternatives for economic growth (Novelli, 2015).

Community-based tourism (CBT) has been defined in different ways, and there is no agreed-upon definition. CBT describes alternative forms of tourism development which maximise local benefits and advocate capacity building and empowerment as a means of achieving community development objectives (Tolkach and King, 2015). It is an approach to tourism development for the sustainable economy that involves the community in decision-making processes, primarily related to the acquisition of income, employment, and the preservation of the environment, and culture of the indigenous people (Sunuantari, 2017). CBT acknowledges the need for the community members to have the opportunity to have a voice in tourism development (Grybovych et al., 2011). Further, it is a community development tool that strengthens the ability of rural communities to manage tourism resources while ensuring community participation (Hamzah and Khalifah, 2009). Because of its ability to generate income for the local community, it becomes a tool for poverty reduction, and it is also aimed at reducing the negative impact that characterises tourism development (Novelli and Gebhardt, 2007).

CBT uses the resource base of the community, both cultural and natural, for tourism activities in order to:

- Promote socio-economic development and provide local people with sources of income;
- Encourage community commitment to conservation of biodiversity and sustainable management of natural resources base;
- Involve people in the process of their own development and give them more opportunities to participate effectively in development activities (Naguran, 1999: 41–42).

The institutional structure in any given country is central to determining how CBT will be allowed to operate and whether rural development is incorporated into the broader development strategy. An institutional arrangement is essential to stakeholders' interaction and partnership as it influences policy directions (Naguran, 1999; Hall, 2007) and the design and implementation of community-based projects (Naguran, 1999). Murphy's (1985) community-based approach to tourism, however, did not address the issues of power distribution to the local community to allow them to participate in tourism development (Hall, 2007). An institutional arrangement is vital as developing countries are characterised by the history of a centralised system of government where only the national government can undertake tourism development (Tosun, 2000; Nelson, 2012). Often what happens is that the community is presented with tourism plans that would have been done by the government which they may not be able to say no to (Arnstein, 1969; Tosun, 1999, 2000; Hall, 2007), rather than allowing them to take ownership of such processes.

Case study

In Zambia, sustainable tourism development has been linked to other relevant ministries, and they all have a role to play in ensuring that the objectives are met.

The driving force behind utilising the community as an appropriate framework for planning for tourism development is because it is assumed to be the closest to the people (Hall, 2007). A general belief that has prevailed is that CBT offers considerable opportunities for marginal communities to participate in the tourism industry (Spenceley and Meyer, 2012) and to benefit from tourism projects (Thompson et al., 2010). CBT gives opportunities for the local community to gain economic benefits, alternative livelihood and affords them the opportunity to participate in decision-making (Novelli, 2015).

CBT can be a means for meeting the needs and aspirations of the community through their active participation in tourism planning and development processes (Oriade and Evans, 2011). When local communities are involved in the planning process, it ensures that development plans respond to their needs and such plans will receive the support of the community in project implementation (Grybovych et al., 2011). Also, the CBT approach to development facilitates community support for tourism development. When tourism planning does not take into consideration the needs of the host community, they are likely to frustrate the implementation of tourism projects (Grybovych et al., 2011).

Notwithstanding the benefits of CBT as highlighted in the literature, it is not without its own criticisms as an approach to development. Tosun and Jenkins (1998) argue that planning approaches that advocate community participation were formulated for the developed world, and may not apply to the situation in the developing world (Tosun and Jenkins, 1998). Further, the likelihood of implementing community participation has been doubted by researchers for reasons such as being time consuming, difficult to achieve with lack of education, lack of financial assistance and conflicting vested interests of those who participate (Okazaki, 2008). Again, such an approach is often ineffective due to the high transaction costs involved in getting the programme started and also maintained (Okazaki, 2008). To this end Malek et al. (2017) conclude that the development of tourism with regards to local community involvement is indeed a complex and delicate process because of the inherent fragility of territorial environment, socio-economic and cultural balances.

With CBT, power is not often distributed evenly within a community as some individuals have the ability to exert greater control over tourism planning than others through their access to knowledge, finance, time resources and expertise to be involved in such processes (Hall, 2007). Again, communities are unlikely to benefit from tourism if they do not have sufficient understanding of how the industry functions, or how to attract tourists and manage the industry (Spenceley and Meyer, 2012). This necessitates that local communities need to be trained to enable them to manage tourism activities. According to Tosun (2000), for local people to participate actively in tourism, training is an essential element, which must be tailored to the needs of the community and the type of CBT project to be developed.

Although authors criticise community participation for the high operation costs in terms of time and financial resources, what is more obvious is a dearth of experience and/or education among planners and other industry stakeholders on how to involve local communities in tourism development (Hamzah and Khalifah, 2009; Lindström and Larson, 2016). Despite the mixed views on the benefits of CBT and its practical applications, CBT continues to be promoted as a tool for poverty reduction, environmental conservation and community development (Novelli, 2015).

Community participation and empowerment

For long-term sustainability of tourism, it is essential that local community members participate and are empowered. Also, because community participation is an integral part of CBT development and management a crucial element for CBT, success is management and empowerment of local community members. CBT often requires community participation in the decision-making process, management and distribution of tourism-related activities and operations, and it ensures a degree of ownership by the community in the development process and operations (Naguran, 1999; Timothy, 1999; Dodds, 2007). Local community participation is inevitable in sustainable tourism development (Mowforth and Munt, 2009). A CBT project can be successful when it fosters community participation, equilibrium and cohesion (Kibicho, 2008). Through CBT, community members can become more united as they all work together to achieve a common goal.

Empowerment is much broader than local community involvement because it gives control to the local people. One essential benefit of a CBT approach to development is that it empowers the local community (Dodds et al., 2016). Empowerment of local communities in tourism development is crucial to realising sustainable tourism development that takes into consideration the socio-economic and political environment of communities (Sofield, 2003). Community-based conservation and sustainable management can empowerment the poor and provide incomes for them (Thompson et al., 2010).

In empowerment discussion, what is uncertain is the degree to which the local communities should be self-reliant for it to be said that empowerment has occurred. Some authors believe the community should be in total control on one end of the spectrum, others on the other end believe the control should be with minimal outside involvement. However, a challenge in community tourism development in developing countries where communities lack the resources and capacity to help themselves is that such programmes may fail without assistance from the national government (Sofield, 2003), the private sector, civil society bodies, non-governmental organisations (NGOs), research and educational institutions (UNWTO, 2013). This shows the need for stakeholders' participation. The role of government in supporting CBT is critical given the vulnerability of poor communities, and many factors that constrain them (Novelli, 2015). To facilitate CBT, the stakeholders in the public sector, NGOs, the private sector and the local communities should work together (López-guzmán and Sánchez-cañizares, 2011).

A community can be economically empowered when their incomes are being enhanced, and lasting employment is generated, where the economic benefits of tourism development are shared equitably among the community as a whole, and where the local community retains access rights to the community's resource base (Garrod, 2003).

Scheyvens (1999, 2002) provided some dimensions of community empowerment that tourism development can bring to the local community; they include economic, psychological, social and political (Scheyvens, 1999, 2002). For the economic dimension, tourism development should bring lasting economic gains to the entire local community; cash earned through tourism should be shared between many households in the community (Scheyvens, 2002). Psychological empowerment refers to the increased self-esteem of community members as a result of developing pride in their culture and natural resources. Social empowerment is when cohesion and equilibrium of the local community are enhanced through working together to promote tourism and the money earned is used to improve living conditions of the people, for example to build schools and other amenities in the community. Finally, political empowerment allows community members to be involved in the tourism decision-making (Scheyvens, 2002).

Tourism resource base

CBT development is based on the assets of the local community: their natural environment, infrastructure, facilities, and unique cultural events or festivals (Murphy, 1985; Sunuantari, 2017). Most tourist products are developed around the natural resource base, the cultural product, the family product and other affordable attractions (Van Der Merwe & Van Niekerk, 2013). Tourism development depends ultimately upon the environment (Holden, 2000). CBT projects should be oriented towards protecting and managing the resources in local communities. Therefore, the cooperation of the host community is essential to access and develop these assets appropriately (Murphy, 1985; Sunuantari, 2017).

In CBT projects it is essential to maintain and take proper care of the tourism resource base. One cannot ignore the resource base which forms the raison d'etre for tourism if it is to be understood and managed for the benefit of the society (Murphy, 1985). Tourism development must strive to protect its attractions to make visitor experiences enjoyable, whether they be natural or human-made (Murphy, 1985). In fact, the competitiveness of destinations in developing countries depends on a combination of the natural resource base, which makes a destination attractive to visitors in the first place, and the ability of the destination to effectively mobilise and deploy this resource base (Crouch 2000 cited in Scheyvens and Russell, 2009). The resource base is more important if the major attraction is a public amenity, used for the public good (Murphy, 1985).

Because of the dependence of tourism development on the natural and cultural resources of local communities, the need to maintain resources sustainably in developing a CBT project becomes inevitable. The subject of sustainable development is the focus of the next section.

Sustainable development

As most CBT projects are small scale, they encourage sustainable development and local community involvement. Tourism activity is integral to the development of rural areas, and if developed carefully, CBT can generate alternative revenue in a non-extractive and sustainable way (Novelli, 2015). The environmental, economic, and socio-cultural impacts of tourism have led to increasing concerns towards sustainable tourism development. Sustainable development is aimed at offering people both social and economic growth and protecting the environment (Holden, 2000). Sustainable tourism is maximising the positive tourism impacts and minimising the negatives, thereby addressing the needs of hosts and guests without compromising the wellbeing of future generations and of the physical environment (Tolkach and King, 2015). When local communities participate in tourism development projects and they realise economic benefits from the natural or cultural resources in their locality, they become motivated to protect and manage sustainably.

Indeed, sustainable tourism development in a sense has become predicated on the notion that incorporating community support in tourism development is a key component to its success (Mair and Reid, 2007). The natural resource base is fundamental to the goals of sustainable development, and it needs to be recognised by all of those whose activities have impacts on these resources (Garrod, 2003). CBT shares the goals of sustainable development; this is because it strives for the long-term socially equitable, ecologically sound and economically viable development (Dodds et al., 2016). In fact, CBT is crucial to sustainable tourism development (Naguran, 1999; Beaumont and Dredge, 2010; Bojanic, 2011; Lindström and Larson, 2016).

International organisations such as World Commission on Environment and Development (WCED) and World Tourism Organisation (UNWTO) have paid much attention to the issues of sustainable development in general and specifically for tourism. Following the World Commission on Environment and Development (1987: 8), community participation has been recognised as important to achieving sustainable development:

> Humanity has the ability to make development sustainable, to ensure that it meets the needs of the present without compromising the ability of future

generations to meet their own needs. . . . Meeting essential needs requires not only a new era of economic growth for nations in which the majority are poor but an assurance that those poor get their fair share of the resources required to sustain that growth. Such equity would be aided by political systems that secure effective citizen participation in decision making.

Community involvement that allows the local people to have control in tourism projects, the way their natural resource is utilised and the outcomes of those processes is a critical element of sustainability (Scheyvens, 2002).

Since the beginning of the new millennium, there are arguments to support CBT as having the ability to play a central role in community-based development, conservation and rural diversification in sub-Saharan Africa (Novelli, 2015). One main output of the Quebec Declaration on Ecotourism was that to develop sustainable tourism, the active participation and agreement of local communities in the management of such projects on a continuing basis are vital (UNWTO, 2004). The seventeen sustainable development goals (SDGs) and one-hundred and sixty nine targets to be achieved by 2030 also noted the significance of addressing the economic, social and environmental dimensions of sustainable development in a balanced and integrated manner (UNESCO, 2015). CBT can contribute to achieving some of the SDGs in developing countries.

Bramwell and Lane (2000) suggest that the local community in destinations should be perceived as part of the tourism resources and partners in sustainable tourism development. Uncoordinated planning and management can hinder sustainable development, thereby reducing local benefit sharing and, ultimately, nature conservation (Hübner et al., 2014).

Planning process and outcomes

As a result of the negative impact of tourism in local communities that host tourism resource base, and the fact that they are often left behind in the process of decision making, community participation in planning processes is being promoted in the body of literature to involve the local communities in decision-making (Murphy, 1985; Tosun, 2000) and empowerment (Scheyvens, 2002; Sofield, 2003). A way of involving local communities in the planning process is through community-based tourism management (Murphy, 1985; Tosun, 2000; Mair and Reid, 2007; Grybovych et al., 2011). When local communities are not involved in the decision-making, it may result in the inability of government to implement vital policies and ensure effective development. The problem of disenfranchisement can only be resolved through community empowerment (Sofield, 2003). Oriade and Evans (2011) observe that each stakeholder within the tourism system makes decisions and contributions affecting corresponding parts of the system; however, the breadth of control needed to achieve sustainability is generally beyond the individual stakeholder acting in isolation. Community participation and empowerment in tourism development is both a function of the process of involving local communities in decision-making and an outcome of policy implementation and realising benefits from tourism development (Sofield, 2003). When some stakeholders are excluded from the process and outcome of tourism development, it results in adverse actions (Sofield, 2003).

Resource allocation

Central to the philosophy of sustainable tourism and CBT is responsible resource use, which informs the basis of allocating resources and consequently dictates most approaches employed in managing visitors and/or visitors' use of tourism resources (Oriade and Evans, 2011). Despite the increased awareness and importance of tourism development and its resultant impacts, many developing countries' governments have not embraced and included appropriate sustainable principles in their political programme and so do not devote resources to it compared to other sectors (Sofield, 2003). The community-based approach requires the involvement of local residents, tourism entrepreneurs, other relevant business actors, government representatives, planners, and developers as they all form part of the social structure of the community, and their involvement or lack of participation influences the course of tourism development (Lindström and Larson, 2016). Given the fragmented nature of tourism and the multiplicity of stakeholders involved, there is a need for stakeholder coordination and systematic allocation of resources. Tourism is a political phenomenon, so the structures involved in establishing institutions responsible for development and allocation of resources must understand the mechanics of the politics required. Fundamental to resource allocation is also the method of resource audit and classification, as these enable destinations to take stock and categorise their resources and know where attention is required. Whatever approach employed to allocate resources, the focal point should be on the spread of development and avoidance of waste.

Case study of the Kawaza village tourism project in Zambia

The National Tourism Policy for Zambia has highlighted sustainable tourism development as important to contribute to sustainable economic growth and poverty reduction by 2030 (Zambia Ministry of Tourism and Arts [ZMTA], 2015). The strategies set for achieving these objectives are to facilitate tourism-related income-generating activities in local communities for poverty reduction (ZMTA, 2015).

The Zambian tourism policy widely supports local community participation in the management of sustainable tourism development projects. Because it can improve their livelihood of the community members and build their capacity to be able to support tourism projects,

> Local communities should share in the management and revenues of Eco-tourism in order to enhance for the protection of the environment and all fauna and flora. Community involvement, participation and collaboration

with stakeholders should be continually encouraged to enhance local capacity and improve livelihoods.

(ZMTA, 2015: 15)

The policy document also recognised the need to train the local people on local management of tourism so that they can be involved in sustainable tourism planning and management of natural and cultural heritage (ZMTA, 2015).

Further, the policy highlighted the need for local community empowerment in tourism development and advocated that local community members should be trained to develop skills to establish, own, and manage tourist-related small and medium-sized enterprises (ZMTA, 2015). Also, to stimulate local entrepreneurship, ownership and investments in opportunities are needed, such as local cultural experiences and stays in local lodging, traditional ceremonies, storytelling and local crafts, local tours, tourist guide services, security, food and beverages, and souvenirs (ZMTA, 2015: 23). Additionally, the policy acknowledges the importance of creating public awareness and educating local communities. Plans to do this are to raise public awareness, and sensitise and educate the local communities about tourism issues and how they can benefit from tourism by disseminating information to the communities on positive and negative attributes of tourism and organising capacity-building programmes for local communities (ZMTA, 2015).

Kawaza Village Tourism Project (KVTP) is located in Upper Lupande, about 20 km from the Mfuwe gate to South Luangwa National Park. KVTP started in 1997, with support from the Robin Pope Safaris (RPS) team who took tourists to visit the village school. This worked well, and RPS suggested to the community that they develop a tourism project for RPS clients to experience village life. Hence the KVTP project was the primary outcome of those visits. The cultural tourism project was to meet the needs of tourists who are not only interested in experiencing wildlife but are also keen to stay overnight in the village to meet the local people and to learn the Kunda culture (Pope, 2007; Schlesinger, 2018). The Kawaza Villagers responded and were happy to share their culture with tourists as they saw the initiative as one that could be beneficial to them to help raise money for other community development projects and the school (Pope, 2007).

At the start of the project, the community members were trained in financial management by the Zambia Wildlife Authority in 1997 (Dixey, 2005; Watt, 2012). Within two months, five chalets were already constructed with advice from RPS (Dixey, 2005; Expert Africa, 2011). The traditionally styled architecture chalets were built with mud and thatch rondavels (Dixey, 2005). A traditional summerhouse known as *Insaka* was also constructed (Dixey, 2005). The project was supported by the Danish Association for International Cooperation who donated the sum of US$250 for the purchase of mattresses for the chalets to get the project started (Dixey, 2005). The chalets were equipped with two beds with mosquito nets fitted Schlesinger, 2018. Also, an open shower surrounded by a reed screen was constructed for tourists, and community members lent their basins to them to take their bath. Finally, toilet facilities in the form of pit latrines were provided (Dixey, 2005; Schlesinger, 2018).

KVTP is managed by some elected committee from the village, with seventeen members (seven men and ten women). However, they get support in the form of technical advice from the Danish Association for International Cooperation volunteer and driver guides (Dixey, 2005). The Robin Pope Safaris (RPS) team continues to play a vital role in the survival of the project by providing the village with logistical support by marketing the project internationally through RPS website, tour operators and acting as their booking agent. The RPS team also advises the local managers (Pope, 2007; Expert Africa, 2011).

The Kawaza Village Tourism Project has become a CBT success story which serves as a benchmark for similar initiatives worldwide (Watt, 2012). It is marketed by many operators and receives most of its clients (85%) through cooperating tourism companies. Approximately 60% of visitors are up-market international fly-in tourists who book through RPS. About 20% are tourists on overland trucks and the remainder comprise of backpackers (5%) on mobile safaris, self-drive tourists (5%), development workers (5%) and overseas educational groups (5%) (Dixey, 2005: 36).

Process/activities

When tourists arrive at the community, they draw up a plan for them based on their request. The KVTP offers village tours to various locations in the village such as the school, church, clinic and the local traditional healer's place. They provide tourists with traditional food, entertain them through cultural activities such as storytelling and cultural music and dance (Dixey, 2005; Pope, 2007).

Through the Kawaza Village CBT project, the community has significantly improved, including benefits in the form of employment for community members, for example, three guides working full time (Dixey, 2005). The project also employs cooks, guides, dancers, drummers and more, up to twenty people in total (Africa Travel Resource, 2018).

Profits from the first year of the project were ploughed back into the tourism venture without anyone taking a salary (Schlesinger, 2018). For the subsequent years the community has utilised the profit to buy books and other school supplies to run the institution (Pope, 2007; Schlesinger, 2018). Kawaza School now has a reputation in Zambia of being a great example of how tourism can improve a community and support education.

Proceeds from the CBT project have also been used to build other facilities in the village such as water pump, and to take care of the vulnerable members of the community such as the sick, older adults and orphans. Profits also go into a community fund, and each year the community group decides collectively what will be done with the money in order to continually improve their community and to supports the villagers (Pope, 2007; Schlesinger, 2018).

Kawaza Village Tourism Project emerged the winner of the prestigious Silver Otter Award, given for the Best Overseas Tourism Project by the British Guild of

Travel Writers, and is now a role model for other community-owned and managed cultural tourism enterprises in Africa (RPS, 2018).

The importance of planning was revealed in the case study both from the private and public sector. For example, Robin Pope Safaris is one of the main supporters of the KVTP, and they are committed to responsible tourism that benefits the environment, protects natural wildlife areas, alleviate poverty through good employment practices and contributes positively to the local community (RPS, 2018). They do these by ensuring that neighbouring local communities benefit from their presence through grassroots sustainable community development initiatives. They understand the interdependence between local communities and the wildlife and natural resources that tourism depends upon. Their commitment to poverty reduction interventions has been recognised through the winning of international responsible tourism awards (RPS, 2018). Robin Pope Safaris believes that investing in education provision in the local community is one of the best contributions they can make to their neighbouring communities. Education is key to ending the cycle of poverty in rural African communities.

The Kawaza School Fund has become one of the biggest success stories in the Luangwa Valley and has inspired both guests and other safari operators in the area to work together to change lives through improved education provision. It has not only developed the standards of school buildings in the area but has been an avenue for getting educational materials. This fund, amongst other things, has enabled children to benefit from smaller class sizes and more classroom time with qualified teachers (RPS, 2018).

The outcomes of the KVTP aligns with the broad aim of tourism development in Zambia, as highlighted in the tourism policy that tourism development should be economically, culturally, socially and environmentally sustainable, to maximise socio-economic benefits, job creation and local investment opportunities for Zambian livelihoods and national heritage (ZMTA, 2015). Further, that tourism will generate opportunities for job creation, income generation, entrepreneurship, education and stimulating creativity for Zambians across the country (ZMTA, 2015).

Conclusions

This chapter noted the importance of broader development plans having strategies for tourism development in local communities. By including tourism development in rural areas in the National Tourism Policy, it can facilitate the development of CBT projects in local communities with tourism potential. The KVTP processes and outcomes align with the Zambia tourism policy.

This chapter has discussed some of the issues that can hinder successful operations of CBT. Given the vulnerability of poor communities and the limited capacity of local communities to help themselves, the role of government and other stakeholders are critical to supporting CBT. To continually sustain CBT projects the broader institutional structure in Zambia must continue to encourage active local community participation in sustainable tourism development. It was evident from the KVTP that the local community members were supported by the private and public sector to make the CBT project a success. It is essential to have linkages with the public sector, private sector and NGOs who can assist local communities.

The case study revealed the way that CBT can support communities by improving their education system, providing resources needed to run local schools, employment opportunities for community members and provision of amenities in the community, as well as supporting vulnerable members of the village.

The potential of CBT to contribute to achieving some of the SDGs in developing countries such as alleviating poverty through economic development potential, promoting equality through community participation and conservation benefits which are enhanced when the local community have control over the resources used for developing tourism projects was also discussed.

References

Arnstein, S. R. (1969) 'A Ladder of Citizen Participation', *Journal of the American Planning Association*, 35(4), pp. 216–224. doi: 10.1080/01944366908977225.

Beaumont, N. and Dredge, D. (2010) 'Local Tourism Governance a Comparison of Three Network Approaches', *Journal of Sustainable Tourism*, 18(1), pp. 7–28.

Bojanic, D. (2011) 'Using a Tourism Importance Performance Typology to Investigate Environmental Sustainability on a Global Level', *Journal of Sustainable Tourism*, 19(8), pp. 989–1003.

Bramwell, B. (2004) 'Partnerships, Participation, and Social Science Research in Tourism Planning', in Lew, A. A., Hall, C. M., and Williams, A. (eds) *A Companion to Tourism*. Oxford, UK: Blackwell Publishing, pp. 541–554.

Bramwell, B. and Lane, B. (2000) 'Collaboration and Partnerships in Tourism Planning', in *Tourism Collaboration and Partnerships: Politics, Practice and Sustainability*, vol. 2. Bristol: Channel View Publications.

Burgos, A. and Mertens, F. (2017) 'Participatory Management of Community-based Tourism: A Network Perspective', *Community Development*. Routledge, 48(4), pp. 546–565. doi: 10.1080/15575330.2017.1344996.

Dixey, L. (2005) 'Inventory and Analysis of Community Based Tourism in Zambia', In *Production, Finance and Technology (PROFIT) A USAID Private Sector Development Programme*, (November), p. 93.

Dodds, R. (2007) 'Malta's Tourism Policy: Standing Still or Advancing towards Sustainability?', *Island Studies Journal*, 2(1), pp. 47–66.

Dodds, R., Ali, A. and Galaski, K. (2016) 'Mobilising Knowledge: Determining Key Elements for Success and Pitfalls in Developing Community Based Tourism', *Current Issues in Tourism*, 21(13), pp. 1547–1568.

Garrod, B. (2003) 'Local Participation in the Planning and Management of Ecotourism: A Revised Model Approach', *Journal of Ecotourism*, 2(1), pp. 33–53.

Grybovych, O., Hafermann, D. and Mazzoni, F. (2011) 'Tourism Planning, Community Engagement and Policy Innovation in Ucluelet, British Columbia', in Dredge, D. and Jenkins, J. M. (eds) *Stories of Practice Tourism Policy and Planning*. Farnham, Surrey: Ashgate, pp. 79–104.

Hall, C. M. (2007) 'Tourism Governance and the (Mis-)location of Power', in Church, A. and Coles, T. (eds) *Tourism, Power and Space*. Routledge London, pp. 247–268.

Hamzah, A. and Khalifah, Z. (2009) *Handbook on Community Based Tourism "How to Develop and Sustain CBT"*. Asia-Pacific Economic Cooperation Secretariate. Singapore: I Print Solution.

Holden, A. (2000) *Environment and Tourism*. London and New York: Routledge.

Hübner, A., Phong, L. T. and Châu, T. S. H. (2014) 'Good Governance and Tourism Development in Protected Areas: The Case of Phong Nha-Ke Bang National Park, central Vietnam', *Koedoe*, 56(2), pp. 1–10. doi: 10.4102/koedoe.v56i2.1146.

Kibicho, W. (2008) 'Community-based Tourism: A Factor-cluster Segmentation Approach', *Journal of Sustainable Tourism*. doi: 10.2167/jost623.0.

Lindström, K. N. and Larson, M. (2016) 'Community-based Tourism in Practice: Evidence from Three Coastal Communities in Bohuslän, Sweden', *Bulletin of Geography. Socio-Economic Series*, 33, pp. 71–78.

López-guzmán, T. and Sánchez-cañizares, S. (2011) 'Community – Based Tourism in Developing Countries: A Case Study', *Tourismos: An International Multidisciplinary Journal of Tourism*, 6(1), pp. 69–84.

Mair, H. and Reid, D. G. (2007) 'Tourism and Community Development vs. Tourism for Community Development: Conceptualizing Planning as Power, Knowledge, and Control', *Leisure/Loisir*, 31(2), pp. 403–425.

Malek, A., Carbone, F. and Alder, J. (2017). 'Community Engagement, Rural Institutions and Rural Tourism Business in Developing Countries', in Oriade, A. and Robinson, P. (eds.) *Rural Tourism and Enterprise: Management, Marketing and Sustainability*, 145.

Mowforth, M. and Munt, I. (2009) *Tourism and Sustainability: Development, Globalisation and New Tourism in the Third World*. London: Routledge.

Murphy, P. E. (1985) *Tourism: A Community Approach*. New York and London: Methuen.

Naguran, R. (1999) 'Community Based Tourism in Kwazulu Natal: Some Conceptual Issues', in Reid, D. G. (ed.) *Ecotourism Development in Eastern and Southern Africa*. University of Guelph, pp. 39–57.

Nelson, F. (2012) 'Blessing or Curse? The Political Economy of Tourism Development in Tanzania', *Journal of Sustainable Tourism*, 20(3), pp. 359–375. doi: 10.1080/09669582.2011.630079.

Novelli, M. (2015) *Tourism and Development in Sub-Saharan Africa: Current Issues and Local Realities*. doi: 10.4324/9780203069325.

Novelli, M. and Gebhardt, K. (2007) 'Community Based Tourism in Namibia: "Reality Show" or "Window Dressing"?', *Current Issues in Tourism*, 10(5), pp. 443–479. doi: 10.2167/cit332.0.

Okazaki, E. (2008) 'A Community-based Tourism Model: Its Conception and Use', *Journal of Sustainable Tourism*, 16(5), pp. 511–529. doi: 10.1080/09669580802159594.

Oriade, A. and Evans, M. (2011) 'Sustainable and Alternative Tourism', in Dieke, P. U. C.; Robinson, P. and Heitmann, S. (eds.) *Research Themes for Tourism*, Oxford: CABI pp. 69–86.

Scheyvens, R. (1999) 'Ecotourism and the Empowerment of Local Communities', *Tourism Management*, 20(2), pp. 245–249. doi: 10.1016/S0261-5177(98)00069-7.

Scheyvens, R. (2002) *Tourism for Development: Empowering Communities*. Harlow: Prentice Hall.

Scheyvens, R. and Russell, M. (2009) *Tourism and Poverty Reduction in the South Pacific*. Palmerston North, New Zealand: Massey University.

Sofield, T. (2003) *Empowerment for Sustainable Tourism Development*. London: Emerald Publishing Limited.

Spenceley, A. and Meyer, D. (2012) 'Tourism and Poverty Reduction: Theory and Practice in Less Economically Developed Countries', *Journal of Sustainable Tourism*, pp. 297–317. doi: 10.1080/09669582.2012.668909.

Sunuantari, M. (2017) 'Tourism Communication in Community Based Tourism Regarding Dieng Culture Festival in Dieng Community in Central Java, Indonesia', *Binus Business Review*, 8(2). doi: 10.21512/bbr.v8i2.1894.

Thompson, P., Sultana, P. and Arthur, R. (2010) 'Integrating Biological Conservation into Management: Community Adaptive Learning in the Wetlands of Bangladesh', *Biodiversity*, 11(1–2), pp. 31–38. doi: 10.1080/14888386.2010.9712644.

Timothy, D. J. (1999) 'Participatory Planning: A View of Tourism in Indonesia', *Annals of Tourism Research*, 26(2), pp. 371–391.

Tolkach, D. and King, B. (2015) 'Strengthening Community-Based Tourism in a New Resource-Based Island Nation: Why and How?', *Tourism Management*. Elsevier Ltd, 48, pp. 386–398. doi: 10.1016/j.tourman.2014.12.013.

Tosun, C. (1999) 'Towards a Typology of Community Participation in the Tourism Development Process', *Anatolia*, 10(2), pp. 113–134. doi: 10.1080/13032917.1999.9686975.

Tosun, C. (2000) 'Limits to Community Participation in the Tourism Development Process in Developing Countries', *Tourism Management*, 21(6), pp. 613–633. doi: 10.1016/S0261-5177(00)00009-1.

Tosun, C. and Jenkins, C. L. (1998) 'The Evolution of Tourism Planning in Third-World Countries: A Critique', *Progress in Tourism and Hospitality Research*, 4, pp. 101–114. doi: 10.1002/(SICI)1099–1603(199806)4:2 < 101::AID-PTH100 > 3.0.CO;2-Z.

UNESCO (2015) *UNESCO Science Report: Towards 2030*. UNESCO Reference Works Series. Paris, France: UNESCO Publishing.

UNWTO (2004) I*ndicators of Sustainable Development for Tourism Destination: A Guide Book*. Madrid: World Tourism Organization Publications.

UNWTO (2013) *Sustainable Tourism for Development Guidebook Enhancing Capacities for Sustainable Tourism for Development in Developing Countries*. Available at: http://cf.cdn.unwto.org/sites/all/files/docpdf/devcoengfinal.pdf.

Van Der Merwe, J. H. and Van Niekerk, A. (2013) ''Application of Geospatial Technology for Gap Analysis in Tourism Planning for the Western Cape'', *South African Journal of Science*, 109(3–4), pp. 1–10. doi: 10.1590/sajs.2013/1226.

World Commission on Environment and Development. (1987) *Our Common Future: Report of the World Commission on Environment and Development*. Oxford: Oxford University Press.

Websites

Africa Travel Resource (2018) Kawaza Village Available at: www.africatravelresource.com/kawaza-village/ (Accessed 23.09.18).

Expert Africa (2011) Kawaza Village Available at: www.expertafrica.com/zambia/south-luangwa-national-park/kawaza-village/in-detail (Accessed 27.09.18).

Pope, J. (2007) Kawaza Village Available at: http://aborinet.cefe.cnrs.fr/spip.php?page=article&id_article=468&lang=en (Accessed 23.09.18).

RPS (2018) Responsible Tourism Available at: www.robinpopesafaris.net/responsible-tourism.php (Accessed 03.10.18).

Schlesinger, V (2018) Gonomad Kawaza Village Tourism Project: Authentic Village Visits Available at: www.gonomad.com/2764-kawaza-village-tourism-project-authentic-village-visits (Accessed 23.09.18).

Watt, S. (2012) This African Encounter Is up Close and Personal Available at: www.independent.co.uk/travel/africa/this-african-encounter-is-up-close-and-personal-7166358.html (Accessed 24.09.18).

Zambia Ministry of Tourism and Arts (ZMTA) (2015) National Tourism Policy 2015 Available at: https://www.mota.gov.zm/?wpfb_dl=70 (Accessed 13.08.2019).

9 'Meet the locals'

Community tourism – an approach to combat over-tourism in Malta and Gozo

Andrew Jones and Julian Zarb

The research evaluates the current ongoing 'Meet the Locals' project and assesses how effective community-based tourism has been in providing alternative forms of tourism based upon community, heritage and culture. It also demonstrates how such an approach can help offset the increasing problems being encountered from mass and over-tourism on the islands. In turn it evaluates some of the key lessons that can be learnt from community engagement in tourism activities. The study is based upon action research and a qualitative research approach using three local villages on the Maltese islands – Zurrieq, Qrendi and Kirkop.

Introduction: 'Meet the Locals': discovering Malta and Gozo through its people and culture

The importance of tourism as a tool for social, cultural and economic development has been widely emphasised in the past (Murphy, 1985; Pearce et al., 1997). This research is focused on the evaluation of alternative approaches to tourism with a focus on the role that local communities have in their contribution to the tourism experiential and learning experience. The research is based upon a current ongoing project titled: 'Meet the Locals: Discovering Malta and Gozo through its people and culture'. The project concept initially originated from the Ministry for Tourism, the Environment and Culture in 2011 which established the development of a number of village tour itineraries for communities which were considered to be on the periphery with regard to mainstream tourism, but which nonetheless showcased the real and authentic experience of the Maltese Islands. In this context itineraries and tour guides were prepared for the following localities: Bormla (Cospicua), Gudja, Għarb, Ħ'attard, Ħal Tarxien, Ħal Kirkop, Ħaż-Żabbar, Mqabba, Naxxar, Qrendi, Safi, Santa Venera, Żebbuġ (Gozo) and Żurrieq.

The 'Meet the Locals' project was initiated to support these initial actions. As such, the project outcomes aim to produce, at more depth, a number of specialist tourism experiences, such as community heritage and cultural resource audits, cultural trails, pilot tours and, in turn, encourage strategies that development local tourist craft enterprises and 'cottage' industries. The aim is to disseminate or spread the benefits of tourism (which in Malta are currently very much based upon major coastal tourism resorts) to smaller, more outlying village communities and associated disparate local stakeholders who might otherwise be excluded from the current wealth and benefits that tourism brings to the Maltese Islands.

Through 'Meet the Locals' the development of community-led tourism and associated tours of village communities aim to be very different to the mainstream 'holiday experience' that is presently offered across Malta and Gozo as part of mainstream tourism activities. This alternative approach is very much based upon capacity building of local communities, where the emphasis and focus is on meeting and interacting with the host community, learning about traditions, history, legends and folklore from the locals themselves.

In this context the research builds upon work already undertaken and evaluated by, for example, Jones and Zarb's assessments (2017) of the same project in 2015–2016 and provides an up-to-date and current review of issues and challenges for 2017 and the future. As such, this research evaluates the issues and challenges of the project thus far. It evaluates how effective current community-based tourism has been, particularly the successes and failures, in attempting to rekindle host-visitor interaction and in the development of local cultural tourism resources and enterprises. In broader terms it assesses the effectiveness of this more sustainable, interactive and responsible approach to encourage local tourism and evaluates some of the key lessons that can be learnt. The key objectives of the study have set out to:

- Introduce the concept of community-based tourism to the islands of Malta and Gozo,
- Work with local stakeholders to develop and promote an experiential tourism experience that is culturally unique, culturally authentic and benefits all local stakeholders,
- Manage and monitor the development of community-based tourism and evaluate issues and challenges for local implementation and stakeholder engagement, and
- Provide alternative responses to increasing pressures being created from mass tourism and over-tourism on the islands.

Background: community tourism and tourism stakeholder theory

The literature provides a discourse of key critical issues for community-based tourism which tend to focus on issues and challenges associated with consultation, interactivity, communication, stakeholder theory and ultimately community ownership and capacity building. These are notions that are particularly relevant to the Maltese Islands and the future direction for tourism growth. Authors such as Murphy (1985) and Pearce (1997), the work of Van der Stoep (2000), Richards and Hall (2003) or more recently, for example, by Moscardo (2008) or Messer (2010) provide the theoretical framework and backdrop for the study. The concept is a simple one; it embraces the principles of sustainable and responsible tourism and provides a method for implementing those principles effectively, by involving the key local stakeholder groups working together. The literature suggests that tourism needs to be considered as a socio-cultural activity rather than just an economic industry; it is not just about quantifying the industry in terms of tourist arrivals, bed-nights and revenue; but rather it is about enhancing the host-visitor interaction through an intercultural dialogue, communication and sharing experiences.

The prime concept suggests that community-based tourism is an alternative development approach to a destination, region or locality. In this respect it is not a process which works from the top down but from the bottom up. Again, early approaches and assessments of such notions have also been identified by Veal (2010: 219), who referred to Arnstein's (1969) work regarding the 'The Ladder of Citizen Participation' which consists of 13 levels of stakeholder participation ultimately culminating in 'citizen power'. These are concepts that can, in theory, be applied to the Maltese islands where geography and socio-political structures can offer and facilitate new approaches for tourism development based upon community actions.

Hall and MacArthur (1998) describe this as a shift from the 'expert' view and policies to a more integrated and holistic involvement of the local community who should be the real owners of local tourism, heritage and culture. Moscardo (2008: 10) refers to this as 'building community capacity' and demonstrates the importance of linking community-based tourism to local stakeholder involvement. The author also defines this community capacity as 'the community's awareness of, and education in, tourism development'. By understanding the community with its needs, culture, traditions and characteristics Moscardo asserts that this will help nurture a sense of pride and engender local tourism enterprise within local communities. More recent work by, for example, Freeman et al. (2010) has referred to the concept of 'Stakeholder Management Theory' and states that tourism planning is about stakeholder relationships and the dynamic relationship that exists between stakeholder groups.

Local community tourism has achieved positive results in a number of localities over the last decade or so. Calvia, Mallorca (Spain) is a case in point. In Calvia, the project has been based on four key principles: the principle of environmental sustainability, the principle of local economic development, the principle of quality tourism and the principle of citizen participation (November, 1994). Pedersen (2002: 32–33) supports such notions and suggests that community tourism needs to be seen as a process working from within the community and together, evolving a complete strategy that offers the visitor a holistic experience of living history, cultural integration and social interchange. It is the key principle that the project 'Meet the Locals' closely adheres to.

Hall and MacArthur (1998), however, cite a number of issues that prevent full stakeholder involvement due to institutional malaise. Krutwayso and Bramwell (2004: 685) cite a number of implications for community tourism project implementation and stakeholder engagement. Their research revealed various dialectical relations between policy implementation and the socio-economic, political, governance and cultural contexts. Dodds and Butler (2010) also consider a number of critical themes that can be identified in the literature, ranging from power clashes between political parties at a national level to lack of stakeholder involvement and accountability at the local level (Dodds and Butler, 2010: p. 41). The idea of 'citizen power', as Arnstein (1969) coined in his last stage of the ladder of citizen participation, is pertinent in this context. The need to understand and avoid the repercussions that are so common today in top-down tourism planning or stalled efforts in community participation are key notions that need to be further explored and understood. This is certainly the case if community tourism is to provide realistic alternatives to mainstream tourism developments for the future. They are also certainly issues that provide some salutary indicators for the future success or failure for community tourism development across the Maltese islands.

In summary, the literature for community tourism is now firmly established in the dialogue of tourism practitioners and policy makers. There are good examples of how community-based tourism can aid tourism diversification, help innovate local community capacity and enterprise and help contribute to alternative forms of sustainable tourism based upon local culture and heritage. There are nevertheless challenges to such approaches to tourism which are clearly highlighted by several authors. In this respect the challenge of sustaining community engagement in tourism activities is one that remains critical to the wellbeing of such approaches for alternative tourism and destination development. It is a challenge that must try to ensure the convergence of sustainable tourism principles and practices as opposed to the often diverging interests that would appear characteristic of more traditional tourism and destination management operations. These are issues and challenges that are fully explored in the 'Meet the Locals' community tourism project.

Tourism in Malta: building an alternative community-based tourism model

Malta as a traditional Mediterranean package tour destination (sun, sand and sea) has increasingly put pressure on Malta's infrastructure. (Lockhart, 1997; Attard and Hall, 2004). Today tourism has attained year on year growth. Arrivals increased from 1.4 million visitors in 2012 to over 2.3 million in 2017, up 16.4% from 2016, with an expenditure estimated to be above 2 billion euros up 13.9% from 2016 (MTA, 2018). The balance between an increase in tourist arrivals and a rise in earnings offset against increasing resource pressures, particularly societal and environmental, has increased debate on the future direction for tourism in Malta. These debates and concerns are now increasingly focusing on over-tourism (Micallef, 2018; Costa, 2018).

This continued growth in tourism numbers, particularly in the peak summer period, is already creating environmental strains which are now leading to carrying capacity issues, resource, waste and pollution impacts, congestion, environmental degradation and local community unease. Indeed 2017 also saw news headlines from across Europe including Barcelona, Dubrovnik, Mallorca and Venice which highlighted growing disquiet, anger and sometimes conflict which has emerged between host communities and visitors. Primarily, these concerns have been attributed to mass tourism and the perceived lack of local benefits for such communities (Kettle, 2017).

Tourism in Malta and Gozo has traditionally focused on traditional coastal resorts of Sliema, St Julians, Buggiba, Qwara and Mellieha and key cultural icons which include Mdina, Valletta, the Grand Harbour, the prehistoric temples and Gozo (MTA, 2016) This has been the mainstay of the tourist 'offer' over the past fifty years or more and has created a somewhat 'narrow' tourism image of the Maltese islands. This, in turn, has been used by the various main tourism stakeholders and authorities as key symbols of the 'traditional tourist package' for tourism on the Islands.

In this respect the Ministry for Tourism's recent National Tourism Strategy 2015–2020 (MTA, 2016) is now increasingly focusing on ensuring sustainable growth and has emphasised the development of tourism based upon cultural, community and resource assets placing the growth of community tourism and the development of associated local tourism industries at the forefront for new alternative strategies for tourism growth.

As an example the development of 'community-based tourism' has been piloted since 2011 when the Government of Malta first took practical steps to add value to the visitor experience. As already stated, the primary tasks undertaken included the creation of itineraries for sixteen local councils listing the attractions and services that were identified and on offer by local municipalities. Initially, the rationale was to provide visitors with alternative, tailor-made locally sourced and based community and cultural tourism experiences. It has been a project with mixed results (Ministry for Tourism and Culture, 2007). Nevertheless, the refocusing of strategies through 'Meet the Locals' to include 'outlying villages and nontraditional tourism areas' has been an interesting policy change in this respect and one which continues to present real opportunities and challenges for continued and future local community engagement.

'Meet the Locals': research approach

As Freire stated in (1982) research can be attributed to 'Learning to do it by doing it'. In this context the methodology adopted for this project has and primarily continues to be based on a critical participative action research approach supported by qualitative techniques used for data collection. This has involved local stakeholder focus group participation, personal interviews with both locals and visitors, scoping meetings and local village-based seminars.

Kemmis and McTaggart (1988) describe action research as a six-step process – plan, reflect, replace, act, observe and reflect. These descriptions express the benefit of applying a participatory action research process to this study, since this can take a continuous and cyclical format. Action research models such as the work of Kumar (2012) as well as other authors such as Kemmis, McTaggart and Nixon (2014) and McIntyre (2008) indicate that participatory action research, in practice, can provide insightful data and can act as a key motivator and incentive to stakeholders engaged in research. The 'Meet the Locals' project looks at developing this process and the implementation of tourism community development at a local or 'grassroots' level by using such models, while also focusing on the principles for sustainable development.

Critical participatory action research has two basic objectives according to Kemmis et al. (2014). These primarily focus upon opening up space to dialogue and bringing about change. It is a process that helps all the participants and stakeholders work together to 'meet the criteria of rationality, sustainability and justice' (Kemmis et al., 2014, p. 23). Phillmore and Goodson (2004, p. 285) consider the advantages of action research from the point of view of a more reliable and representative study since it involves the actual participants in a direct and sincere discussion rather than the more rigid method of interviews.

The framework for 'Meet the Locals' research followed a participatory staged approach for developing community tourism which was programmed between 2013–2019.

'Meet the Locals': Stage 1: Scoping meetings: 2013–2015: This stage involved working with local councils to identify the strengths and weaknesses for tourism activity in the locality. Here the project started by targeting local councils in Malta and Gozo and developing itineraries and tourist maps for their respective localities. The itineraries did not follow the traditional 'programme-based' set lists of sites and places of interest but were more a compilation based upon local knowledge of those historical, cultural, religious and social sites that each community felt important to promote. These were, in turn, developed and offered to visitors. The intention was to provide a set of alternative and unique local experiences tailored to in-depth local community knowledge at a given locality.

'Meet the Locals': Stage 2: Pilot projects: 2015–2016: This stage aimed to identify those localities that would be prepared to develop the concept of a community-based experience for visitors through the development of local guides and village tours. The key objective aimed to develop local authentic cultural experiences where the visitor and the host communities were given the chance of interacting, learning from each other and where opportunities availed, secure economic benefit from the experience. Five localities (Zurrieq*, Qrendi, Mqabba, Safi and Kirkop) were included in the pilot project stage.

'Meet the Locals': Stage 3: Project implementation, promotion and initial feedback: 2016–2017: In collaboration with local destination management organisations (DMOs), this stage considered two objectives: i) to provide the logistical framework to establish and kick-start community tourist guides/tours which aimed to provide visitors with authentic local tourism experiences based upon local culture and heritage and opportunities to meet 'the locals' and ii) to analyse initial feedback from the pilot projects in terms of understanding key source markets (including demographics and qualitative data concerning the experiences and perceptions from visitors).

'Meet the Locals': Stage 4: Project reflection: 2017–2019: Stage 4 aims to analyse the promotion and implementation process for the community-based operations using both a quantitative and qualitative analysis method. This aims to provide key data to evaluate the current and future needs of the project. This stage remains ongoing for the foreseeable future.

Current research outcomes

The implementation of the community-based operations within the three pilot villages has presented a number of research issues and challenges. These have included a number of discourses and lessons learnt. On the positive side there have been those outcomes that relate to the socio-cultural dimension of the study: by and large the reaction by the key local stakeholders has been positive and supportive. In this respect Freeman's work (2010) on 'stakeholder management theory' highlights the synergies that can occur when local community projects are executed successfully. Such concepts would seem pertinent for this project. Such an approach appears to encourage a more integrated, inclusive approach to support alternative forms of tourism development based upon community, heritage and culture. Evidence from the study thus far also demonstrates that involving local stakeholders tends to develop a rapport between all interested parties which can produce consistent and unique community and cultural experiences for a visitor and tangible benefits for a local host community.

The development of the community-based operations and activities has required strong participation by all the key local stakeholders. There is clear evidence from the project, however, that local communities can enhance the host–visitor interaction through the development and dissemination of knowledge for local or more intangible cultural heritage. This aspect has been referred to by authors such as Norkunas (1993: 218) as preservation of local culture by promoting 'A sense of themselves through orally transmitting family stories and through celebrations and rituals performed inside the group'. The richness of such an approach has certainly contributed to valued visitor experiential learning and beneficial community experiences within the three pilot villages.

As well as opportunities for developing new strategies and models for alternative tourism development the study has also shown that key benefits to the local community and visitors can accrue positive outcomes in a number of other ways. For example, the three-village project has provided opportunity to revive local heritage and culture and establish a unique brand potential for nontraditional tourism areas across Malta. The project has also had potential to create new demand and encourage the development of new tourism economies and off-season opportunities. In this respect the project has offered growth for new community tourism businesses based on crafts, events, accommodation and associated hospitality enterprises. There has also been some scope to encourage environmental enhancement and small-scale infrastructure investment. These benefits are very much concepts and advantages explored by Messer (2010) and Moscardo (2008) in their work on community tourism.

At a more challenging level there have been some outcomes that need further consideration. The concept of stakeholder fatigue and maintaining consistent involvement and consultation throughout each stage of the project has been a challenge in this respect. The situation of 'fatigue' has been described by Dodds and Butler (2010) as one of the key challenges. This has also led to delays for the implementation of key project stages particularly for the development of village guides and tours.

Two key factors would seem apparent here: i) ownership and ii) consistency in participation. The political aspects that tend to govern the local council administration in Malta has led to a situation that ownership has generally not been developed through any commitment across councils or municipalities. Instead it has tended to be very dependent on individuals and individual passion for the project. In this context participation, ownership and consequent 'stakeholder fatigue' has been very much determined by changing local council priorities and functions. Pedersen (2002) has highlighted such problems for the continuity of like projects. He has stated that there is need to work inclusively from within and across communities in order to ensure that there is a complete inclusive strategy. Such an approach, he suggests, offers the visitor and local community a holistic experience of living history, cultural integration, social interchange and economic benefit.

This general 'patchwork' of participation has sometimes challenged established local stakeholder relationships and in some instances caused friction and anger. This has certainly pointed to a need to encourage or to enforce a stronger synergy between stakeholder partners in order to avoid delay or discord as Pedersen (2002) suggests.

Dodds and Butler (2010) also suggest that challenges to the implementation of community strategies are tensions that occur between how stakeholders perceive tourism either as a socio-cultural activity or tourism as a socio-economic industry. In this respect, most still perceive tourism growth usually in quantitative terms and within short-term return dimensions. In this respect the project thus far has to some extent suffered from the 'short-termism' of the local political representatives, whose period of office is normally between three to four years. This is also exacerbated by the fact that local councils and the local business community expected an immediate result or economic return from time and investment spent. It is an interesting notion. Hall and MacArthur (1998) support such notions by suggesting that stakeholder involvement cannot ignore the fact that prime motivations are driven through politics and popularity rather than a genuine desire to involve and achieve the stakeholder participation and the community sense of ownership. It is a pertinent point.

Lai et al. (2006) mention barriers that concern the issue of management and planning that are important for a balanced stakeholder approach to project implementation. The study certainly had its challenges in this respect. Action research focusing on three pilot areas experienced plenty of situations which involved 'trial and error' and presented a real learning curve for balancing the often diverging rather than converging interests between academic, host community, visitor and business concerns and interests.

At a more operational level the project has identified some disquiet expressed by some stakeholders in the development of the broader project objectives. These have tended to relate to perceived negative impacts and barriers for future sustained development. Concerns regarding village gentrification and the potential removal of traditional working and living practices through tourism commercial exploitation have been expressed in some community quarters. Barriers in promoting alternative cultural guides and tours through a perceived all-pervasive institutional dominance of 'mass tourism' has been another. The divergence or fragmentation of stakeholders within each village community together with general perceived levels of strategic dis-coordination are sentiments widely held. Some also felt that the poor quality of local infrastructure and perceived low quality of hospitality services remained key barriers for sustained future development. The need for community capacity building, in this context, remains a real challenge and one that is clearly relevant today by sentiments expressed by authors such as Moscardo (2008). See Figures 9.1 and 9.2.

Figure 9.1 Research outcomes – community tourism: the positives
Source: Author

Figure 9.2 Research outcomes – community tourism: the negatives

Source: Author

Conclusions

The research is ongoing and will continue, through a monitoring process, to understand and evaluate ongoing stakeholder contributions, commitment and needs. The research contributes in developing a broader understanding of development and policy approaches for community tourism. This can be used to stimulate a more sustainable, responsible and alternative tourism approach for local communities and in-turn assist with diversifying traditional tourism destination economies and in turn offer some alternatives to the recent phenomena of over-tourism.

Key lessons can be learnt from the project to date. To conclude, therefore, lessons illustrate that community-based tourism can provide a strong basis for community integration and alternative forms of tourism development which is primarily focused on local and unique community and visitor cultural experiences. That said, lessons have shown that the project has experienced, in terms of sustainability outcomes, both convergent and divergent results. In this respect the project illustrates that it has been largely dependent on key 'champions', 'drivers' or 'individuals' and that there is a risk that these can be short-lived, thus threatening project continuity and sustained growth. Overriding principles for successful outcomes also suggest that building community tourism operations that meet with all stakeholders' needs is paramount to ensure both ownership and continuity. In this context lessons suggest that the promotion of community-based tourism activities generally needs a different approach to the more 'commercial' or traditional mass tourist experiences and one which needs to be much more sensitive to local needs such as local carrying capacity limits and sensitive approaches to support and encourage community engagement.

In summary indictors from the results emphasise the need for involving all stakeholders in building community capacity for local tourism projects. This approach is identified as important in sharing knowledge and best practice that will enhance both the visitor experience and benefit local communities in socio-economic and environmental outcomes. The research also points to a need for a continuous and consistent process of consultation, monitoring and engagement with the key stakeholders in order to ensure that projects remain on a sustainably sound footing and do not become irrelevant or outdated.

The results advocate that future directions for community tourism should recognise convergent sustainable outcomes and how these can be maximized or capitalised upon and where divergent sustainable 'gaps' exist how these can be minimised and addressed. The 'Meet the Locals' project demonstrates that such an approach can form a platform or paradigm that can be used as an effective technique to encourage medium- to long-term alternative sustainable tourism strategies for the Maltese Islands and in turn provide broader lessons for community-based tourism.

References

Arnstein, S. R., 1969. A ladder of citizen participation, *JAIP*, vol. 35, no. 4, July, pp. 216–224.

Attard, M. and Hall, D. 2004. Transition for EU accession: the case of Malta's restructuring of tourism and transport sectors. In Hall, D. (ed). Tourism and transition, governance transformation and development. Wallingford. UK: CAB International, pp. 119–132.

Costa, M., 2018. Even in Malta, the fight against mass tourism starts gathering steam, *Malta Today*, Valletta, 13 July. online https://www.maltatoday.com.mt/environment/environment/88092/even_in_malta_the_fight_against_mass_tourism_starts_gathering_steam#.XYCtV2ZS_IU. Accessed 17.09.2019.

Dodds, R. and Butler, R., 2010. Barriers to implementing sustainable tourism policy in mass tourism destinations. *Tourismos, International Multidisciplinary Journal of Tourism*, vol. 5, no. 1, Spring, pp. 35–53.

Freeman E. R., Harrison, J. S., Wicks, A. C., Parmar, B. L. and De Colles, S. 2010. *Stakeholder Theory – The State of the Art*, Cambridge University Press, Cambridge.

Freire, P. 1982 Creating alternative research methods: learning to do it by doing it, in B. Hall, A. Gillette & R. Tandon (Eds) *Creating Knowledge: a monopoly?*, pp. 29–37. Khanpur, New Delhi: Society for Participatory Research in Asia.

Hall, S. and Macarthur, C. M., 1998. *Integrated Heritage Management: Principles and Practice*, John Wiley & Sons, Chichester.

Jones, A. and Zarb, J., 2017. Developing community-based tours for greater stakeholder benefit and commitment, *International Journal of Tourism Policy*, vol. 7, no. 3, pp. 250–267.

Kemmis, S. and McTaggart, R. (Eds.), 1988. *The Action Research Planner*, Deakin University Press, Victoria.

Kemmis, S., McTaggart, R. and Nixon, R., 2014. *The Action Research Planner. Doing Critical Particpatory Action Research*. Springer Science+Business Media. Singapore.

Kettle, M. 2017. Mass tourism is at tipping point but we are all part of the problem, *The Guardian*, 11 August, www.theguardian.com/commentisfree/2017/aug/11/tourism-tipping-point-travel-less-damage-destruction. Accessed 25.10.2017.

Krutwayso, O. and Bramwell, B., 2010. Tourism policy implementation and society, *Annals of Tourism Research*, vol. 37, no. 3, pp. 670–691.

Kumar, R., 2012. *Research Methodology: A Step-by-Step Guide for Beginners*, Sage Publications, London.

Lai, K. Feng, X. and Yiping, L., 2006. Gap between tourism planning and implementation: A case of China, *Tourism Management*, vol. 27, pp. 1171–1180.

Lockhart, D. 1997. Tourism to Cyprus and Malta. In D. Lockhart, & D. Drakakis-Smith (Eds.), Island tourism: Trends and prospects (pp. 152–178). London: Pinter.

Malta Tourism Authority (MTA), 2016. National Tourism Strategy 2016–2017. Valletta.

Malta Tourism Authority (MTA), 2018. National Tourism Statistics 2017. Valletta.

McIntyre, A., 2008. *Participatory Action Research – Qualitative Research*, Methods Series 52 (pp. 5, 84), Sage, Thousand Oaks, CA and London.

Messer, C., 2010. *Community Tourism Development*, 3rd edition, University of Minnesota Extension Service. Minneapolis.

Micallef, K., 2018. Hoteliers sounds warning of 'over-tourism' Calls for carrying capacity study, *Times of Malta*, Valletta. 18th May. Online https://timesofmalta.com/articles/view/mhra-tourism-warning.679389. Accessed 17.09.2019.

Ministry for Tourism and Culture, 2007. *Tourism Policy for the Maltese Islands 2007–2011*, Ministry for Tourism and Culture, Valletta.

Moscardo, G., 2008. *Building Community Capacity for Tourism Development*, p. 10, CABI, Oxon.

Murphy, P. E., 1985. *Tourism – A Community Approach*, Routledge, Oxon.

Norkunas, M. K., 1993. *The Politics of Public Memory – Tourism, History and Ethnicity in Monterey, California*. State University of New York Press, Albany.

Pearce, P. L., Moscardo, G. M. and Ross, G. F., 1997. *Tourism Community Relationships (Tourism Social Science Series)*, Emerald, Bingly.

Pedersen, A., 2002. *Managing Tourism at World Heritage Sites – A Practical Manual for World Heritage Site Managers*. UNESCO, Paris.

Phillmore, J. and Goodson, L., 2004. *Qualitative Research in Tourism, Ontologies, Epistemologies and Methodologies*. Routledge, Oxon.

Richards, G. and Hall, D., eds., 2003. *Tourism and Sustainable Community Development* (Vol. 7). Psychology Press.

Van der Stoep, G. A., 2000. Community tourism development, In *Trends in Outdoor Recreation, Leisure and Tourism*, pp. 309–321.

Veal, A. J., 2010. *Leisure, Sport and Tourism, Politics, Policy and Planning*, 3rd edition, CABI, Oxon.

10 Reviewing the background to success in communities developing tourism

An evaluation through participant observations

Peter Wiltshier

Introduction

Perceptibly, in the past forty years, tourism consumption and production has moved towards experiential and existential modes. These modes have been conceptualised by many theorists, including leading academic commentators such as Dean MacCannell (2013), Valene Smith (2012) and Erik Cohen (1979), reviewing and revising philosophical approaches to tourism consumption trends (see for example chapter 5 of Apostolopoulos et al., 1996). Modes of consumption and production are predicated on skills and attributes held by new destination management champions. At the same time, central government policy is designed to empower individuals, and to ensure that public funds are used to deliver growth opportunities to entrepreneurs and innovators in various public, private and not-for-profit sectors (Kleinman and Piachard, 1993; Liebfried and Pierson, 1995). A government focus on allowing markets to determine patterns on production and consumption, rather than allowing suppliers to determine these, now exists (Hills and Stewart, 2005; 219). Of course the constant is change in that values, beliefs and actions by consumers have consistently become unpredictable and chaotic (Krippendorf, 1987: 87; Russell and Faulkner, 1999; McKercher and DuCros, 2002).

The background to success includes such factors as service delivery, product innovation, strategic business planning, service quality evaluation and issues to do with marketing and brand and image congruity, as have been identified in the literature developing experiential marketing (Dimanche, 2008; Frochot and Batat, 2013). This report identifies those indicators and competencies that can be used to validate the effectiveness and quality of relationships between service provider – in this context usually a family-run small business (SME) – and consumer in the twenty-first century. It uncovers the skills and training needs anticipated by clients as visitors, the expectations and perceptions of those visitors and the exemplars of skills and competencies matched to consumer satisfaction.

SME management issues contribute towards a measure of success in managing consumer satisfaction and improving productivity and sustainability (McGehee et al., 2015; Otto and Ritchie, 1996; Mok et al., 2013). The author acknowledges that these identified factors are in no way unique to the location, nor does the research exhaustively pursue causal factors. The project does however prioritise issues for suppliers in a demand-driven, neo-liberal economy. The project also makes recommendations for a diversified local economy based around satisfaction indices for products consumed by a wide range of consumers from local residents through to international visitors.

Matrix of place, people and process

In the Peak District the public sector through local government, both a local territorial authority and the National Park Authority have a lead role as they enable integrated developers of people for tourism operations. They periodically undertake a review of the skills, capabilities, resources, certification, and quality and risk minimisation undertaken within the Peak community to achieve both a socio-economic return to the Peak and consumer satisfaction.

At the heart of the public sector is the need to find a democratic approach to the development of communities. Developing communities through networking, resourcing, negotiating, information gathering and sorting, analytical skills developing and communicating has been identified and discussed and is built into the model that this concludes with (Taylor, 2003; Taylor et al., 2000). To undertake these developmental processes, communities require a range of stakeholders from public, private and volunteer contexts. All stakeholders have responsibilities in terms of social, economic and environmental outcomes and their outcomes are in general more focused on sustainable outcomes that are to be measured in effectiveness of project, business, employment generation, space and place protection and productivity. Marketeers will add a dimension of scarce resources and competitiveness in this and then there is the need for quality in process and evaluation. More so in the twenty-first century is a focus on delivery to satisfied consumers by entrepreneurs with a sustainable consumption orientation, as opposed to a production focus. Individual suppliers need to work collaboratively to please their customers.

The sustainable tourism paradigm embodies the set of skills and competencies required to deliver destination management according to the precepts of the Rio Declaration and Local Agenda 21 (Jafari, 2000). The provision of concerted, integrative skills in formal and informal education and training is future-proofing sustainable development at destinations. Adapting a systems approach to future-proofing will also develop integrative and adaptive thinkers to support entrepreneurs and innovators in their endeavours to obtain client satisfaction and a demand-led set of experiences in tourism. It will move these suppliers, mostly engaged in small businesses, beyond the current rather linear and binary oppositional approach of the developers and the conservators in sustainable destination management. Communities need to explore and exploit, with permission given by these innovators, the entrepreneurial dimensions to successful destination management (see for example, Gibson, Lynch and Morrison, 2005). Visionaries help to unlock the stores of ideas and practices identified in various factors including finance, culture, knowledge and the technology interface and commercialisation of services and products for leisure and recreation (Smallwood and Obiamiwe, 2008).

It is this focus on adaptive, creative and innovative individuals that the future of tourism destinations depends (Nunkoo and Ramkissoon, 2011). It is on training and skills acquisition for the integrative approach that destinations can align their costs and expect their incomes. It is the responsibility of informed practitioners, and of public sector strategists, to make clearly visible the trend towards more integrative and holistic learning informing the visitor experience. This approach towards education in the tertiary sector is becoming more apparent in the design and re-engineering of tourism management courses (Botterill and Tribe, 2000; Flohr, 2001; Stuart, 2002). To perform at the level required by an informed public, who now have a wide range of alternative and substitute products available, a tourism supplier will need access to transparent and highly visible training and skills at many levels and incorporating multiple factors for innovation (Uyarra, 2007). This research identifies how those skills, coupled with the appropriate training and levels of knowledge required in this complex market, allows suppliers to provide experiences that the consumer can relate to and will value.

Tourism in the Peak District is representative of the East Midlands' regional tourism trends towards increasing numbers of day visitors (currently at 32 million per annum with a worth to the economy of £5.3 billion) and a smaller number of overnight and international visitors (1.1 million international visitors estimated contribution £365 million). The regional economy has developed over the past decade an emerging and specific strategy for managing day, international and overnight visitors through a destination-specific series of themes and associated promotional campaigns which are relevant to this research and to strategies to engage market share (East Midlands Tourism, 2003; personal communication D. Eagar, 2016).

Antecedents can be built around using existing brand and identity strategy where suppliers cooperate in articulating Pine and Gilmore's (1999) six key step model employing experiences marketed through product and service cohesion, clusters and networks forming and norming, a brand and identity that focuses consumers to avoid distraction, providing appropriate collateral evidence, a complete sensory overload, monitoring and responsiveness to feedback.

Methodology

This research approach is built upon the planning systems theory approach and is developed from a framework that focuses on the supply and demand and interventions current in English planning approaches (Gilg, 2005). The objectives are defined by key stakeholders and elaborated in the literature; the outputs and outcomes are to be developed by local government in tandem with community consultation; the impacts and evaluation will be addressed through management responses to initiatives and interventions recommended in this report. The inductive soft-systems approach espoused by Checkland and Scholes (1990) is therefore considered an appropriate paradigmatic and epistemological choice for this investigation. Bowen (1989) considers participant observation appropriate in terms of building the human interaction experience in everyday life through interpretation of its meaning. To understand motivation and drivers of choice in tourism consumption we can identify that the focus has shifted from work and productivity to leisure and highly complex consumption options. We anticipate less order and certainty of 'goodness of fit and fitness for purpose' in this chaos and that to objectively study the phenomena of experience tourism through quantitative data collection would create difficulty in assigning role and responsibility in the numerous indicators we wish to consider in model development and analysis (Roberts, 2004; 2). Consumers elect their lifestyles and make choices accordingly in time and space.

Between 2005 and 2016 a series of unstructured interviews were conducted with business leaders, public sector specialist consultants in the service sector development arena (mainly in farming diversification, tourism, marketing and creative arts, performance, events and festivals) and consultants working alongside specific projects for community development, service and product design and development (Food and beverage production). Participant observation is a relevant paradigmatic perspective as the researcher was often involved in all aspects of these stakeholders' groups' research through the following process and rationale. As a researcher, the focus was on input to stakeholders' perspectives on development through knowledge transfer partnership, primarily unstructured in terms of financial exchange but frequently engaging the work-related learning paradigms of a university (Taylor et al., 2004; Rae, 2007).

Discussion

Clients' & partners' expectations

In the project there are several key components selected from supply, demand and intermediary aspects. In managing the consumer's experience the involvement and participation of the consumer as a willing and informed stakeholder is widely discussed (Prentice, 1993; Lash and Urry, 1994; Gabriel and Long, 2006). The supplier must acknowledge the changed position that a demand-led economy creates for component small businesses and their effective management, endogenous strategic planning and sustainability (Simchi-Levy et al., 2003; Diamond and Liddle, 2005; Leitch, 2006). Crouch et al. (2007) identifies the consumer as an active and privileged producer and through conceptual individualism and doing lives, effectively the customer relationship activity is less pre-determined. Suppliers need to understand the customer's motivation, needs and wants more effectively than has been possible in the past using indicators for experience-led success, and learn how to manage the experience for long-term profit. We can accept that there is evidence of post-Fordist consumption trends that are predicated on consumerism, choices on methods of communication, greater involvement and less passivity in acceptance of products and services and chaotic uncertainty on repeat purchase decisions leading to a need for greater involvement in the psyche of the consumer (Gabriel and Long, 2006). This report does not critique the existing neo-liberal, market-forces, and third way models of sustainable development but does acknowledge the related governance, democracy and socio-cultural specific contexts for grounding indicators and issues (Tonnies, 1974; Michael and Plowman, 2002; Powell and Geoghegan, 2005).

This conceptual chapter identifies where the gaps are in skills and knowledge about the consumer's experience and the response from the producer and the community at the destination. This has been illustrated with five case studies that have informed where interventions determined the skills gap, capacity building issues and shortfalls identified in various projects that the university has agreed to share as research and practice-based projects. This has implications for training and skills acquisition particularly at higher education and the extent of the gaps in our knowledge. Indicators and parameters derived from the model of SME experience will clarify current exemplars of expertise in what the consumers' needs look like and how to manage for extraordinary achievement.

Mascarenhas et al. (2006) offer suggestions for building a total customer experience around product differentiation and interactive relationships. Berry et al. (2002) discuss more the managing of the total customer experience through each component of the experience and from the perspective of competing on and with other experiences. They talk of organising, orchestrating clues to those experiences. Pine and Gilmore (1999) identify the following six factors, which will be considered for the discussion in this research:

- Possessing a cohesive theme
- Forming impressions
- Eliminating distractions
- Providing memorabilia
- Ensuring that all senses are engaged
- Feedback for continuous improvement

These factors have been considered in the emerging model and can be used for subsequent collection of evidence through case studies (a summary is contained in Table 10.1).

Sustainable tourism development

This project is underscored by the importance of sustainability and operator/supplier compliance with the long-standing and global agreement on responsible and sustainable tourism development as exemplified by the Rio Declaration Earth Summit and subsequent adoption of LA21 (Jafari, 2000; Gabriel and

Table 10.1 A start point for consumer-driven success: characteristics of successful experience-led entrepreneurs

Supplier Characteristic and Literature	Example	Case Study
Planning Pine and Gilmore (1999) Osborne et al. (2002) Gilchrist (2004) Ledwith (2005) Crouch et al. (2007) Wittmann and Reuter (2008)	Links to innovation and intuition. Strategic thinking Setting a theme to the product Creating memorabilia Engaging the senses Finding funds and fighting for support	Building identity in Matlock Bath Telling the relevant stories to underpin identity and brand
Network/ Team player/ Shared Values Granovetter (1983) Csikszentmihalyi (1992) Ray (1998) Taylor et al. (2000) Prahalad and Ramaswamy (2004) Von Friedrichs Grängsjö (2003) Gibson et al. (2005) Gibson (2006) Szreter and Woolcock (2004)	Building links with supply chain Seeking out like-minded partners	Market Towns Initiative encouraging Emulation of successful projects
Visionary/ Relationship Management/Nurturing/ Empathy, intuitive/ Early adopter/ Innovation in practices Kleinman and Piachard (1993) Prentice (1993) Drucker (1994) Outhwaite (1994) Liebfried and Pierson (1995) Pine and Gilmore (1999) Brooker and Joppe (2014) Page et al. (2017)	Personal skills possessed by serial entrepreneurs Capturing impressions and moods from that theme Sharing knowledge with others – mentoring them Being aspirational and proactive	Ongoing success of New Opportunities Wirksworth
Risk Minimisation/ Informed decision making Faulkner and Tideswell (1997) Lowe and Talbot (2000) Simpson (2001) Taylor (2003) Choi and Sirakaya (2005)	Adapting and adopting business planning essentials and taking advantage of public sector funding Getting feedback Getting recognition for a job well done	Buxton Town Team setting the scene for A sustainable travel plan

Long, 2006; Wittmann and Reuter, 2008). Tourism is at the centre of many community development and regeneration agendas (Okazaki, 2008; Timothy and Tosun, 2003; Joppe, 1996; Simpson, 2001). The learning community and tourism development, or how to build social capital in communities that are prepared to espouse sustainable tourism development is an economic and social community base pre-requisite (Haskins, 2003; Egan, 2004; Leitch, 2006).

Case study 1

Farmers on film

At the request of an entrepreneur my university elected to deploy students to undertake research into the viability of contemporary farming in the twenty-first century diversification and development model. Were farmers sufficiently engaged, skilled and possessed of the capacity required to branch out into added-value products and services for the sophisticated new consumer? Students were given appointments to interview farmers and shopkeepers with relevant food and beverage products at their places of business and film the interventions that appeared to best meet a competitive and diversified supply chain and consumer market. This highly enjoyable project produced outputs that were emulated by other universities, and were indeed, emulated in the United States and Australia by the entrepreneur. New knowledge about the relative difficulty and skills, resources and capacity to innovate was created and stored on film. Students that engaged with the project developed excellent new communication and knowledge transfer skills and were excited by a different type of real-world learning and problem-solving activity occurring outside of the classroom and producing new confidence in learners in skills that had scarcely been touched by university academic programmes previously. The entrepreneur developed a high profile in the agriculture, food and beverage sectors and reflected upon the business that had been at the core of this innovation. Additional benefits included market collateral for all research subjects and for the entrepreneur. At the same time the identity, brand and skills resources for diversification and competitive capacity were sharply refocussed by all stakeholders with renewed confidence to tackle a sometime very difficult market environment with many external factors impacting this sector.

Sustainable tourism development incorporates elements of stakeholder theory, of endogenous planning and devolved responsibility to destinations and their local communities to commit to integrated and community-based model of development (Joppe, 1996; Jamal and Getz, 1995; Andereck and Vogt, 2000; Simpson, 2001 etc.). An empowering local and central government provides the necessary support to destinations and communities intending to lead on community-based and led tourism development through experience-led entrepreneurs. This model incorporates community initiatives and new services and products designed by 'destination champions' to widen consumers' choices and cognate demand sets. Active participation by community champions, using public choice theory approach (Michael and Plowman, 2002). To successfully model tourism development led by champions and developed by entrepreneurs, experiential tourism support is also recommended for skills in leadership, networks, resources for projects, negotiation, information gathering, analysis and communication and dissemination (Thomas and Long, 2001; Saxena, 2005; Dunne et al., 2016; Fernández-Morales et al., 2016). The empowerment of SMEs through concerted public sector funded projects and improved resources for sustainable tourism development will unlock the potential of entrepreneurs and regenerators in the Peak District. Organisational changes may be required at both public sector and local government levels to acknowledge poor knowledge sharing and intellectual capacity development within the SMEs that typify the product/supply source in the location.

Pine and Gilmore (1999) indicate that to unlock skills and potential for experiential tourism marketing a range of themes, impressions, and memorabilia engaging all senses and some feedback are required. Community-led destination development requires planning through an array of factors which may include a matrix of places, people and processes to validate those factors and link them with key indicators of successful service and product development. People factors might include sustaining clusters of like businesses and partners to share knowledge and skills (Page et al., 2017). Mentoring is seen as contributory to providing new skills as well as developing psychosocial bonds between partners in clusters. Experiential-led tourism is aspirational and proactive suppliers will seek people with interests and aptitudes similar to their own. To achieve the success anticipated in planning for development and sustainability a one-stop-shop approach to public sector support is deemed essential.

Experience-led entrepreneurs

Drucker (1985) identified seven sources of innovation and four strategies employed by entrepreneurs more than two decades ago. The Drucker framework constructed around consistent achievement, 'creative imitation', leadership and specialisms, may still be used for determining the experiences required for success in the development of experiential tourism management in the twenty-first century (Drucker, 1985: 203). Getz et al. (2006) identified several barriers to growth which can be construed as opportunities which included the existence of a business plan, vision and purpose shared with others in the network or cluster, poor access to capital, unclear market planning and implementation and failure to compete. Connected to this are poor support from the public sector advisory services, low uptake of best-practices and insufficient monitoring of strategies. Getz et al. (2004) considered sustaining and developing of family business where many barriers and opportunities are demonstrably the outcome of poor knowledge sharing.

SMEs will undoubtedly benefit from knowledge sharing and mentoring. Mentoring has been valuable to communities in terms of knowledge creation and business growth (Page et al., 2017). These mentor/protégé relationships have provided resources to regenerate communities through the largely informal and invisible relationships that have become established in the Peak District (Wiltshier, 2007). Farmers have become traders in organic produce. Former service workers have become independent small business operators such as bed-and-breakfast accommodation owners. The active encouragement of mentors has been instrumental in encouraging such entrepreneurial activities (Brooker and Joppe, 2014). Knowledge transfer and learning through mentoring alongside public sector business support will also be considered in this study. Between 2003 and 2008 over £6 million per annum was spent in uncoordinated, haphazard and duplicated business support in the region, through 31 different schemes (Parker, 2005). Whilst acknowledging the need for such business support it is imperative that transparent and effective support is offered to sustain innovation against a political background of devolved responsibility.

Case study 2

New Opportunities for Wirksworth

After a renewed interest within this small market town comprising 5000 residents in tourism, marketing, and the creative arts including festivals and performances, the local council was successful in the early twenty-first century in obtaining seed funding for a new project to coordinate and take forward a short-term project to enhance the skills, capacities and re-focus the public and private sector stakeholders on contemporary strengths to bolster a somewhat lacklustre brand, identity and out-of-focus community for the future. New Opportunities for Wirksworth (NOW) was created some twenty years ago and remains a vital part of the community today. The keys to success include a buy-in to key values and beliefs held dear by the community and an agreement to support the project into the twenty-first century with resources shared by the same sectors – public, private and volunteer – with the arts, tourism, education, tourism and marketing. Although not always financially prudent and viable, NOW has taken this community from its fledgling role in tourism and festivals to a healthy performing and creative arts sector on a regular basis with a profile recognised locally and nationally. Key to this case study is the regular and ongoing assertion to skills, capacity building in the agreed areas of development by NOW and guaranteed support from county and town council.

Informal networks of mentors and protégés, which have come into being alongside endogenous planning, policy creation and development, and the public sector's encouragement of local and devolved responsibility from the public to the private sector is well documented (Selman, 1998; Taylor, 2003; Uyarra, 2007). We have seen a rapid increase in postwar baby boomers contemplating retirement and early retirement. What is of concern and interest is the economic and socio-cultural contribution that entrepreneurs can make to communities and regions. A 1998 survey of baby boomers conducted by the American Association of Retired Persons (AARP) revealed that 80 percent of respondents planned to work beyond retirement age, and 17 percent of those planned to launch new businesses (Bridgeland et al., 2008). Further evidence from the United Kingdom comes from a report released by Barclays Bank entitled 'Third Age Entrepreneurs – Profiting from Experience'. Older entrepreneurs are responsible for 50 percent more business start-ups than 10 years ago which amounts to around 60,000 business start-ups in 2006 alone. Third-age entrepreneurs worked hard to build their business with nearly 49 percent working an average of 36 hours or more a week (Bridgeland et al., ibid.).

Older innovators may possess advantages over their younger counterparts with familiarity with business and sector-specific organisational structure and with bureaucracy in general. They may also manage rivalry and competing aims more easily than younger entrepreneurs and be more attuned to the needs of succession planning and 'keeping innovation within the family' (Getz et al., 2004). Despite the emerging empirical evidence to convey adaptation to an entrepreneurial work force and the wider sharing of new and different practices, there are still tensions between planned and ad hoc approaches, between social awareness and the need for new organisational structures and abandoning of obsolete policy (Bridge et al., 2003; Smallwood and Obiamiwe, 2008: 4; Brooker and Joppe, 2014). There are questions around tax and fiscal rewards for innovation and the lagging adoption of continuous and embedded learning in the community.

Skills and training

Embedded within a public sector funded approach to experience economy is the partnership between a diverse range of students and teachers involved in learning in higher education. One size does not fit all and a wide array of skills is required to meet the needs of operators and consumers to ensure a close match between demand and supply. Without doubt current experience-led entrepreneurs have much to share with new start-up SMEs and a new platform with this focus on consumption built into the curriculum will support work-based learning and create work-ready and sensitised suppliers that can fully participate in the staged performance and absorbed involvement with the consumer's values and choices (Csikzentmihalyi, 1992; Prahalad and Ramaswamy, 2004).

Morrison et al. (1999) refer to lifecycle and pioneer an unplanned, formalised structure. They identify phases of development like survival, consolidation and control and control and planning. Getz et al. (2006) offer us a business family ownership model which is developmental and based upon low barriers to entry and a concomitant relatively low level of professionalism, and attention to quality management experiences and practices. They further refine their model by drawing attention to setting, demand, lifecycle, environmental factors that impact upon success and highlight pre-conditions for success as motivation, vision, communication, finance, shared values, laws, strategic planning, networks, supply chain, gender imbalance and seasonality. We cannot pursue all of these but will be mindful of them in the emergent exploratory model.

Case study 3

The market towns initiative

Early in the current century the university was invited to take part, through student engagement, in face-to-face research on a Market Town Initiative that was designed to build skills, capacity and enterprise to develop aspects of declining rural towns' retail and tourism attractiveness components. A project manager developed several interview instruments to measure consumers' preferences for visits to market towns and the availability of key services (transport, car parking and retail). Students engaged with the research and provided an overview of residents, visitors and business perceptions and expectations in respect of capacity to meet and exceed consumers', residents' and business owners' perceptions of barriers and enablers for growth. A series of market towns' 'health' maps was created which reflected the capacity and enthusiasm for development into the twenty-first century. Not only did the project utilise destination communities that were truly and clearly attractive to all but comprehensively reviewed those communities which had hitherto been ignored for any attractiveness for visitors and engaging new business and related innovations and enterprise. In conclusion, three sectors – public, private and voluntary – benefitted from the funded project and on review, all sectors agreed that the project had benefitted their communities and by turn, skills, capacity and orientation to success in meeting diverse needs for the future.

Case study 4

Buxton Town Team – transport committee

Central to the rejuvenation and re-development of any town is the focus on capacity to manage transport services, congestion on public access and difficulties perceived in parking private vehicles in the town. A committee, a sub-branch of the local lobby non-government organisation, was established to identify more sustainable forms of transport in, around and to/from the town. More sustainable options included electric transport for both public and private transport users and a renewed interest in cycling, walking and reduction in the use of private fossil-fuel vehicles by residents, business owners and their employees, places of education and visitors. The current events conducted include seminars and public meetings designed to refocus all stakeholders on alternative and sustainable transport methods and a focus on the local council using the Buxton Town Team members to build a travel plan for all stakeholders with use of university students and volunteers to gather data on perceptions and expectations relevant to the project brief. Thus far the project has some visibility within the town; the aim is to develop a sustainable travel plan that can be rolled out to other destinations and thereby give some credibility to the project team.

Case study 5

Matlock parish council

The local parish council in the remarkably well-known yet tiny inland resort destination of Matlock Bath is the subject of many criticisms and occasional joyous recognition of its existence as an early spa and thermal water destination in the limestone gorge of the River Derwent in Derbyshire. The resort has a plethora of rather cheap and somewhat tawdry attractions with a spectacular gorge setting and an aerial gondola taking visitors from the Derwent's gorge to the top of a peculiarly named cliff top 'Heights of Abraham'. It is a place of stories, of literary connections, of archaeological and historical connections that have, over many years, been lost to the community who lament a credible image and brand within the regional identity and now seek to resurrect tourism as a viable option for future community prosperity and a cornerstone of the regeneration activity now planned (see, for a Portuguese example, Vieira et al., 2016). Staff and students from the university engaged in a variety of tasks to uncover the appropriate brand and identity informed by beliefs and values of a range of stakeholders in the community. Consumer feedback was also solicited in respect of attractions, infrastructure, accommodation and transport, parking arrangements. A rather boisterous series of stakeholders meetings did eventually lead to the promulgation of a tourism development plan led by key stakeholders who were observed to volunteer for roles within the community with this particular rejuvenation and refreshing of brand and identity at the front of these endeavours. Partnerships, networks and collaboration are immediate outcomes for the community stakeholders and new skills and capacity areas have been identified within the community and ongoing involvement of the university is acknowledged to support plans.

Conclusion

There are many factors and indicators that can be used to identify excellence in consumer-led tourism development and then management. The soft skills and aptitudes required of suppliers to lead and harness resources have been considered in the model in Table 10.1. There are many commentators from the social sciences and humanities in addition to a proliferation of critical tourism management and tourism studies research conducted in the past two decades that both underpin the background to success in experience management and marketing (Stylidis et al., 2014; Middleton et al., 2009; Waligo et al., 2013; Prebežac et al., 2016; Wiltshier, 2017). The research engaged in this project will lead to data collection and analysis from demand and supply perspectives. It can reaffirm the current passion for enterprise and initiative generated from services delivered in a competitive arena. It is still important to see that cognition and attitudes toward development are as central to success as the affective components from networks, emotional ties, and aptitude of aspirational leaders in supply. Situation, culture, ideology and pre-disposition all factor in for the consumer experience to improve in future. There are implications for further empirical work as has been outlined.

References

Andereck, K. & Vogt, C. (2000). The relationship between residents' attitudes toward tourism and tourism development options. *Journal of Travel Research*, 39(1): 27–36.

Apostolopoulos, Y., Leivadi, S. & Yiannakis, A. (1996). *The sociology of tourism: Theoretical and empirical investigations*. London: Routledge.

Berry, L. L., Carbone, L. P. & Haeckel, S. H. (2002). Managing the total customer experience. *MIT Sloan Management Review*, 43(3): 85–89.

Botterill, D. & Tribe, J. (2000). The national curriculum for tourism higher education. *National Liaison Group for Higher Education in Tourism: Guideline No. 9*, NLG, London.

Bowen, D. (1989). Consumer thoughts, actions and feelings from participant observations in the service industries. *The Services Industries Journal*, 28(10): 1515–1530.

Bridge, S., O'Neil, K. & Cromie, S. (2003). *Understanding enterprise, entrepreneurship and small business*. Hampshire: Palgrave Macmillan.

Bridgeland, J. M., Putnam, R. D. & Wofford, H. L. (2008). *More to give: Tapping the talents of the baby boomer, silent and greatest generations*. American Association of Retired Persons (AARP).

Brooker, E. & Joppe, M. (2014). Entrepreneurial approaches to rural tourism in the Netherlands: Distinct differences. *Tourism Planning & Development*, 11(3): 343–353.

Checkland, P. & Scholes, J. (1990). *Soft systems methodology in action*. New York: John Wiley & Sons.

Choi, H. S. C. & Sirakaya, E. (2005). Sustainability indicators for managing community tourism. *Tourism Management*, 27(6): 1274–1289.

Cikszentmihalyi, M. (1992). *Flow, the psychology of optimal experience*. London: Harper Collins.

Cohen, E. (1979). A phenomenology of tourist experiences. *Sociology*, 13(2): 179–201.

Crouch, D., Jackson, R. & Thompson, F. (2007). *Media and the tourist imagination: Converging cultures*. London: Routledge.

Diamond, J. & Liddle, J. (2005). *Management of regeneration*. London: Routledge.

Dimanche, F. (2008). From attractions to experiential marketing: The contributions of events to new tourism. In *Change management in tourism: From 'old' to 'new' tourism*, 173–184. Berlin: Erich Schmidt Verlag.

Drucker, P. F. (1985). *Innovation and entrepreneurship: Practice and principles*. London: Heinemann.

Drucker, P. F. (1994). The theory of the business. *Harvard Business Review*, 72(5): 95–104.

Dunne, T. C., Aaron, J. R., McDowell, W. C., Urban, D. J., & Geho, P. R. (2016). The impact of leadership on small business innovativeness. *Journal of Business Research*, 69(11): 4876–4881.

East Midlands Tourism (2003). *Destination East Midlands; East Midlands tourism strategy 2003–2010*. Nottingham: East Midlands Tourism (EMT).

Egan, J. (2004). *The Egan review: Skills for sustainable communities*. Office of the Deputy Prime Minister/HM Government Printing Office.

Faulkner, B. & Tideswell, C. (1997). Framework for monitoring community impacts of tourism. *Journal of Sustainable Tourism*, 5(1): 3–26.

Fernández-Morales, A., Cisneros-Martínez, J. D. & McCabe, S. (2016). Seasonal concentration of tourism demand: Decomposition analysis and marketing implications. *Tourism Management*, 56: 172–190.

Flohr, S. (2001). An analysis of British postgraduate courses in tourism: What role does sustainability play within higher education? *Journal of Sustainable Tourism*, 9(6): 505–513.

Frochot, I. & Batat, W. (2013). *Marketing and designing the tourist experience*. Oxford: Goodfellow Publishers Limited.

Gabriel, Y. & Long, T. (2006). *The unmanageable consumer*. London: Sage.

Getz, D., Carlsen, J. & Morrison, A. (2006). *The family business in tourism & hospitality*. London: CABI.

Gibson, L. (2006). *Learning destinations: The complexity of tourism development*. Karlstad: Karlstad University Studies.

Gibson, L., Lynch, P. & Morrison, A. (2005). The local destination tourism network development issues. *Tourism & Hospitality Planning & Development*, 2(2): 87–99.

Gilchrist, A. (2004). *Community cohesion and community development: Bridges and barricades?* London: Runnymede.

Gilg, A. W. (2005). *Planning in Britain: Understanding and evaluating the post-war system*. London: Sage.

Granovetter, M. (1983). The strength of weak ties: A network theory revisited. *Sociological Theory*, 1: 201–233.

Haskins, C. (2003). *Rural delivery review: A report on the delivery of government policies in rural England*. London: Department of the Environment, Food and Rural Affairs (DEFRA).

Hills, J. & Stewart, K. (2005). *A more equal society*. Bristol: The Policy Press, University of Bristol.

Jafari, J. (2000). *Encyclopaedia of tourism*. London: Routledge.

Jamal, T. & Getz, D. (1995). Collaboration theory and community tourism planning. *Annals of Tourism Research*, 22(1): 186–204.

Joppe, M. (1996). Sustainable community tourism development revisited. *Tourism Management*, 17(7): 475–479.

Kleinman, M. & Piachard, P. (1993). *A European welfare state? European Union social policy in context*. Houndmills: Palgrave McMillan.

Krippendorf, J. (1987). *The holiday makers*. Oxford: Butterworth Heinemann.

Lash, J. & Urry, S. (1994). *Economies of signs and space*. London: Sage.

Ledwith, M. (2005). *Community development: A critical approach*. Bristol: Policy Press.

Leitch, S. (2006). *Leitch review of skills*. London: HM Treasury.

Liebfried, S. & Pierson, P. (1995). Semi sovereign welfare states: Social policy in a multitiered Europe, in Liebfried, S. & Pierson, P. (eds.), *European social policy. Between fragmentation and integration*. Washington, DC: The Brookings Institution.

Lowe, P. & Talbot, H. (2000). Policy for small business support in rural areas: A critical assessment of the proposals for the small business service. *Policy Review Section' Regional Studies'*, 34(5): 479–499.

MacCannell, D. (2013). *The tourist: A new theory of the leisure class*. Oakland: University of California Press.

Mascarenhas, O., Kesavan, R. & Bernacchi, M. (2006). Lasting customer loyalty: A total customer experience approach. *Journal of Consumer Marketing*, 23(7): 397–405.

McGehee, N. G., Knollenberg, W. & Komorowski, A. (2015). The central role of leadership in rural tourism development: A theoretical framework and case studies. *Journal of Sustainable Tourism*, 23(8–9): 1277–1297.

McKercher, B. & Du Cros, H. (2002). *Cultural tourism: The partnership between tourism and cultural heritage management*. Abingdon on Thames: Routledge.

Michael, E. & Plowman, G. (2002). Mount Stirling; the politics of process failure. *Journal of Sustainable Tourism*, 10(2): 154–169.

Middleton, V. T., Fyall, A. & Morgan, M., & Ranchhod, A. (2009). *Marketing in travel and tourism*. London and New York: Routledge.

Mok, C., Sparks, B. & Kandampully, J. (2013). *Service quality management in hospitality, tourism, and leisure*. Abingdon on Thames: Routledge.

Morrison, A., Rimington, M. & Williams, C. (1999). *Entrepreneurship in the hospitality, tourism and leisure industries*. Oxford: Butterworth Heinemann.

Nunkoo, R. & Ramkissoon, H. (2011). Developing a community support model for tourism. *Annals of Tourism Research*, 38(3): 964–988.

Okazaki, E. (2008). A community-based tourism model: Its conception and use. *Journal of Sustainable Tourism*, 16(5): 511–529.

Osborne, S. P., Williamson, A. & Beattie, R. (2002). Community involvement in rural regeneration partnerships in the UK: Key issues from a three nation study. *Regional Studies: The Journal of the Regional Studies Association*, 36(9):1083–1092.

Otto, J. E. & Ritchie, J. B. (1996). The service experience in tourism. *Tourism Management*, 17(3): 165–174.

Outhwaite, W. (1994). *Habermas: A critical introduction*. Cambridge: Polity.

Page, S. J., Hartwell, H., Johns, N., Fyall, A., Ladkin, A. & Hemingway, A. (2017). Case study: Wellness, tourism and small business development in a UK coastal resort: Public engagement in practice. *Tourism Management*, 60: 466–477.

Parker, K. (2005). *Rural funding programmes: A case study in the Peak District*. Peak District National Park Authority and Countryside Agency (CA).

Pine, B. J. & Gilmore, J. H. (1999). *The Experience Economy*. Brighton: Harvard Business Press.

Powell, F. & Geoghegan, M. (2005). Beyond political zoology: Community development, civil society, and strong democracy. *Community Development Journal*, 41(2): 128–142.

Prahalad, C. K. & Ramaswamy, V. (2004). Co-creation experiences: The next practice in value creation. *Journal of Interactive Marketing*, 18(3): 5–14.

Prebežac, D., Schott, C. & Sheldon, P. (Eds.). (2016). *The tourism education futures initiative: Activating change in tourism education*. Abingdon on Thames: Routledge.

Prentice, R. (1993). *Tourism & heritage attractions*. London: Routledge.

Rae, D. (2007). Connecting enterprise and graduate employability: Challenges to the higher education culture and curriculum? *Education+ Training*, 49(8/9): 605–619.

Ray, C. (1998). Culture, intellectual property and territorial rural development. *Sociologia Ruralis*, 38(1): pp. 3–20

Roberts, K. (2004). *The leisure industries*. Houndmills: Palgrave McMillan.

Russell, R. & Faulkner, B. (1999). Movers and shakers: Chaos makers in tourism development. *Tourism Management*, 20(4): 411–423.

Saxena, G. (2005). Relationship networks and the learning regions: Case evidence from the Peak District National Park. *Tourism Management*, 26(2): 277–289.

Selman, P. (1998). Local Agenda 21: Substance or spin. *Journal of Environmental Planning and Management*, 41(5): 533–553.

Simchi-Levy, D., Kaminsky, P. & Simchi-Levy, E. (2003). *Designing and managing the supply chain*. New York: McGraw Hill.

Simpson, K. (2001). Strategic planning and community involvement as contributors to sustainable tourism development. *Current Issues in Tourism*, 4(1): 3–41.

Smallwood, C. & Obiamiwe, L. (2008). *Improving Employment Prospects for the over 50s*, Prince's Initiative for Mature Enterprise in Wales (PRIME).

Smith, V. L. (ed.). (2012). *Hosts and guests: The anthropology of tourism*. Philadelphia: University of Pennsylvania Press.

Stuart, M. (2002). Critical influences on tourism as a subject in UK higher education: Lecturer perspectives. *Journal of Hospitality, Leisure, Sport and Tourism Education*, 1(1): 5–18.

Stylidis, D., Biran, A., Sit, J. & Szivas, E. M. (2014). Residents' support for tourism development: The role of residents' place image and perceived tourism impacts. *Tourism Management*, 45: 260–274.

Szreter, S. & Woolcock, M. (2004). Health by association? Social capital, social theory, and the political economy of public health. *International Journal of Epidemiology*, 33(4): 650–667.

Taylor, D. W., Jones, O. & Boles, K. (2004). Building social capital through action learning: An insight into the entrepreneur. *Education+Training*, 46(5): 226–235.

Taylor, M. (2003). *Public policy in the community*. Houndmills: Palgrave McMillan.

Taylor, M., Barr, A. & West, A. (2000). *Signposts to community development* (2nd ed.). London: Community Development Foundation.

Thomas, R. & Long, J. (2001). Tourism and economic regeneration: The role of skills development. *International Journal of Tourism Research*, 3(3): 229–240.

Timothy, D. J. & Tosun, C. (2003). Arguments for community participation in the tourism development process. *Journal of Tourism Studies*, 14(2): 2.

Tonnies, F. (1974). *On social ideas and ideologies*. New York: Harper & Row.

Uyarra, E. (2007). Key dilemmas of regional innovation policies. *Innovation the European Journal of Social Science Research*, 20(3): 243–261.

Vieira, I., Rodrigues, A., Fernandes, D. & Pires, C. (2016). The role of local government management of tourism in fostering residents' support to sustainable tourism development: Evidence from a Portuguese historic town. *International Journal of Tourism Policy*, 6(2): 109–135.

Von Friedrichs Grängsjö, Y. (2003). Destination networking: Co-opetition in peripheral surroundings. *International Journal of Physical Distribution & Logistics Management*, 33(5): 427–448.

Waligo, V. M., Clarke, J. & Hawkins, R. (2013). Implementing sustainable tourism: A multi-stakeholder involvement management framework. *Tourism Management*, 36: 342–353.

Wiltshier, P. (2007). Visibility from invisibility: The role of mentoring in community-based tourism. *Tourism*, 55(4): 375–390.

Wiltshier, P. (2017). Community engagement and rural tourism enterprise, Ch 4 in Oriade, A. & Robinson, P. (eds.), *Rural tourism and enterprise: Management, marketing and sustainability*, Wallingford: CABI.

Wittmann, R. G. & Reuter, M. (2008). *Strategic Planning*. London: Kogan Page.

11 The path

From agricultural country to popular travel destination

Akmal Rakhmanov and Nutfillo Ibragimov

Introduction

Uzbekistan has a population in excess of 33 million and is the size of the US state of California in the middle of Central Asia. Physically, it is 85 percent steppes adjoining both the Pamir and Tyan Sian mountains in the South and the East. It has a dry, subtropical climate. It separated from Russia with the demise of the Soviet Union and is now a sovereign republic with borders with Kazakhstan, Kirgizstan, Turkmenistan, Tajikistan and Afghanistan.

However, it is renowned for its ancient nomadic civilization with artifacts found from the Bronze Age. The great empires of China, Persia and India helped local tribes to use the opportunity to connect one to each other. One of first Europeans to reach Uzbekistan, Macedonian Alexander who discovered the Sogdiana, once led his troops to Bactria. Uzbekistan was once the location of a path from Europe to East Asia for almost two millenniums. Across this path merchants, travelers, invaders, scientists, researchers and diplomats naturally made the heart of Central Asia one of significant crossroads of the biggest civilization exchange, known today as Great Silk Road. Along with main commodities traffic, silk from east to west and pearls, jade and lapis lazuli from west to east, Bukhara and Samarkand became also centers of religious encounter in different periods. In terms of religion Uzbekistan is considered as the first monotheistic beliefs; Zoroastrianism with its strong cultural traditions used to dominate from 5th century BC. The Nestorians traveled through to the East during the time while Buddhist monasteries in central Asia were widely sending their missionaries to the East and West. Obviously Islam, as the last and strongest culture within two hundred years, became the main faith of the governing dynasties here that followed the Renaissance of Islamic culture lasting from the 10th century till the 15th century and brought the masterpiece of Islamic architecture. The latter is considered to be the "post cards" of Uzbekistan tourism attracting most travelers in the first place.

The formation of state committee of the Republic of Uzbekistan for tourism development

In Uzbekistan, economic reforms are gradually being implemented in the tourism sector. According to expert opinion, the first stage of economic reforms in this

Map 11.1 Location of Uzbekistan

Source: U.S. Central Intelligence Agency; www.geographicguide.net/asia/caucasus-map.htm

area began as far back as 1992 (Ibragimov, 2014). At this particular time the "Republican council for tourism and guided tours", branches of the State Committee for International Tourism "Goskomintur"(State Committee for International Tourism) located in Tashkent, Samarkand and Bukhara had been established, and the National Company "Uzbektourism" set up in the framework of the youth tourist organization "Sputnik" based on the Decree of President I.A. Karimov (see Figure 11.1).

The decree was adopted in order to create a tourism system in Uzbekistan that meets the requirements of international standards, to improve the management of this area, and increase economic efficiency.

After becoming a member of the World Tourism Organization (WTO) in September 1993, the following year "Uzbektourism" NC in cooperation with the UN and UNESCO held the world tourism international seminar "The Great Silk Road" in Tashkent. At the meeting held on Registan square, the Samarkand Declaration for the Great Silk Road project implementation was adopted:

- 1996 – Two large hotel complexes "BuxoroPalace" and "Afrosiyob Palace" were set up.
- 1997 – "Uzbektourism" NC was elected to the WTO Executive Committee and its international activities were recognized by Uzbekistan, France and

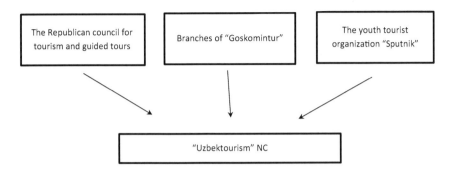

Figure 11.1 Directions of foundation of the national company "Uzbektourism" (Ibragimov, 2014)

Source: Author

Italy at the 12th General Assembly of the World Tourism Organization, which was held in Istanbul.

- 1998 – Association of private tourism organizations was established pursuant to the Resolution of the Cabinet of Ministers of the Republic of Uzbekistan No.346 "On improvement of the activities of tourism organizations" in order to promote the participation of small and medium-sized tourism organizations in market of travel services.
- 1999 – The Law of the Republic of Uzbekistan "On Tourism" is adopted. Decree of the President "On the State Program for the Development of Tourism in Uzbekistan until 2005" was signed.
- 2000 – The Republican Scientific and Consulting Center of "Uzbektourism" NC was established in order to train personnel and implement measures on personnel advanced training, retraining and certification in tourism. The faculty of international tourism was established at the Tashkent State University of Economics.
- 2003 – Provision on licensing of tourist activities is approved by the Resolution of the Cabinet of Ministers of the Republic of Uzbekistan No.497 of November 11, 2003, in accordance with article No.5 of the Law of the Republic of Uzbekistan "On licensing of certain types of activities".
- 2004 – Resolution of the Cabinet of Ministers of the Republic of Uzbekistan No.360 of July 28 "On further improvement of the activities of "Uzbektourism" NC" is adopted in order to ensure an effective management system in the field of tourism.
- 2006 – "Uzbektourism" NC started the implementation of measures for the gradual restructuring of the tourism sector in 2006–2010 in accordance with the enactment of the Cabinet of Ministers of the Republic of Uzbekistan.
- 2007 – Decree of the President of the Republic of Uzbekistan "On additional measures for acceleration of the development of the service sector in the

period up to 2010" is issued with a view to further developing the service sector and providing the population with modern and high quality services.
- 2009 – "Program for development of tourism and improvement of the quality of services in the Republic of Uzbekistan until 2015" was approved by the Prime Minister of the Republic of Uzbekistan Sh. M. Mirziyoyev.
- 2010 – The Cabinet of Ministers of the Republic of Uzbekistan adopted a Resolution "On approval of the State program for the protection, preservation, promotion and use of intangible cultural heritage in 2010–2020".

The Deputy Prime Minister of the Republic of Uzbekistan E.M. Ganiev approved the "Program of goal-oriented measures for the development of tourism in 2011–2012 and the export potential of tourism services by regions".

The marketing project "Mega-info-tours"–"Arrangement of study tours" is being implemented for representatives of foreign travel companies and mass media.

In 2015, there were 1,977,600 foreign visitors to Uzbekistan who received services, and at that time there were more than 900 travel-oriented companies in the country, including over 400 hotels and 500 travel agencies.

80% of the stream of tourists is accounted for in the developed tourist regions of the country – the Bukhara, Samarkand, Khorezm, Tashkent regions and Tashkent city.

Tourist areas of the Fergana Valley, Jizzakh, Kashkadarya and Surkhandarya regions, constituting 20% of the total stream, are of great interest to foreign tourists.

As one of the main countries of the Great Silk Road, Uzbekistan is increasingly attracting foreign partners and tourists for its centuries-old history, unique culture and traditions.

Another important feature unique to Uzbekistan is that the national craftsmanship is highly developed and carefully preserved. Currently, over 1,500 craftsmen are engaged in the manufacture of gifts (souvenirs). These are porcelain, ceramic goods, national knives, shahisuzani, skullcaps, knitted and carpet articles and many others. According to experts, tourists spend about 30% of their money on commercial goods (clothing, folk crafts and other souvenirs) in the places where they travel. Thus, the revival of folk crafts will give an additional impetus to the further growth of the export potential of Uzbekistan.

According to the State Committee of the Republic of Uzbekistan for tourism development, today there are 795 tour operators and over 886 hotels in Uzbekistan (State Committee of the Republic of Uzbekistan for tourism development, 2019). In 2018, there were 222,000 employees in this area, which is 0.8% of the total employment. In view of multiplier effect (Safarova, 2014) of the tourism industry, it is 577.2 thousand people which accounts for 2.6% of total employment. This statistical data shows that the tourism infrastructure in Uzbekistan is developing rapidly.

It should be noted that tourism in the economy of the Samarkand, Bukhara, Khiva and Shakhrisabz regions is widely known due to high attractiveness from the tourist point of view. The contribution of the Tashkent International Economic University, the Samarkand Institute of Economics and Service, and the Bukhara State University, as well as five secondary and specialized educational institutions is invaluable in the training of personnel in the field of tourism.

Uzbekistan has great tourism potential. First of all, these are unique cultural monuments of our country being the main representations of the history of many thousand years of Uzbekistan, as well as major cities of the Great Silk Road: Samarkand, Bukhara, Khiva, Shahrisabz and others. In addition, the location of our country in the center of Central Asia is geographically advantageous. Uzbekistan has a vast natural and climatic attractiveness. In addition, our republic is highly well located in terms of geography, in other words, in the core of the Central Asia. Uzbekistan has vast natural and climatic notable places. There are different climatic zones: sandy deserts, crags, oases of valleys, beautiful and unique mountains and even subtropics. Bioclimatic conditions of the country create favorable conditions for the active use of tourism. During the year, one can go in for sports and restore health.

There are ninenature reserves protected by the state, recreation parks, monuments of nature, dendrological and botanic gardens. This indicates a great potential for the development of ecotourism.

140 health centers are built for the development of mountaineering and ecotourism in the nature areas of Chimgan and Charvak, which will allow for recovering the health of 28,000 visitors a year, that is, to promote recreational tourism.

Over 20,000 private summer cottages are transferred to their owners, which allow more than 16,000 local visitors a year to relax in nature. All these events create favorable conditions not only for the development of cultural tourism, but also other types of tourism, such as mountaineering, ecotourism, and recreational tourism.

However, cultural tourism is the main type of tourism for Uzbekistan. According to the State Committee of the Republic of Uzbekistan for tourism development, there are 4,134 architectural and archaeological monuments in Uzbekistan, of which 501 are used for tourist purposes (see Table 11.1). There are 1,548 architectural objects and 2,586 archaeological monuments of historical and cultural value in Uzbekistan. However, only some cities have the status of tourist place. Others, however, are still unable to address issues of effective use of their tourism potential and remain in the form of a remarkable geographical location that has neither advantages nor harm.

There is potential for the development of tourism and attraction of tourists to densely populated parts of the architectural monuments of Bukhara, Samarkand, Khiva, Shakhrisabz and Tashkent, which have the status of tourist place and are known as tourist cities in the world market, but are in poor repair, far from the main tourist sites, and in an insufficiently explored state from a historical point of view, as well as being insufficiently known to the developers of tourist packages.

It should be noted that it is not appropriate to use only 13% of the existing potential in cultural tourism, and the issue of developing effective ways to use them should be of paramount importance to workers of this sector.

Since 2016, the Uzbekistan tourism sector has experienced dramatic changes. The following regulatory acts form a legal framework for these changes: "On

Table 11.1 Number of historical and cultural monuments in Uzbekistan

No.	Cities and regions of Uzbekistan	Architectural monuments		Archaeological monuments	
		The republican	*The regional*	*The republican*	*The regional*
1	Tashkent city	158	16	6	31
2	The Tashkent region	24	19	207	0
3	Andijan	17	90	62	196
4	Bukhara	186	112	88	410
5	Jizzakh	3	0	59	50
6	Kashkadarya	86	81	205	0
7	Republic of Karakalpakstan	23	3	104	0
8	Namangan	17	50	79	31
9	Samarkand	101	223	148	660
10	Surkhandarya	36	6	151	0
11	Syrdarya	4	0	1	0
12	Fergana	51	105	68	0
13	Khorezm	120	17	8	22
	Total	826	722	1186	1400
	Total	1548		2586	

Source: State Committee of the Republic of Uzbekistan for tourism development

Measures to Ensure the Accelerated Development of Tourism Sector of the Republic of Uzbekistan" dated 2016;"On Arrangement of Activities of the State Committee of the Republic of Uzbekistan for Tourism Development" dated December 2, 2016;"On Measures for Accelerated Development of Tourism Potentials of Bukhara and Bukhara region for 2017–2019" dated May 19, 2017; "On Priority Measures for Development of Tourism Sphere for 2018–2019"; "On Introduction of Amendments and Additions into the Consular Fees Tariff of the Republic of Uzbekistan" dated December 4, 2017; "On Establishment of "Charvak" Free Tourism Zone" dated December 5, 2017; "On Further Managerial Procedures to Create an Enabling Environment for the Development of Tourism Potential of the Republic of Uzbekistan" dated February 3, 2018; "On Measures for the Development of Inbound Tourism" dated February 6, 2018;"On Measures for Further Improvement of Activities of the State Committee of the Republic of Uzbekistan for Tourism Development" dated February 6, 2018; "On Measures to Ensure Accelerated Development of Domestic Tourism" dated February 7, 2018; and tourism development concept for 2019–2025 has been adopted.

On January 5, 2019, the following regulatory acts essential for tourism sector were passed: Decree of the President "On Measures for Accelerated Development of Tourism in the Republic of Uzbekistan".

- These regulatory acts determine the major strategic directions for tourism sector development and set objectives. Thus, priority directions for tourism sector development are defined as follows: improvement of regulatory and legal framework in the field of tourism activity, implementation of international regulations and standards aimed at the establishment of enabling environment for tourism sector development.

- In this direction, an objective was set to ensure harmonization of domestic regulatory and legal framework with international standards and regulations, to establish enabling environment for tourism sector development, to ensure the efficient use of economic resources in order to enhance the role of this sector in the economy, including, to reach US$2.2 billion tourism export growth by 2025.
- Development of tourism and related infrastructures in all regions of the republic with account of needs and demands of tourists. Therefore, the following shall be provided for: tourism infrastructure development in accordance with international standards by increasing the number of tour operators from 860 to 1,676 and of other tourism sector actors, by increasing the number of means of accommodation from 900 to 3,000; ensuring the versatility, quality and increase in the volume of tourism services export, attracting the major representatives (brands) of world market and increasing the inflows of foreign investments.
- Development of transport logistics expansion of external and domestic routes, improvement of transport services quality. In particular, the following shall be achieved: expansion of international flight geography and direct flights, including, to historical cities of the country, improvement of the quality and reduction of cost of air travel; insuring comfortable and affordable transport logistics, that includes air, rail and road transport, arrangement of comfortable conditions for traveling to the regions and foreign countries, transformation of the country into a major regional transport hub in passenger transportation field.
- Adoption of complex measures aimed at the reduction of the influence of seasonal factor by diversification of tourism product and services, focused on various segments of tourism market. In this direction, the following targets are set: improvement of the attractiveness of proposed tours by filling them with events and combining different types of tourism, increasing the average duration of tours around the country for at least two days, bringing it to 8 days, and around the cities to 3 days from 1.5–2.0 days.
- Ensuring sustainable tourism development and achievement of follow-up visits to the country.
- Development of domestic tourism, providing encouragement for high performance of tourism actors aimed at satisfaction of needs in tourism services within the Republic. In this direction, the following objectives are set: to efficiently use domestic resources to develop high quality tourism products, to reduce the dependence on seasonal factors and increase hotels occupancy, especially during low season months.
- To expand the domestic tourists flow between the regions and increase the number of tourists from 14 million. to 25 million people per year.

- Promotion of tourism product of the Republic of Uzbekistan for domestic and external tourism market, improvement of country's image as safe destination for travel and recreation.
- It is necessary to build an image of a country with a developed tourism industry and rich tourism potential, as well as a safe destination for travel and recreation, to ensure development of new promising markets, to increase in the number of foreign travelers from 5.3 million to 9.1 million people per year, as well as to engage foreign partners in attraction of tourists to Uzbekistan.
- Improvement of a system for highly skilled specialists training, retraining and further training of service providers shall be provided to establish an integrated system for professional personnel training, to increase the quality of education and services provision, and to meet the demand for highly qualified managers, administrators, operators, receptionists and chefs.

Results

Over the past 3 years, International Openness Index of Uzbekistan has suffered major changes and currently the following results have been achieved:

- As of February 1, 2019, 30-day visa-free regime has been introduced for citizens from 45 states. Now, the total number of countries of citizens are allowed visa-free entry into Uzbekistan has reached 64;
- As of February 1, 2019, the list of countries approved by the State Committee for Tourism Development, the Ministry of Foreign Affairs, and the National Security Service, of which citizens are allowed to receive electronic entry visa has been expanded to include over 100 countries;
- As of March 15, 2019, a system of electronic visas (two-time and multiple entry visa), valid within 30 days has been introduced, as well as additional visa categories for certain groups of foreign citizens (academic visa, student visa, pilgrim visa, vatandosh visa, medical visa);
- Simplification of registration system for all type of visitors(backpackers, business travelers, package/group travelers, relative visitors) in different categories of accommodations including hostels, 2-3-4-5 star hotels, home stays, family visits, camping, and yurt accommodations by online application via www.e-mehmon.uz.

As a result of progress in the sector, competition among entrepreneurs arose. These innovators began to expand services outside of the major visited cultural centers. They acknowledged the need to diversify experiences for visitors beyond agriculture and introduce them to the main treasure of the nation: exploration of Uzbek rural life. The country lifestyles had been "terra incognita" due to inaccessibility. Any tourism offers of less sophisticated rural locations during visits help visitors to learn more about the region. *Rustam Aka's*(brother) house outside of Bukhara could be a perfect example of such a successful project. Being professionally educated in tourism, involved in both accommodation and gastronomy, his son Doston, who has been living in Bukhara city for a long time, initiates a day trip to his motherland *Nayman* village. Along with telling the story of a small community, its origins, and its daily life, he includes familiarization with the economy, standards, and the communications inside. Moreover, with the assistance of his friendly neighborhood, guests have the opportunity of a "hands on" experience to be a local. While ladies, traditionally for them in this region, invite volunteers to give a hand with cooking and baking, men are involved in some physical activities in privately owned gardens as well as animal husbandry. Since owning or renting land and animal breeding businesses are tightly linked to each other, the hosts suggest with pleasure that their guests walk to one of the nearby close farming lands to help with seasonal physical work, as they say, "there is always some job needed to be done on the spot".

At the beginning of the local tourism project only one hosting family participated and prepared appropriate facilities to receive guests from abroad. Now, not only visiting farms run by independent entrepreneurs, but also visits to the imam of the mosque and school visits are commonplace. Eventually, from season to season as more local people join in, more community stakeholders are encouraged as they explore new ideas and actions for extra income.

Perhaps the most successfully operating projects in the community-based tourism of Uzbekistan is the visit of traditional workshops in less remote areas, where the main purpose is getting acquainted with local handcrafts (see Figure 11.2).

The Narzullaev's family from Gijduvan, considered as the representatives of old ceramic school, were regularly visited by travelers taking the highway between Samarkand and Bukhara. Typically for such a workshop, Olimjon and Obidjon's well as their father and another five previous generations are busy making their iconic pottery. Their newly reconstructed workshop, which is also their own home, permits them to provide guided tours in a foreign language with the demonstration of the product given in each step separately for each group. Even though selling ceramics to visitors is the main income for three generations of the family the most common additional service is providing fresh home food prepared and served by other family members and neighbors, keeping both guests and staff busy.

Conclusion

Being involved in this industry practically as the professional tour operators for regional and international tourism also, the authors are aiming to continue scientific and practical experiments with their own input into creation of new segments as well as opportunities to develop sustainable models of growth. As we see the very obvious role of state before and especially after the designed reforms in this "new" industry, we believe that further facilitating long-term operations should not only accurately protect national cultural values for its

Figure 11.2 Masterclass from master (author: Master's collection)
Source: Author

original and unique preservation but also step-by-step inference of its physical influence in liberalization.

As the main goal to increase an attractiveness of destination by providing safety and accessibility (financial and distance) along with different type of activities for various categories of travelers, we believe that the young but still fast-growing population of Uzbekistan saves its great achievement, tolerance, that plays perhaps one of major roles for integration in a high competing 21st-century world.

References

Ibragimov N.S., (2014) Destinatsion menejment: davlat miqyosida turizmni bozor usulida boshqarish san'ati. (Destination management: The art of managing tourism in market style throughout the country). "Turon zamin ziyo", Toshkent.

Nilufar Safarova, (2014) Tsepnaya reaktsiya turizma (Chain Reaction of tourism). J. "Ekonomicheskoye obozreniye", http://review.uz/ru/article/855[15.08.2014].

National Statistics Committee of Republic of Uzbekistan, 2018. www.stat.uz/tourism [10.10.2018]

State Committee of the Republic of Uzbekistan for tourism development, (2019). http://uzbektourism.uz/ru/research. (accessed 05 March 2019).

12 Community-based tourism

The Romeiros Way in São Miguel Island in Azores/Portugal

Vitor Ambrósio

Introduction

"Community-based tourism is becoming a priority for destinations throughout the world". This sentence was the challenge received for writing this book chapter. Bearing it in mind the author decided to explore a potential tourist product which exists in São Miguel Island in the Azores Archipelago (Portugal).

In this island the Lent Pilgrimages take place every single year. At the end of a pilgrimage day the locals welcome the pilgrims in their houses, providing them dinner and accommodation.

On the one hand the 250 km (approximate) pilgrimage route along the coast (natural patrimony), crossing the small towns and passing by all churches where there's a Virgin's image (built patrimony), could become a great tourist product; on the other, the services now offered to pilgrims could become a tourist supply delivered by the host communities to tourists, allowing locals to have an extra incoming at the end of the year.

As commonly known, tourist supply and tourist demand are the two pillars of tourism products and tourism destinations. On the side of the tourist demand will be discussed the type of tourists who could better fit in the proposed product and on the tourist's supply side will be debated both the characteristics of the tourist destination and how the locals can become part-time tourist agents (without changing their usual economical sustenance/profession).

The research supports the idea that a tradition with over four centuries of existence may become a starting point and a good example of a community-based tourism that would strengthen at same time sustainable development and sustainable tourism.

Methodology

Working on a report/research requested by an Azorean Tourism Organization for improving religious tourism in the Azores, more specifically in the main island São Miguel, the author had to look for all its religious traditions.

Although in the report it was necessary to refer to the main religious manifestations on the island, before starting it, it was already acquired that the best-known religious festivity is the Feast of Ecce Homo (which takes place in the fifth week after Easter). Besides the Feast as a moment of deep religious experiences/practices for the islanders it is also a gathering occasion for the Azorean diaspora (mainly the ones living in the US and Canada), with this Feast for many São Miguel inhabitants being even more important for the family's congregation than Christmas. For the referred to reasons this event is one of the island's strongest tourism products, not only among the Azorean immigrants but also among the mainland Portuguese.

Amidst the other religious manifestations there was one that called the author's attention – the Lent Pilgrimages. In the subsequent research, an interview with a regular pilgrim/*romeiro* in the Lent Pilgrimages offered the opportunity to participate in the pilgrimage. In fact, answering the question about the emotions felt by pilgrims during the pilgrimage, the interviewed stated that no verbal description would be enough to transmit the pilgrims' feelings. Only by joining a group would it be possible to reach the question's understanding.

To be part of the *romeiros'*/pilgrims' group constituted the opportunity to implement direct observation considering the physical realities of the way, the group's behaviours, the hosts' conduct, and the services organized and offered by the locals to the *romeiros*/pilgrims.

In the report/study for the Azorean Tourism Organization, it was underlined the potential that that pilgrimage road had to become a tourist product, and how it could complement the tourism supply of the probably most important tourism product in the Azores, nature tourism. The final recommendations focused on the creation of a 250 km route; for that it would be necessary to rethink the land management of some municipalities by improving the existing trails and the rural and forest paths and mainly by replacing/turning the asphalt tracks into nature trails.

Though the required study was above all to find solutions for increasing religious tourism, already during the pilgrimage it become evident for the author that the creation of the Romeiros Way could also trigger different kinds of tourism products.

In fact, the 8 days experience lived, and the observation of the elements comprehended in the Lent Pilgrimages (either material or immaterial) allows to state that most of those elements accomplish the essential variables for the construction of a solid community-based and sustainable tourism product. This is the point of view which will be defended along this chapter. For that it is necessary to provide the description of the Lent Pilgrimages (pointing out spiritual and material characteristics), to review and to select the existing resources according to the intended proposal's tourism supply, to define the segments that can fit in the proposal's tourist demand and last but not least to suggest how all elements and agents should interact to achieve the desired community-based tourism project in São Miguel island.

The tradition – Lent Pilgrimage in São Miguel/Azores (Portugal)

The origin of the pilgrimage dates to the XVI century when seismic crisis affected São Miguel Island. The destruction and the many deaths caused impelled the locals to organize pilgrimages in order to seek divine protection against those events and obtain forgiveness for their own and everyone else's sins. Since then, every year groups of men, called *romeiros*, bond in pilgrimage around the island (Visit Azores, 2016).

The Lent Pilgrimage takes place in the period between Carnival and Easter (in a period of about 5 to 6 weeks). Men of all ages and social status (women are not allowed to join the pilgrims' groups) get together in groups and walk about 250 km around the island for 8 days. The brothers (as the pilgrims are called) must all dress alike and follow very strict rules such as not holding mobile phones, cameras, sunglasses or shave during the whole pilgrimage (it seems that blade shaves were forbidden to prevent occasional bloody fights). Each pilgrim contributes with a varied small amount of money for logistical issues. The groups of pilgrims are on average made up of 40–50 men, being each group always accompanied by the spirit/presence of the Holy Family – St. Joseph, the Virgin Mary and Baby Jesus (Ambrósio, 2011).

Most groups start the pilgrimage at their parish church on a Saturday, and end on the following Saturday, again at the same parish church (the first groups leave on the weekend after Ash Wednesday and the last groups return to their home parishes on Holy Thursday). The groups round the island, walking clockwise, and ensure the visit to churches and chapels in which there is a statue of the Virgin (altogether there are about 100). As there's no signage on the way or books with the itinerary, it is only possible to walk this pilgrimage road when accompanied by a guide (in the Lent Pilgrimage, two pilgrims lead the group).

The purposes inherent to this tradition are mainly religious and spiritual, being structured in a penitential basis – one of the pilgrims named the prosecutor of the souls receives the prayers sought by the islanders and requests the master to have them prayed when he finds it more convenient (Ambrósio, 2011). The pilgrimage's day lasts around 15 hours and a good part of that time is reserved for praying – along the way the pilgrims recite the rosary, chant prayers and stop at the entrance of churches and chapels to sing their salves and prayers or go inside the temples to kneel before the Blessed Sacrament.

Logistics regarding meals and accommodation are planned in advance. A few weeks before the day of departure, pilgrimage participants meet once a week. These weekly meetings serve two goals: on the one hand, to provide spiritual/religious guidance, and on the other hand, to plan the stops, during the 8 days, regarding the meals and places where they will stay overnight.

The beginning of the day is usually around 4 a.m. and the day of pilgrimage ends only at sunset. The main mealtimes take into account the rhythms of the pilgrimage. The first main meal is served at 4:30 a.m., consisting of hot drinks (milk, tea, coffee) and cheese or ham sandwiches; the second, at 9 a.m., is a hot meal with soup, main course and fruit or dessert; the third one, at 2:00 p.m., is identical to the previous one – between these meals, rest stops can also become comfort-stops. Meals during the day are offered by the locals (as the result of residents' initiatives) and are served in parochial centres, in local associations or in picnic parks (when by meal time the pilgrims' group is far from a town). On the second and fifth day the noon meal is brought by the pilgrims' families – that is a moment for sharing emotions and to replace dirty laundry with washed laundry. The last warm meal (the night one) is offered by the families that welcome the pilgrims in their houses.

In fact, one of the characteristics of the Lent Pilgrimages is that local communities shelter the pilgrims. The pilgrims' walking day ends at a town's parish church; there, pilgrims and local community attend a mass. At its end each family takes home two to three pilgrims/brothers. After a warm and relaxing shower, all (pilgrims and family members) share a rich meal and some prayers. For those families is very important to offer what they have best (either food or accommodation); it's their way of thanking the pilgrims for the sacrifices that they make to obtain the celestial protection for the whole island.

> Whoever receives these pilgrims of peace does not hide a huge pleasure in the hospitality, in its noblest sense. They share their home – and in most cases, offering the pilgrims their own bedroom – with those men who trudge hundreds of kilometres carrying on their shoulders the sins of the community.
>
> (Coutinho et al., 2006: 85)

Although this tradition/pilgrimage is deeply based in religiosity and spirituality, the fact is that it's possible to find in it the basic tourism elements. On the one hand, we have the attractions of a tourist destination, in this case, rails/paths along the Atlantic coast, surrounded by beautiful landscapes of volcanic origin and luxuriant vegetation; on the other, we may find the main tourist supply's components, lodgement and food/beverages.

Any tourist product must be planned bearing in mind that apart from having transport to reach the destination and apart from the tourist destination's attractions, tourists must also have a place to sleep and the possibility to have meals served. Another question is the variety of tourism supply options, swinging from the humble to luxurious conditions.

In São Miguel Island, with exception made for its capital (Ponta Delgada), the most part of small towns crossed by the pilgrims don't offer anything close to luxurious/comfortable commodities, meaning that (future) tourists who look for them will not fit in the case study explored in this chapter. This issue leads to a set of very important questions: what the destination attributes are, considering the patrimony (natural and built resources) and commodities, and what are the types of tourists that can become the public/demand for this kind of tourist proposal.

The proposal's tourist supply

Pilgrimage roads are becoming quite important tourist attractions, the Santiago Camino being the best-known example. The correct management of a pilgrimage route induces local and regional development. This is a reality attested by many studies and academic works, focusing some of those the efforts and investments often made by different stakeholders to enhance the pilgrimage route's features and to augment visitors'/pilgrims' experience (Murray and Graham, 1997; Devereux, 2003; Richards and Fernandes, 2007; Ambrósio, 2015; Fernandes et al., 2017; Ambrósio, 2017).

A pilgrimage route cannot be artificially created. It is only possible to think of a pilgrimage way as a tourist product if for decades and/or centuries believers have walked the same road to reach a certain sanctuary. More important than the natural beauty and built patrimony along the way (tangible elements), it is the spirituality left by many thousands and even by millions of pilgrims who have trudged that same road (intangible elements). Pilgrims' emotions and feelings are not visible, but their strength/energy is felt by those who walk along one pilgrimage path.

Bearing in mind this assumption, only the pilgrimage routes still in use and, in some cases, those that existed but have been no longer used, can be considered for the creation or improvement of this type of tourism product.

Besides the referred, it is also important to underline that routes (in general) serve to link attractions that would independently not have the potential to attract visitors. Using a synergy effect, a route creates a greater pulling power and seems to be a good opportunity for less mature areas with cultural/heritage resources that appeal to special interest tourists (Meyer, 2004).

Regardless of the cultural resources, in any tourist destination, it is essential to structure the supply for satisfying the respective tourist demand. In the present proposal, as it regards a pilgrimage route to be used not only for religious proposes but also as a tourism product, the following elements must be considered as essential for its success: spirituality of the pilgrimage road; route in nature trails and/or rural roads; built heritage (such as churches, oratories, etc.); accommodation with possibility of washing laundry at site (preferably in humble places such as the pilgrim hostels or locals' houses); restaurants and cafes along the way; safety and security; medical assistance (in case of need); local population's welcome and varied support to pilgrims.

Based in the experience in the field (the direct and participative observation as pilgrim) and supported by conversations with locals and pilgrims/walkers from different pilgrimage routes (Santiago Camino, Fatima Way, Romeiros Way, etc.) it is plausible to describe the stage of the raised variables. However, only with thorough research is it possible to inventory the real variables and their weighted importance to the overall framework of the proposed tourism product.

The spirituality of the road – stage, very high – the island of Sâo Miguel (Azores/Portugal) is renowned in terms of religious belief of its people. A great part of the culture of this island is displayed through the legacy of people's religious traditions (Visit Azores, 2016). Probably the best-known religious festivity is the Feast of Ecce Homo (which takes place in the fifth week after Easter) but the Lent Pilgrimages have no less importance and are probably lived in a more participant and intimate way.

The route in nature trails and/or rural roads – stage, high – if only the natural beauty of the pilgrimage way was taken into account, the classification would be very high – "The eerie beauty of the Azores calls the mystical and transcendent" (Coutinho et al., 2006: 133). But in this variable, it must also be considered that many kilometres of the route are along asphalt roads. For improving the situation, the local authorities must replace the asphalt tracks by creating bicycle and/or pedestrians' paths parallel to the referred tracks.

Built heritage (such as churches, oratories, etc.) – stage, high – although there are no temples of great monumentality, most of the more than one hundred sites that constitute the built heritage of this pilgrimage route are in good condition and reflect well the strong religiosity of the people. Exceptions could be overcome with incentives from the private sector or with EU funds – if considered as a heritage and cultural tourist interest, the Romeiros Way could facilitate access to development funds, especially as the Azores are considered a peripheral region.

Accommodation with possibility of washing laundry at site (preferably in humble places such are the pilgrim hostels or locals' houses) – stage, medium-high – this variable is the most difficult to classify without deepening the research. However, it is possible to advance that in the participant observation, it was found that in most houses where the author was housed by the local population, there are conditions to accommodate the potential Romeiros Way's tourists/walkers. Although the facilities are not luxurious, the houses are comfortable and with good sanitary conditions. In addition, some rural municipalities could invest on the rehabilitation of abandoned buildings, turning them into small hostels.

Restaurants and cafes along the way – stage, medium – this variable is also difficult to classify due to the differences in population density areas. In the most densely populated regions, south, south-east and part of the north of the island, cafes and restaurants are regularly found; the opposite happens in the north-east and south-east of the island. Since the number of tourists/walkers in this project will not be high (nor is it the intention) it is not justifiable to open those kinds of establishments in those regions. Tourists/walkers will have to stock up on food and drink in the localities they cross.

Safety and security – stage, very high – these are two of the most striking features of the island. The complaints of tourists registered in the police regarding safety and security are few and almost all related to incidents occurring in larger cities. In any case, it is prudent to increase the policing on the most remote trails so that this degree of safety will continue.

Medical assistance (in case of need) – stage, medium- high – again there is a difference between regions. In the most densely populated regions, there is good medical assistance and well-equipped hospitals. In the less densely populated regions, when locals have serious health problems they must be transported to bigger towns/cities; the same will also have to happen to more severely injured tourists/walkers of the Romeiros Way.

Local population's welcome and varied support to pilgrims – stage, high – in addition to participating in the Lent Pilgrimage, the author carried out other researches on religious tourism in the Azores. Some included interviews with locals who host pilgrims and others involved interviews with parish councils' presidents. In both cases, the receptivity to receive future tourists/walkers of the Romeiros Way was big, not only for being active agents in a new tourism product but also because the rent of rooms will improve the families' monthly income.

The proposal's tourist demand

Tourists are surrounded by the social environment when visiting a destination. In fact, they cannot avoid interactions with local residents and those influence tourists' attitudes and behaviour (Fan et al., 2017). Although true it's also a fact that when tourists are aware of this fact, they play an important role in the decision process about the region they want to visit and what kind of interaction they want to have while visiting the destination.

According to the referred authors there are numerous studies exploring tourist typology, such are the ones from Cohen (1972, 1979), Plog (1974, 2001), Smith (1989) and Pearce and Lee (2005). Additionally, Aditya Ranjan (n.d.) also refers to Perreault et al. (1979), Westvlaams Ekonomisch Studiebureau (1986), Dalen (1989), Gallup and American Express (1989) and Smith (1989).

Independently from each author's proposals/divisions, the typologies found vary basically from organized travel mass tourist to very independent travel.

The tourists belonging to the first group (organized travel mass tourist) are characterized by Cohen (1972) as the ones who buy a package holiday to a popular destination and largely prefer to travel around with a large group of other tourists. Westvlaams Ekonomisch Studiebureau (1986) designate this typology as traditionalists or in other words the tourists who value safety and security and try to avoid surprises by sticking with familiar destinations and types of holiday. Smith (1989) presents mass tourists as the ones who expect the same things they are used to at home, adding to this group the charter tourists who have little or no interest in the destination itself providing that the holiday gives them the entertainment and standards of food and accommodation they expect. Fan et al. (2017) name this kind of tourist dependent, its most distinguishing characteristic being its dependent nature. Apart from the features pointed out by the previous referred authors, they still underline that this typology has relatively few travel experiences and that they

> have limited interactions (and little desire to contact) with the locals due to their limited language competence, age, personality or other constraints. ... As in Cohen's (1972) and Jaakson's (2004) description, the social separation is like an environmental bubble or tourist bubble, which creates a protective wall for the tourists from the host communities.
>
> (Fan et al., 2017: 361)

Having in mind the experiences and observations in the Lent Pilgrimage (as an actual participant) and the characteristics of organized mass tourists travel it is possible to state that this typology of tourists doesn't fit at all in a community-based tourism project as the one that will constitute this chapter's proposal.

Speaking about more independent tourists, authors have some difficulties in classifying them in a single typology. Most researchers opt for intermediate categories pointing out the tourists' features in each of the proposed divisions.

As the community-based tourism proposal in the Azores is based on specific realities (those presented in the previous point), here will only be presented the categories/typologies that might fit in it.

Cohen (1972) defines the explorers as the tourists who make their own travel arrangements, avoiding contact with other tourists, and looking for meeting local people, expecting, nevertheless, a certain level of comfort and security. The same author, in 1979, adds to his list the experiential tourist (looks for authentic experiences) and the experimental tourist (wants to be in contact with local people).

Plog (1974) named allocentrics those tourists who are outward-looking people who like to take risks and seek more adventurous holidays. The same author, in 2001, enlarged the number of types, adding the near allocentric whose characteristics are named by other researchers as explorers, being those more suitable for the Azores community-based project.

Perreault et al. (1979) point out a category, adventurous tourists, that can also be considered acceptable for the project; they are described as well-educated and affluent and show a preference for adventurous holidays. Westvlaams Ekonomisch Studiebureau (1986) include in its typology the contact-minded holidaymakers and the nature viewers. The first value making new friends on holiday and being hospitably received by local people, the second want to be well received by the host population while enjoying very beautiful landscapes.

For Gallup and American Express (1989), adventurers are independent and confident and like to try new activities; dreamers are fascinated by the idea of travel and they read and talk a lot about their travel experiences and different destinations. In the same year, Smith (1989) proposed a new typologies list including in it the off-beat tourists and the unusual tourists: the first aim to get away from other tourists, the second make side trips from organized tours to experience local culture. In any of those four cases, the present community-based project could become a challenge.

No doubt in the 70s and 80s of the 20th century the tourists' behaviours and typologies were widely researched and are still influencing the authors who write about these subjects. In the 21st century some authors, having in mind tourism development in the last decades, came back to these themes adding new motivations/behavioural lists to the existing ones. Pearce and Lee (2005), in their 14 factors division, point out some which might be considered interesting for the Azores proposal: novelty, autonomy, nature, self-development (host-site involvement) and self-actualize. In the first are included features such as having fun, experiencing something different, feeling the special atmosphere of the vacation destination, visiting places related to self-personal interests; in the second, being independent, being obligated to no one, doing things in one's own way; in the third, viewing the scenery, being close to nature, getting a better appreciation of nature, being harmonious with nature; in the fourth, learning new things, experiencing different cultures, meeting new and varied people, developing own knowledge of the area, meeting the locals, observing other people in the area, following current events; in the fifth, gaining a new perspective on life, feeling inner harmony/peace, understanding more oneself, being creative, working on own personal/spiritual values.

In the present decade, Fan et al. (2017) contributed with a new list of tourist types having in mind their social contacts. Two of the five types of tourists considered might also be interesting as focal groups for the Romeiros Way project, the explorers and, in a way, the belonging seekers. For the authors, explorers are experienced travellers, they interact with the local residents and seek to know more about the locals' life via casual and profound contacts, they attend some local events, visit the non-tourism areas, and approach non–tourism-related natives to experience something novel and exciting. These contacts may change their original images of the destinations or of the hosts in the destinations and enhance their cross-cultural competence. The belonging seekers contact with natives for social purposes, they like to associate with the natives by deep communications and mutual sharing, participating in their daily life; via contacts with the locals, they make some local friends and feel that they are part of the hosts' social groups.

After having discussed, in the previous point, the tourist destination's characteristics, considering its patrimony (natural and built resources) and the commodities which might be provided by the locals, and after having analyzed, in this point, the types of tourists that would best suit this community-based project, it is time to move on to the project's proposal, the Romeiros Way in São Miguel Island in Azores/Portugal.

São Miguel/Azores community-based tourism's proposal

The World Tourism Organization considers a local tourism destination as

> a physical space that includes tourism products such as support services and attractions, and tourism resources. It has physical and administrative boundaries defining its management, and images and perceptions defining its market competitiveness. Local destinations incorporate various stakeholders, often including a host community, and can nest and framework to form larger destinations. They are the focal point in the delivery of tourism products and the implementation of tourism policy.
>
> (WTO, 2002: n. p.)

Let's start by the physical and administrative boundaries. Bearing in mind the first, as the Romeiros Way circulates the whole island, the Atlantic Ocean tends to be the natural limits of the tourist destination and of the tourist attraction in study; the second are formed by a set of all six island municipalities that are crossed by the Pilgrimage Way and by the policies emanated by the regional government. This leads to an important issue, who are the agents who must set/define the paths of the Romeiros Way. The priority should be given to the Romeiros Association because the pilgrims are the ones who have walked the same paths for over four hundred years, passing by all churches where there's a Virgin's image. In fact, the Romeiros Way has been defined along the centuries by faith and tradition (as it happened also in other pilgrimage ways as for example the Santiago Camino). The next phase would consist in mapping the Romeiros Way, establishing which routes would involve a safe walking trail away from the major roads. To replace the asphalt tracks by creating bicycle and/or pedestrians' paths would strengthen efforts to rethink the land management of some municipalities (Ambrósio, 2011). After having defined the Romeiros Way each municipality should be responsible for signalling the way and for preserving the signage and good track conditions. The island's Tourism Board should create an additional app with all the Camino's tracks and should also promote this tourism product in the right communication channels.

Considering the support services variable mentioned in the WTO quote, it is necessary to point out how the tourism product in question could be structured. As referred before, to provide accommodation is a must for almost all tourism destinations; here, apart from the bigger towns crossed, the stakeholders would have to be the private landlords. At first, the Azorean Tourism Board would have to regulate what should be the minimum conditions for hosting walkers/tourists – in this case, the foreseen tourism segment for the Romeiros Way is not too demanding. Also advisable is to set a fixed price for overnight per person as it happens in the official Santiago Camino's albergues/hostels; the amount to be charged for accommodation and dinner should be discussed among the stakeholders and the different parish council boards, never forgetting that hiring a room and serving dinner and breakfast to these walkers/tourists should be considered an extra income and not a main family's monthly income.

In case this tourist product, the Romeiros Way, becomes quite popular, the parish councils would have to think about complementing the accommodation. Bearing in mind the good practices from their congeners in the North mainland (crossed by the Santiago Camino) probably the best solution would be to convert abandoned or ruined buildings into albergues/hostels.

Also following the good practices in either the Portuguese or in the Spanish Santiago Caminos, the restaurants' landlords of the Romeiros Way should get together for establishing the price of the pilgrim's menu which consists usually in a soup, main dish, dessert, coffee and a drink.

Regarding images, perceptions and destination's market competitiveness, the Romeiros Way could easily incorporate the international/European and the national pilgrimage ways' net, as for instance the already referred Santiago Camino (France, Portugal, Spain, among others), the Fatima Ways (Portugal), the Via Francigena (Italy and several European countries) or the Tro Breiz (Bretagne, France). In fact, the contact with walkers/pilgrims who experience the spiritual benefits of a pilgrimage way (regardless of whether it is) allows to state that "one should not forget that those who walk with satisfaction along one religious path will seek others in the future." (Ambrósio, 2011: 28).

Although each pilgrimage route has its unique characteristics, it is also true that many share common features. On any pilgrimage route the walker/pilgrim travels both ways, doing an interior journey and an exterior one. In the first situation, the differences in the physical paths don't interfere much in the inner journey once it is the time for oneself and the effects of bodily exhaustion that counts. The opposite is the case in the second situation; the greater the landscape's beauties, the better are the walkers/pilgrims' positive comments in edited books or in social networks.

Unquestionably, the 250 km Romeiros Way along the coast, being almost always lined with lush vegetation, will hardly be beaten by other pilgrimage routes. Also, the fact that the overnight is spent in locals' homes establishes a quite unique characteristic among the former referred pilgrimage roads.

For many walkers/pilgrims, mainly for the ones named by different academicians as explorers, allocentrics, adventurers, or belonging seekers, to spend the night, to have dinner and to contact directly with locals becomes an added value in choosing this pilgrimage way.

To walk all the way of a pilgrimage route is a physical and spiritual challenge for everyone. Due to that reason, most walkers/pilgrims feel the necessity of taking back home their memories to remember how persevering they were, overcoming each day's difficulties. For sure the easiest ones to get and sometimes the only material souvenirs that are possible to bring back home are the pictures (usually taken with their own mobile phone). In Santiago Camino the proof of having achieved the final goal is the compostela (certificate of having completed the pilgrimage). To get the compostela the walkers/pilgrims must show (at Santiago de Compostela) their passport and the various stamps on it to certify that he/she has walked at least 100 km. For the Romeiros Way a certificate should also be created but instead of copying the Santiago Camino's stamps format, an alternative should be found. As one of the reasons for the existence of the Azorean pilgrimage way is to ensure the visit to churches and chapels in which there is a statue of the Virgin (in together they are about 100), the passport should provide the same number of spaces for sticking the stickers which could only be found in each of those about 100 religious spaces.

Bearing in mind all characteristics and strategies described in this point for the creation of the Romeiros Way there's no doubt that most variables for achieving a sustainable tourism product are foreseen. On the one hand, all proposed measures are in line with respect for nature – it is also important to underline that this tourism segment is among those that show more respect for nature – and on the other, the procedures to be followed respect the communities, their traditions and ways of life. Tourist contacts in this study are anchored in the positive aspects of tourism: to understand better the others and oneself without jeopardizing the existing social structure.

Summary

The brightest tourism products of a destination many times overshadow other potential tourism products from the very same destination. Considering the religious tourism in São Miguel island in the Azores the best well-known tourism product is the Ecce Homo Festivity, meaning that all other religious-based tourism products are placed in a secondary stage. This tourism product/event, apart from being concentrated in the fifth week after Easter, takes place in the largest island's city, its capital, Ponta Delgada. During that weekend all hotels are fully occupied and some lodging units from the suburban area also register full occupancy.

Bearing in mind another religious tradition that could allow a continued tourism afflux it is proposed in this chapter the creation of the Romeiros Way. Besides the importance of spreading tourism to less-searched island areas it is also a concern to propose a tourism product anchored in community-based tourism.

On the one hand, the structured tourism product presented, the Romeiros Way, accomplishes the editors' challenge for creating a product supported by local traditions and economically exploited by the locals; on the other, it should also be contemplated as a tourism product which obliges tourists staying for a longer period, shortening in a way travel opportunities and at same time reducing their carbon emissions by repetitive air travel.

Also, according to Lew and McKercher (2006: 409) "Time spent in a destination area is arguably the single most influential criterion shaping tourist behaviour because it can directly constrain or expand the number and range of potential activities available and the depth at which individual activities can be experienced". In fact, for walking the whole Romeiros Way the walkers/pilgrims had to plan at least two weeks stay. The first day is for arrival, the following 10/12 days for hiking about 21 to 25 km daily, and the last two days for resting and preparing for departure. During their sojourn the contact with the residents, although present throughout the day, will be privileged at evening when lodging and eating in the locals' homes.

Concerning the different tourism agents in this sustainable tourism project, the major role at the project's launch must be played by the institutional agents, but after attaining cruising speed, the main actors will be the local communities.

Regarding the regional government, it must be stated that in the last decades tourist promotion of the archipelago has been mainly focused on the discovery and enjoyment of nature. For sure this project will further enhance this type of tourism, improving the tourists' contact with the natural and built heritage (namely the religious one). When pilgrims must walk along asphalt roads it is because there isn't any alternative, either for them or for the tourists or residents. By providing better path conditions, with the Romeiros Way, all will benefit from the future 250 km nature way.

Along with the Azorean regional government, in a first stage, the parish counties and the pilgrims' associations must work for defining the pilgrimage way and for fixing the rules of this community-based tourism project. Afterwards it will be the locals who will lead this tourism process by providing the facilities to the walkers/pilgrims who will come to experience the Romeiros Way.

A last word must be always given to the residents. By accompanying and taking part in the tourism process, they will be, in a way, monitoring the community-based tourism project. Bearing it in mind the communities should meet regularly to decide if the development brought by tourism is interesting and profitable for them to keep it going on or, by the contrary, if tourism is changing their traditions and their social structure and, in that case, to reduce the number of tourists or even to end the tourism project.

The contact with the communities, either during the Lent Pilgrimage, or while leading other tourism projects in São Miguel, allows saying that the Azorean are very friendly towards foreigners. Likewise, the money raised by accommodating walkers/pilgrims will be welcomed by most host families. If this community-based tourism project is implemented almost for sure it will become a successful example of sustainable tourism and fieldwork for further researches.

References

Aditya, R. (n.d.). *Tourist Behaviour.* Retrieved from www.academia.edu/9460333/Tourist_behaviour_TYPOLOGIES_OF_TOURIST_BEHAVIOUR

Ambrósio, V. (2011). Religious tourism and the lent pilgrimages in São Miguel, Azores. *International Journal of Business and Globalisation, 7*(1), 14–28.

Ambrósio, V. (2015). Sacred pilgrimage and tourism as secular pilgrimage. In R. Raj and K. Griffin (Eds.), *Religious Tourism and Pilgrimage Management – An International Perspective* (2nd ed., pp. 130–145). Oxfordshire: CABI.

Ambrósio, V. (2017). Circuitos Turísticos Religiosos e Culturais. In F. Silva & J. Umbelino (Eds.), *Planeamento e Desenvolvimento Turístico* (pp. 323–333). Lisboa: Lidel.

Cohen, E. (1972). Toward a sociology of international tourism. *Social Research, 39*(1), 164–182.

Cohen, E. (1979). A phenomenology of tourist experiences. *Sociology, 13*(2), 170–201.

Coutinho, A. et al. (2006). *A Irmandade dos Romeiros.* São João do Estoril: Lucerna.

Dalen, E. (1989). Research into values and consumer trends in Norway. *Tourism Management, 10*(3), 183–186.

Devereux, C. (2003). Spirituality, pilgrimage and the road to Santiago: Questions for cultural tourism. In C. Fernandes, F. McGettigan & J. Edwards (Eds.), *Religious Tourism and Pilgrimage Atlas – Special Interest Group 1st Expert Meeting* (pp. 131–140). Fátima: Tourism Board of Leiria/Fátima.

Fan, D., Zhang, H., Jenkins, C. & Tavitiyaman, P. (2017). Tourist typology in social contact: An addition to existing theories. *Tourism Management, 60*, 357–366.

Fernandes, C., Silva, G. & Gómez-Ullate, M. (2017). Rethinking Safety Issues within the context of Pilgrimage Routes. In R. Raj, M. Korstanje & K. Griffin (Eds.), *Risk and Safety Challenges for Religious Tourism and Events* (pp. 63–76). Wallingford: CABI.

Gallup & American Express. (1989). *Unique four National Travel Student Reveals Travelers Types.* London: American Express.

Jaakson, R. (2004). Beyond the tourist bubble?: Cruiseship passengers in port. *Annals of Tourism Research, 31*(1), 44–60.

Lew, A. & McKercher, B. (2006). Modeling tourist movements, a local destination analysis. *Annals of Tourism Research, 33*(2), 403–423.

Meyer, D. (2004). *Tourism Routes and Gateways: Key Issues for the Development of Tourism Routes and Gateways and Their Potential for Pro-Poor Tourism.* London: Overseas Development Institute.

Murray, M. & Graham, B. (1997). Exploring the dialectics of route-based tourism: The Camino de Santiago. *Tourism Management*, *18*(8), 513–524.

Pearce, P. & Lee, U. (2005). Developing the travel career approach to tourist motivation. *Journal of Travel Research*, *43*(3), 226–237.

Perreault, W., Dorden, D. & Dorden, W. (1979). A psychological classification of vacation life-styles. *Journal of Leisure Research*, *9*, 208–224.

Plog, S. (1974). Why destination areas rise and fall in popularity. *Cornell Hotel and Restaurant Administration Quarterly*, *14*(4), 55–58.

Plog, S. (2001). Why destination areas rise and fall in popularity: An update of a Cornell Quarterly Classic. *Cornell Hotel and Restaurant Administration Quarterly*, *42*(3), 13–24.

Richards, G. & Fernandes, C. (2007). Religious tourism in Northern Portugal. In G. Richards (ed.), *Cultural Tourism Global and Local Perspectives*. New York: The Haworth Press, EUA, pp. 215–238.

Smith, V. (1989). *Hosts and guests: The anthropology of tourism* (2nd ed.). Philadelphia: University of Pennsylvania Press.

Visit Azores. (2016). *Five centuries of religious traditions*. Retrieved from www.visita zores.com/sites/default/files/brochures/diptico-religioso-EN_2016_final%20low.pdf

Westvlaams Ekonomisch Studiebureau, Afdeling Toerislisch Underzoeu (1986). *Toerishische Gedragingen en Attitudes van de Belgen in 1985*. Brussels: Reeks Vakontieanderzaeken.

WTO. (2002). WTO *Think Tank Enthusiastically Reaches Consensus on Frameworks for Tourism Destination Success*. Madrid: World Tourism Organization.

13 Community-based tourism – the kiwi variation

Peter Wiltshier

Background

This chapter is written by a New Zealander who has travelled the world and returned to his home on a regular basis to explore the contribution of local communities to creating tourism destinations of distinction for the present and planned adoption of tourism for future benefit of all stakeholders.

Community-based tourism demands much of key actors and stakeholders and expects increments in capital to plan future CBT. A resource-based view of tourism as a business must accompany plans for community development. The conceptual approach in theorising structure and agency approaches will inevitably place demands on resources in the country, and skills and capacities in its people, to undertake a reflective approach to planning carefully crafted offers to international as well as domestic travellers in New Zealand. New Zealand needs the right skills and trained experts to manage, monitor and measure success in increased tourism. Resources in a nation of 4.5 million people are quite rightly managed carefully and scarce even before competition is factored in. Competition in allocating resources to alternative purposes to tourism; competition in an era of deregulation and an ageing population struggling to fund development issues for communities.

Against a background of universal deregulation in modern democracies underlines New Zealand's need to acknowledge innovation and skills and competitiveness (Dredge and Jamal, 2015). Actor-network theory underpins the growing capacity in knowledge management. The chapter posits that access to exceptional communications networks and distribution channels are a minimum to compete now (Latour, 2004). Data mined and managed for the purpose of CBT depends on quality information provision, of which New Zealand is assured – a test bed for forty years of new intellectual property. Innovation has long been a renowned feature of New Zealand enterprise; as the nation is relatively small but highly educated, the country was perceived to take risks early with these innovations. The new knowledge managed produces useful stores of community-shared social capital that can be realised by communities and enable developments in tourism to be as resilient and transformative as developments in services, manufacturing, merchandising and banking.

Sustainability is a goal for community development and also a goal for community-based tourism.

Structures and resources to support sustainability measures

Shared increased social capital is another frontier that challenges stakeholders to promulgate tourism development plans as the development process is inevitably uneven in response to the vagaries of the international market demand in a relatively remote location in the South Pacific.

To readily develop community-based tourism (CBT), several stages of development may be required. In the 1990s Ray identified the need for a sequential process to ensure that communities, keen to develop tourism as a productive economic base, in some way unified in their attempts to concur on a brand, an identity and relevant images that all residents, in fact all stakeholders, could buy into before continuing the journey to economic development through tourism. What Ray observed was that this process and the journey were not simple, were complex in being phased and each phase (four in total) was time consuming and stakeholder dependent. Stakeholder dependent has been demonstrated as a need for majority agreement on reality and not an imposed perspective of tourism as a saviour and only perceptions of those with vested interests. The Ray perspective encompasses a much wider and evolving approach with a significant temporal component; the evolution of CBT mandated by the majority will not happen quickly. In addition, there is a component of business management and marketing that must be explored to help a community to turn into destination. Marketing and branding, public relations management and the creation of an identity can only occur as components of the CBT and therefore must all be managed as part of the process that Ray described in 1998 (Ray, 1998).

What is exciting in the current millennium is the recognition of shared and new stores of social as well as economic capital. Tourism is not a bequest that comes without complex requirements of the community but as time goes by we are finding it easier to identify resources generated for the mutual benefit of tourism businesses and additionally residents and other stakeholders in the community as will be shown in this chapter through case studies (for example see Garrod et al., 2006 or Macbeth et al., 2004).

Therefore this chapter focuses on the evolution of CBT and exemplars of good practices which other communities can explore for support in the endeavour to diversify community income, to augment social and economic shared capital and to understand the complex development needs of a range of stakeholders; be they 600 people or 60,000. The approach taken is socially constructed and largely based on narratives including participant observation and case studies.

Also considered here is the permeability of boundaries between communities. Visitors, guests or travellers seldom perceive travel or journeys as geographically bound by political issues. A destination may be the ultimate stop on multiple journeys and each destination may have blurry boundaries. The concept is therefore of boundaries and blurring perceptions of absolute borders between destinations and tourism occurring at these boundaries as well as within the core of the community. This managing of boundaries as well as destinations adds complexity to resolving the future of socially and economically successful CBT. Identify shared responsibilities and rights between communities to add value to CBT and destinations may emerge that share these responsibilities and rights by delivering new stores of social and economic capital for the majority of stakeholders.

In 1999 New Zealand prepared to celebrate the dawn of the new millennium – the first nation to see the dawn of 2000 from the Chatham Islands eight hundred kilometres due east of Christchurch and to the East Coast Maori mystic mountain, sky piercer, Mount Hikurangi.

The new millennium may represent a watershed for tourism in New Zealand. The nation had often hosted major international festivals and events – two Commonwealth Games hosted in the previous forty years – and the annual Ranfurly Cup rugby matches – and the Bledisloe Cup matches between Australia and New Zealand. The point is that New Zealand had a thriving social and cultural life in the fifty years leading to the 1999 event. New Zealand entertained visitors with cultural welcomes unmatched elsewhere and performed willingly in major tourist destinations like the Bay of Islands, Rotorua and Queenstown. What it did seem to lack by 1999 was a sense that the component communities of the country seldom offered locally created and owned events and festivals that truly represented those communities that hosted visitors. There was, and still is, a sense of invitation to guests but a far from wholehearted developed invitation that truly reflected the unique nature of community as a true welcoming destination.

Case study 1

The story of Pat Smith

In the late 1990s the world was buzzing with excitement at the prospect of the new millennium. Even the Chatham Islands, a group of volcanic islands some eight hundred kilometres east of New Zealand, was considering a major event to celebrate the dawn of the new millennium as the first land to see the dawn light of the new millennium. The Islands were successful in a bid for funds from New Zealand to support the celebrations and events were duly planned, including a concert at daybreak and parachute drop coinciding with the dawn. These events went ahead and in due course were recounted in New Zealand's national press. Unfortunately the coverage was perceived by some as rather scathing and dismissive of local Chatham Islands' achievements for the momentous occasion. The author duly contacted the local government representative and suggested that rather than annoyance at external commentary the Islands could exploit their own opportunities to perform host duties in future according to resources and preferences sourced locally on the Islands, and that an inventory and exploration of those opportunities could be undertaken by a small team for very modest financial outlay. It is indeed pleasing to see that local stakeholders and the next generation of those that were engaged in tourism in 1999 have accepted the challenge of planning and managing local CBT ever since with evidence of success. This case study is not to recount the successes (these are documented elsewhere) but to acknowledge that with conviction, time and allocation of resources according to local needs and expectations a brand, identity and new infrastructure to support tourism plans have emerged in the past two decades.

Under the accrual of new resources by a new generation of Islanders there is a realisation that locally based stakeholders, their stories and their tacit and explicit belief in sharing is creating a resource for sharing decision making for the contemporary business opportunity and for the future (see for example Lundmark et al., 2014; McGreavy et al., in Maine, 2015 and Puhakka et al., 2014 in Finland). A renewed enthusiasm for agreeing to share resources, termed cohesion, is evident. The locally based airlines, Air Chathams, has renewed energy to seek the extension of the only runway. The travel agents largely responsible for packaging tours (based near Auckland in New Zealand, some thousand kilometres distant from the Islands) has never been more confident in bringing ecotourists, twitchers and sport fishers to the Islands. There is a real sense that after the faltering first steps for the millennium party of 1999, the Islanders have asserted their unassailable rights to consider, produce, offer and reflect on doing tourism the Chathams' way. The immediate benefits may well be sociocultural; the long-term focus will inevitably be grounded on the knowledge stores and resources located on the Islands. It is therefore a model incorporating local and indigenous stories; a model practiced by a previous generation and now being perfected by their children. It can be appraised as a model of accrued new data and performance indicators; a model cohering to older values, beliefs and identity, a model to endure and now needs to be shared in repositories designed to capture useful practices and attempting to learn from costly lessons in the past.

The key is that with concurrence and several contributions to tourism as a socio-economic driver for a future still typically plagued by a falling population and an increasing workload for remaining, and rather older, resident stakeholders, tourism is now an acceptable component of the community development agenda on the Chatham Islands; a success story may be in endogeny.

Case study 2

The Coromandel Coast route

Two hours' easy drive from Auckland International Airport is the beautiful subtropical and volcanic spine of the Coromandel Peninsula extending two hundred kilometres from the burgeoning service and retirement city of Tauranga to the towering cliffs of Mount Moehau overlooking the Pacific Ocean. One could end-lessly describe the features and benefits of this luxuriant and still largely forested peninsula surrounded by ocean on three sides. Deep sea fishing, surfing, swim-ming and new sports like paddleboarding and kitesurfing are possible off exten-sive white sandy beaches anywhere; mountain hiking, yomping, and trail bike riding are all possible from novice to expert levels throughout the spine of the Peninsula. Subtropical fruits like kiwi, avocado, orange, feijoa and banana grow easily and when in season are inexpensive. New Zealanders have enjoyed the destination for more than a century. Past tourism was more of an adventure; road access until forty years ago was challenging across mountain passes to the Pacific Coast. Hardy kiwis travelled for a day or more to camp or stay in small huts, called baches, and the infrastructure and resources for tourism were limited by the capacity to manage small numbers of local Aucklanders and residents of the Waikato District taking annual beach side holidays. Now more than ten million visitors from throughout the globe arrive at Auckland Airport every year. There are increasing numbers of free independent travelers (FIT) from source countries that traditionally only offered package holidays; the China market is now burgeoning. The Coromandel Peninsula is a year-round attractive offer for these FIT. In response to significant increased demand from overseas the local communities had to cooperate with the national tourism strategy precepts and plan to manage the demands of relatively sophis-ticated visitors with prior expectations of service levels, infrastructure and hor-izontal and vertical supply chains. Anecdotally visitors were treating the Coromandel Peninsula offer as if a gift from the heavens, a land of proverbial milk and honey and all on offer for the myriad arriving without any guarantee of income from visitors, more so FIT visitors who may or may not stay overnight in the Coromandel because access, previously taking half a day in the 1950s, is now reduced to two hours on paved highways from Auckland.

Local businesses cooperated, local regional tourism officers marketed hard what was available and attempted to direct visitors towards attractions, events and services that could match the increased sophistication of international vis-itors. Success has followed, but not uniformly. Visitors still 'freedom camp' putting their tents and campervans on roadsides without paying fees for stop-ping. Visitors will still avoid paying for toilet facilities and pollute streams. Vis-itors will demand access to services and facilities paid for by local residents and ratepayers with scant regard for the cost of maintenance and access. Under-standably residents are upset by the relatively steep demand for facilities and services expected by visitors but the key is in this upset. The national tourism organization and regional tourism organisation are working to build an understanding of the costs of tourism and the available income streams from retail, services, accommodation, attractions and events. At present the area is largely without tourist tax imposition in recognition of tourism being a highly competitive international business opportunity and challenge. What has been retained in the Coromandel is the unique and defining offer of the subtropical rain forest and beach experience offer that first attracted resident Aucklanders a century earlier.

Everyone has benefitted from improved access, better standard of services, higher quality attractions and world class events. What has transpired over the past forty years is that sharing economy principles, what is useful, right and valued by residents and hosts is now shared in equal parts with the intended guests. Inalienable resources, attractions and products for visitors and principles based upon norms and values of the host community has turned tourism into a relevant industry for the residents and business owners/operators in the Coromandel. There is an acknowledgement that tourism is as relevant a sector for investment and development just as are farming, forestry and fishing. Tourism is no longer a poor substitute for socio-cultural development by other means. Private inward investment is supported within the region; however, there are occasional lapses of concentration.

The invitation from the host to guests to camp for free with their own recreational vehicles on the beautiful coastline without paying for services used is now challenged (Figure 13.1). Nevertheless, the invitation is still offered and for many, the invitation is of a universal nature; offered to all and accepted by a manageable percentage. Of course, there is a real chance that in future, resource depletion and overuse of water and land may cheapen the invitation but the invitation is genuine, largely willingly shared by the majority and again evidence of shared perspectives, evidence-based for longevity and responsibility and given credibility as an enduring triple bottom-line opportunity for future success (Figure 13.2).

Figure 13.1 Freedom camping prohibited. Tairua Mount Paku
Source: Author

Figure 13.2 Pauanui and Tairua Harbour, Coromandel Peninsula
Source: Author

Conclusion

The creativity of all stakeholders is acknowledged as a basic creed of developing community-based tourism. There is an acknowledgement of scarce resources for community development and the competitive pressures on business but this model is predicated on sharing and learning and not on marketised greed. An understanding of shared social capital within communities that can engender enthusiasm for guests to become regular visitors and ultimately residents and shareholders in common social and economic capital is at the model's heart (McGehee et al., 2010; Falk and Kilpatrick, 2000).

The concept of reflexive stakeholders is also presented and deliverable. Human insights continuously produce new initiatives to benefit the community and improve our social return on investment but also acknowledge the shared need for better health and wellbeing. These health and wellbeing benefits being the apex of our learning from a new shared agenda and legacy from better health and wellbeing is fed into projects for tourism.

Fora designed to share good practices that are enduring and membership, although often fluctuating with demand, is fully representative of the best volunteers and contributors in the community. These may be the youth or the retirees but are still representative of the focus to serve others in a more thoughtful approach to boost resources and skills required for positive outcomes of increasing tourism.

Business development options are perceived as part of the shared planning agenda. Examples from the rural action zones in England lead us to believe that community representatives can support innovation, creativity and diversity within our business offers and these can be shared between wider ranges of stakeholders.

The adoption of new technology can make lives easier and less stressful for keen business people as well as the not-for-profit sectors typical of volunteers, retirees and the University of the Third Age.

Let us take those people who are gifting skills and capacity to expand our contributions into consideration in running training and capacity building programmes built around the availability of entrepreneurs and innovators. A leader can be appointed to help spread the good news beyond the boundaries of community; guests and visitors are usually not respecters of boundaries and see tourism as a seamless adventure through any physical landscape.

Finally in the case studies presented contributions to community development arising from rejuvenation in a visitor welcome and a growing demand from tourists are recognised by the ACES model detailed in the following, with examples in Table 13.1.

Revisit the extent of these features in each case study.

Accrual

Of goodwill from host service clubs and organisations to commit to delivering services to a variety of guests without prejudice or preference.

Table 13.1 The ACES model in practice

Example	Aces	Future Prospect CBT
Chatham Islands	second generation accrue knowledge shared from the experiences of the millennium celebrations	Embedding indigenous values and beliefs in a customised offering dedicated to very specific and niche sectors in the tourism market. Wildlife conservation and observation. Heritage participation and experiences.
Coromandel coast	bountiful resources in environmental protection and a benign and fruitful local climate coupled to unique values in environmentalism and ecosystems	Astrophotography street lighting limited to overcome light pollution. Illume Festival in winter. Food and drink festivals Matarangi and Tairua. Snorkel Marine Reserve Hahei.

Source: Author

Cohesive

Agreeing to work with other public and private sector representatives to secure an identity that can be shared and to avoid hindrance to development of contemporary sector demands (communications, micro-technology, agriculture and diversified production base for new food and beverage products).

Enduring

This has to become the new norm, a quality of offer to visitor experience that we cannot fall back from, a desire to embed new procedures and quality standards in every offer and not shy away from the need for improvement (even self-improvement).

Sharing

The benefits we accrue today are for future generations' social and economic capital accumulation. We need to re-examine competition in light of many discussions around co-opetition in acknowledging the finite nature of resources for which we all compete.

References

Alhaddi, H. (2015). Triple bottom line and sustainability: A literature review. *Business and Management Studies*, *1*(2), 6–10.

Dredge, D., & Jamal, T. (2015). Progress in tourism planning and policy: A post-structural perspective on knowledge production. *Tourism Management*, *51*, 285–297.

Duxbury, N., & Jeannotte, M. S. (2013). The role of cultural resources in community sustainability: Linking concepts to practice and planning. *The International Journal of Sustainability Policy and Practice*, *8*(4), 133–144.

Dwyer, L. (2005). Relevance of triple bottom line reporting to achievement of sustainable tourism: A scoping study. *Tourism Review International*, *9*(1), 79–938.

Elkington, J. (1998). Accounting for the triple bottom line. *Measuring Business Excellence*, *2*(3), 18–22.

Falk, I., & Kilpatrick, S. (2000). What is social capital? A study of interaction in a rural community. *Sociologia ruralis*, *40*(1), 87–110.

Garrod, B., Wornell, R., & Youell, R. (2006). Re-conceptualising rural resources as countryside capital: The case of rural tourism. *Journal of Rural Studies*, *22*(1), 117–128.

Heimtun, B. (2007). Depathologizing the tourist syndrome: Tourism as social capital production. *Tourist Studies*, *7*(3), 271–293.

Latour, B. (2004). On using ANT for studying information systems: A (somewhat) Socratic dialogue. Ch 3, in Land, F. (ed.) *The Social Study of Information and Communication Technology: Innovation, Actors, and Contexts*, 62–76. Oxford: Oxford University Press.

Lundmark, C., Matti, S., & Sandström, A. (2014). Adaptive co-management: How social networks, deliberation and learning affect legitimacy in carnivore management. *European Journal of Wildlife Research*, *60*(4), 637–644.

Macbeth, J., Carson, D., & Northcote, J. (2004). Social capital, tourism and regional development: SPCC as a basis for innovation and sustainability. *Current Issues in Tourism, 7*(6), 502–522.

McGehee, N. G., Lee, S., O'Bannon, T. L., & Perdue, R. R. (2010). Tourism-related social capital and its relationship with other forms of capital: An exploratory study. *Journal of Travel Research, 49*(4), 486–500.

McGreavy, B., Lindenfeld, L., Bieluch, K. H., Silka, L., Leahy, J., & Zoellick, B. (2015). Communication and sustainability science teams as complex systems. *Ecology and Society, 20*(1).

Puhakka, R., Cottrell, S. P., & Siikamäki, P. (2014). Sustainability perspectives on Oulanka National Park, Finland: Mixed methods in tourism research. *Journal of Sustainable Tourism, 22*(3), 480–505.

Ray, C. (1998). Culture, intellectual property and territorial rural development. *Sociologia ruralis, 38*(1), 3–20.

Sherlock, K. (2002). Community matters: Reflections from the field. *Sociological Research Online, 7*(2), 1–16.

14 Community-based tourism engagement and wellbeing from a learning perspective

Giovanna Bertella, Sabrina Tomasi,
Alessio Cavicchi and Gigliola Paviotti

Introduction

This study explores engagement in rural tourism and in particular with reference to wellbeing. Its aim is twofold: on the one hand, this study aims to encourage a reflection on whether it is fruitful to adopt an experiential social learning perspective to explore the aforementioned phenomenon, taking a practice-based approach to tourism as a starting point. On the other hand, it aims to explore how tourism engagement in rural experiences can be relevant to the wellbeing of the individuals involved (tourists, tourism providers, members of host communities).

Tourism is understood as a place-based practice, where the term 'practice' refers to the process through which people engage, both individually and socially, with the world, do things and reflect on them (Crouch, 1999, 2002). The tourism practice is place-based as the destination is a central component: it does not only provide the context for tourism but it also becomes experience. Moreover, tourism is viewed as a multidimensional practice that develops along the tourists' cognitive, emotional and bodily dimensions (Crouch, 2000).

With this underlying conceptualization of tourism, the aim of the study is to investigate engagement in rural experiences and its potential relevance in terms of wellbeing. Some previous studies already highlighted the reciprocal value of tourism experiences, especially in the case of rural destinations, thus making the case for tourists as well as providers and local community members to be included in the study of such phenomenon (Bimonte and Punzo, 2016; Kastenholz et al., 2013; Sherlock, 2001). The main idea is that in order to frame tourism in terms of sustainability it is important to focus on the experiential benefits both tourists and host communities may obtain (Bertella et al., 2018; Tasci and Severt, 2017). Such benefits may result from the host-guest interactions and might contribute to social groups as the ones described by Rihova et al. (2013). Social groups as described previously can vary according to inclusivity (for example, when considering tourists only as the "detached customers" group) and temporality (for example being limited to the duration of the experiences as the "temporary communitas").

One of the benefits principally taken into consideration by this study is wellbeing, which also allows a holistic approach to be considered in the experiential value that goes beyond the aesthetic, entertainment, educational and escapist realms identified by Pine and Gilmore (1998) and broadly adopted in the literature. The focus on wellbeing helps to include and explore the potential transformative aspect of experiences, identified by Pine and Gilmore (2013). Therefore, the concept of wellbeing as defined in the study embraces the fundamental dimensions of human experiences, that is the hedonic and eudaimonic dimensions. Whilst hedonic wellbeing refers to immediate pleasure, eudaimonic wellbeing refers to personal growth and the perception of meaningfulness in relation to oneself and to others (Ryan and Deci, 2001). It can be noted that these concepts are strictly related to each other, as immediate pleasure can be experienced as the result of doing a meaningful thing and also in relation to the sense of belonging to an ideal community (Henderson and Knight, 2012; Waterman, 2008).

While previous studies about tourism engagement adopted a marketing perspective (Bryce et al., 2015; Taheri et al., 2014), this study wants to adopt an approach based on experiential, social learning theories, taking into consideration the close relation between tourism and learning. Furthermore, such an approach can be useful to uncover processes and factors potentially relevant to wellbeing. From this point of view, eudaimonic wellbeing related to learning as a process of individual and collective identity development, as identified in social learning theories, might be particularly relevant.

The theoretical approach of this study is thus based on scholarly contributions related to educational tourism and on central ideas from the practice-based and transformative learning literature. The previously mentioned perspectives are presented in the next section, following an introduction to the concept of tourism engagement. The theoretical framework of the study is then summarized in the next section. The third section describes the method applied to investigate a case study including rural experiences related to one event in the Italian region of Marche. The main findings of the case study are presented in the fourth section and discussed in the following one. Finally, conclusions are drawn, highlighting the contributions and limitations of our work.

Theoretical focus and perspective

Tourism engagement

The concept of tourism engagement is strictly related to the concept of customer engagement, broadly discussed in marketing literature along with other concepts such as involvement, commitment, trust, participation and loyalty (Brodie et al., 2011; Jaakkola and Alexander, 2014; Pansari and Kumar, 2017). The definition by Brodie et al. (2011) describes customer engagement as interactive and dynamic experiences that occur through relationships with a focal agent or object and develop along the cognitive, emotional and behavioural dimensions. We see this closely related to the benefits claimed in this volume for actively developing CBT.

Engagement is therefore context-determined and as the attention is limited to the case of community-based forms of tourism some scholars describe tourism engagement as a state of being involved with and committed to a specific tourism offer/provider/destination and the related cultures and values (Bryce et al., 2015; Taheri et al., 2014).

Tourism and learning

An emblematic expression of the connection between travel and learning can be found in Dante's Divine Comedy, where Ulysses reflects on his journey and tells his crewmates: "Consider well the seed that gave you birth: you were not made to live your lives as brutes, but to be followers of worth and knowledge". This expression shows that the idea of travelling as an opportunity to learn is rooted in our perception of tourism. A good example is the Grand Tour that used to be undertaken by rich or aristocratic European young men as an important part of their education (Towner, 1985). We have yet to see if these meritorious concepts apply systematically at community level.

The learning component is still a central element in some types of modern travelling. It is the case of educational tourism, which can be described in a broad way as including any type of travel where learning can be viewed as the primary motivator to travel and which occurs both formally and informally especially where those experiences are community-based and link in to the planning and development processes (Ritchie, 2003; Ritchie et al., 2003). Examples can be study tours, school and university tourism, ecotourism, and cultural tourism.

Research about tourism as a learning experience is a relatively new field of study (Falk et al., 2012; McGladdery and Lubbe, 2017; Pitman et al., 2010; Stone and Petrick, 2013), which adds to the concept of learning understood exclusively as an organized and mainly cognitive activity. Several outcomes and benefits come from this perspective on travel, such as increase of factual knowledge, problem-solving skills, self-confidence, adaptability, cross-cultural competence and attitude change (Stone and Petrick, 2013). We would note that this learning can be a two-way activity as communities themselves also benefit from these increases in external capabilities as well.

Richards (2011) argues that educational tourism, such as ecotourism, cultural tourism and agritourism, can actually be related to transformative experiences, when also making reference to the revisited framework about experience value by Pine and Gilmore (2013). In the original framework by Pine and Gilmore, education is viewed as one of the four realms of experiences, along with entertainment, escapism and the aesthetic. More recently, education seen as learning and personal growth has been included in the study of experience economy, as described by the authors, and transformation is viewed as the ultimate state of being, more precisely the last developmental phase of value (Mehmetoglu and Engen, 2011; Pine and Gilmore, 2013). Transformative experiences are also widely commented on by Falk et al. (2012). Falk et al. describe learning in tourism as a context-dependent, highly individual, cumulative and lifelong process of constructing meaning. The authors observe that learning through travel can be deliberate, premeditated, incidental and unintentional and can include skills and knowledge as well as practical wisdom. The latter refers to reflexivity about our actions in the specific context and in line with our beliefs about right and wrong.

A practice-based approach to learning and transformative experiences

As mentioned in the Introduction, this study adopts a practice-based approach and explores tourism engagement and wellbeing from an experiential and social learning perspective in a community-based context.

This practice-based approach has been developed on the position by educationists Etienne Wenger and Jean Lave, according to whom learning is a practice of participation in social activities, through which we develop our own identity as individuals and members of one or more groups or communities (Lave and Wenger, 1991). As stated by Wenger (2000), "knowing is an act of participation in complex social learning systems" (225). Lave and Wenger (1991) use the term 'engagement' to refer to participation to social activities, which includes doing things (e.g. engaging in physical activities) as well as communicating (e.g. engaging in conversations). Engagement can vary among the group members, with some taking on more central roles in the communities compared to others. The latter therefore have a peripheral position in the social group, still engaging in participation of being a group member and, perhaps, becoming a more central member afterwards. Moreover, engagement and, consequently, learning are viewed as influenced by and at the same time influencing the context. Learning can thus be described as a situated or located practice.

According to such a concept of learning, engagement has to be accompanied by the process of reification, i.e. the production of tools, words, documents and stories in order to be effective. These artefacts are essential to the alignment of the specific practice towards a shared goal within the specific context (Wenger, 2000) and can be effectively developed in the processes of management and governance.

In addition to participation, communication, reification and alignment, three more elements are central to this concept of learning: imagination, reflection and identity. Imagination is about "creating images of the world and seeing connections through time and space by extrapolating from our own experience" (Wenger, 1998: 173). Imagination refers to the process through which we construct images of the world in order to reflect on our possible position in it. Along with reflection, imagination is relevant to identity development within communities. Ultimately, the practice-based approach adopted regards learning and the previously mentioned relevant processes as a "vehicle(s) for the development and transformation of identities" affecting individuals as well as the members of social groups (Lave and Wenger, 1991: 13).

Some of the elements of this practice-based approach to learning can be found in experiential and transformative learning literature. Experiential learning refers to learning through personal experiences that combine perception, cognition and behaviour (Kolb, 1984). Reflection over experiences, while they occur and after they have occurred, is a key component for learning (Dewey, 1938; Kolb, 1984) long recognised in communities. The adoption of the concept of transformative learning allows some scholars to make a step forward: transformative learning becomes a sort of deep learning through which our assumptions are revisited, so that a shift in our worldview occurs with changes in the cognitive, affective and spiritual perspective on ourselves and the rest of the world (O'Sullivan, 2002). Transformative learning experiences can be related to the aforementioned practical wisdom and the eudaimonic aspect of wellbeing, when such a shift in worldview is perceived as contributing to our self-realization.

Some scholars suggest that travel experiences can potentially contribute to transformations affecting not only the travellers but also the hosts (Coghlan and Gooch, 2011; Morgan, 2010; Stone and Petrick, 2013). Moreover, transformative learning in tourism experiences has been commented on also in terms of global citizenship, with some authors highlighting the possibility that knowledge and first-hand experience could contribute to promote compassion and, ultimately, global peace (McGladdery and Lubbe, 2017) through notions of active citizenship within local communities.

As the practice-based approach to learning identifies processes relevant to learning, the transformative learning literature describes the possible steps towards transformation. Those are summarized by Coghlan and Gooch (2011) in five core elements: prerequisite and context, dilemmas and confusion, dialogue and reflection, self-realization and reintegration in society. According to this position, transformative learning can be favoured by the context, such as in some of the cases of volunteer tourism investigated by Coghlan and Gooch (2011), and the cases commented on by Richards (2011) and mentioned earlier, i.e. ecotourism, cultural tourism and agritourism where there are close links to values and identities of the communities. Again, according to Coghlan and Gooch (2011), transformative learning depends on some prerequisites and, more precisely, originate from the search by individuals for alternative frames of reference that can contribute to solve possible personal dilemmas and confusion. Transformative learning therefore occurs when new frames of reference are created through active dialogue and purposeful reflection and become part of the renewed individual. In their framework, Coghlan and Gooch (2011) use the term 'engagement' in a limited way, referring to the cognitive processes relevant to learning; more precisely it includes learning through readings, lecture, discussion and critical thinking.

Conceptual model of tourism engagement from a learning perspective

The term 'engagement' is used in both the practice-based learning theory by Wenger and Lave (1991) and the tourism study about transformative experiences by Coghlan and Gooch (2011). In the first case, it refers to participation in social activities; in the second case, it exclusively concerns cognitive processes.

Despite their limitations, these scholarly contributions show some important insights in the relevant processes and can be useful to revisit the definition of 'engagement' as derived from the tourism literature mentioned at the beginning of this section. Tourism engagement can be therefore qualified as a located social practice of involvement with and commitment to a specific tourism offer/provider/destination/community culture. The terms 'involvement' and 'commitment' are described through the processes identified in the learning theories presented in the previous section, and in particular those by Wenger and Lave. Involvement and commitment are about:

- participation in activities,
- communication,
- reflection,
- reification,
- imagination, and
- alignment.

With the aim of understanding how tourism engagement can be related to the wellbeing of the tourists, the providers and the members of host communities, the aforementioned processes are explored with reference to their relation to hedonic and eudaimonic wellbeing. Whilst the first type of wellbeing (hedonic) is understood as pleasure, including sensual gratification and entertainment, the second type of wellbeing (eudaimonic) is viewed as a search for alternative and more satisfying frames of reference, as suggested by Coghlan and Gooch (2011). With regard to the latter, possible dilemmas and confusion can be the cognitive and emotional triggers for engagement, leading to a search for meaningful experiences that can contribute to self-development, in particular when they become part of the everyday life once tourists are back home.

Background context

This research outlines a case study about a tourism initiative, more precisely a rural event, organized by a community association, *Agritur-Aso*, founded in 2007 by the owners of six rural accommodation facilities and farms in Valdaso, a valley between the provinces of Fermo and Ascoli (Marche region). The area is characterised by picturesque landscapes with small medieval hill towns, strong culinary traditions and many typical local products.

According to the association's website (www.agritur-aso.it/), the aim of *Agritur-Aso* is to create projects to promote a better quality of life in the local communities based on solidarity and sustainable tourism. *Agritur-Aso* promotes the collaboration between several local stakeholders who operate in rural tourism offering different kinds of gastronomic products and hospitality services in addition to environmental education (Bertella and Cavicchi, 2018). One of their projects is called *Marche in Valigia* (literally: *Marche in your suitcase*), whose aim is to promote the mobility of members such as owners of agrifood facilities, local farmers, and micro-entrepreneurs in the arts and crafts manufacturing sectors. They often organize cultural meetings abroad during the tourism low season, without any economic support from local governments. As explained in Bertella and Cavicchi (2018), the trigger for those meetings is often an invitation by those who travelled to Italy and are keen to share with friends and relatives their holiday experiences and participation in events and festivals in rural areas.

The local tourism initiatives by *Agritur-Aso* are experiences based on a combination of experiential tourism (Sundbo and Sorensen, 2013), relational tourism (Grolleau, 1987), and community-based tourism (Okazaki, 2008) perspectives. From the perspective of the organizers, the aim is to revitalize abandoned places and increase the local community's commitment to actively face the problems and challenges of promoting the value of a place.

Method

The case study presented in the chapter is the *Lavandaso* event organized by the aforementioned association *Agritur-Aso*. The case is investigated by applying an ethnographic approach that offered the opportunity to study *Lavandaso* organizers, residents and tourists participating in their natural setting, using the twin methods of participant observation and in-depth interviews (Brown, 2009; Fetterman, 1998). Furthermore, desk research of newspaper articles and posts from blogs and social media allowed data triangulation to be carried out.

Participant observation

In June 2017, a member of our research team volunteered at *Lavandaso*, together with tourists, members of the local community and international students hosted at the local university. As a PhD student, she helped local organizers to share information and coordinate activities about the event. In her role as a complete participant (Gold, 1957), she was a member of the group being studied. However, as lack in objectivity could be regarded as one of the disadvantages of her role, the participant observation was supported by in-depth interviews.

In-depth interviews

An interpretative narrative approach was adopted to collect additional primary data through 14 interviews. The sample included different targets depending on the role people played during the event: four organizers, who designed and managed the event; four collaborative participants, who helped to organize the event before and during it; four volunteers (three students and one external), who took part in the event and had an active role (speakers, activity providers, etc.); and two tourists.

The interview conducted consists of 21 open-ended questions divided into five sections. The starting section is about the background of the interviewees, with the aim of collecting biographical info and asking them to introduce themselves and talk about daily life, work and free time and motivations/expectations derived from taking part in the event. The second section is about engagement and explores several aspects such as participation to activities, social engagement, and place-based practice (these questions were asked only to those participants who did not come from Marche or who do not live near the destination). The last section sums up the interview and highlights memories and feelings about the event and the personal impact it may have had on the interviewee.

The interview guide aimed to analyze two main aspects related to the event: involvement and commitment, and wellbeing. The analysis focused on participation in activities, communication, reflection, reification, imagination, and alignment. The presence of these aspects in the interview guide was highlighted by using them as categories and subcategories to be further interpreted in findings and discussion.

In addition, two more participants were asked to describe their experience by writing down their memories and feelings using the 'photo elicitation technique' (Andersson et al., 2016). They were sent three photos referring to different moments of the event: the first one showed a group of people harvesting lavender in the field, a reference to the social aspect of the event; the second one showed hands on a table preparing lavender decorations, a reference to the participation to activities; and the last one showed a glimpse of the setting of the event and it refers to the place-based practice and the engagement with the destination. The interpretation of those texts followed the same method of the questionnaire analysis.

Desk research

Secondary data, such as newspaper articles and posts from blogs and social media provided by event participants, were collected. In particular, articles from local online newspapers such as www.cronachefermane.it and www.viver efermo.it, the Facebook pages of the *Lavandaso* event, other local NGOs and the incoming facilities linked with the project were included in the analysis. The findings of the case study are presented in the following section and then discussed adopting the concepts previously identified as relevant.

Findings

When fieldwork was carried out, in Spring 2017, the *Lavandaso* event celebrated its 7th edition. The event is a festival about the production and the uses of lavender. It is a touring event: the first three editions were set in an ancient, abandoned castle in the rural area of Marche, the following two editions took place in an old mill and, in the last two years, the setting has been a small rural village where few people still live (only three in the historical centre). The philosophy of the event is to revitalize those places, promoting local producers and a natural and rural lifestyle. Every year, around 600 tourists from the nearby area and farther afield and some foreigners visit the event.

The *Lavandaso* event is anticipated by some pre-event activities for organizers and volunteers. For example, lavender harvest, the preparation of the decorations for the event and the preparation and consumption of meals together are regarded as very important activities. During the event, other activities include art exhibitions, painting contests, classical music concerts hosted in cultural sites, a street market to sell natural and handmade products, hands-on workshops, and an open meeting focused on the discussion of local development goals, opportunities and challenges.

Adopting the framework outlined, the event-related processes that were particularly relevant to hedonic and eudaimonic wellbeing are described in the following sections and commented on.

Engagement and hedonic wellbeing

In the interviews, interviewees commented on the participation to the events, always talking about common activities. These are often described referring to the pleasure of meeting people, new and already known, and the interaction with them. With regard to the *Lavandaso* event, some of the tourists did not know the organizers or the other tourists, while others had already met someone before the event. With regard to organizers, some of them had a larger network of contacts compared to others, which often included close connections. The pleasure of meeting and spending time with people clearly emerge from the data collected. For example, a tourist who had been invited by a local student volunteering at the *Lavandaso*, said that the event gave him the opportunity to meet "some very friendly and exquisite people, both Italians and foreigners". The organizers and the volunteer students had met some of the event participants beforehand. According to one interviewee, this is a positive element as she felt 'among friends' from the beginning, a feeling that was shared by several people who were involved in casual conversations during the observation of both events.

One of the organizers commented about the 'fantastic people' she had the pleasure to work with, and in particular referring to their willingness to help and create the event together with them. This can be related to the process of alignment, that is enthusiastic individuals directing their efforts toward a common goal.

Communication is an important element strictly related to participation and conviviality. The data, and in particular the notes from the observation process, show that the people involved in the events engaged in numerous conversations that were usually very friendly, casual and informal. Conversations occurred across the different types of participants (organizer, tourist, local community member). The observation helped to highlight some main topics of conversation: local culture, including several aspects such as rural lifestyle and local urban and natural landscape, and the individuals' opinion about the events and their implementation. An Italian interviewee reported some initial difficulties due to the language but specified that they could be easily overcome.

Communication during the events occurred naturally, also through body language. This type of interaction, including smiles, laughs, physical proximity, hugs and similar, was evident during the observation of the events. Some examples can be the sharing of the meals in both events and *Lavandaso* lavender workshops.

With regard to the bodily dimension, the data collected also suggest that the hedonic pleasure that emerged during the events was sometimes triggered by the simple act of being in the countryside and engaging in outdoor activities, feeling a nice temperature on the skin and enjoying the rural landscape. Sensory gratification was also experienced due to the consumption of food and drinks and the handling of lavender flowers in the *Lavandaso* event. The data collected through the interviews and the casual conversations with the organizers and the volunteers of both events suggest that several people experienced the activities as demanding and tiring but, at the same time, worth participating.

The data also suggest that hedonic pleasure is something perceived after the event. Part of the data were actually collected after the events and the people interviewed and those who participated to the photo elicitation explicitly commented on the pleasure to take a trip down memory lane to the time of the events, recalling in particular the friendly atmosphere. Moreover, it can be noted that some interviewees and some of the people involved in the conversation during the events seem to experience hedonic pleasure also in terms of future expectations, thinking about the possibility to join the events in the next years.

Finally, the data indicate that the social processes described here were facilitated by the limited size of the events and the presence of some people as active organizers. With regard to the size, two interviewees, providers of activities at the *Lavandaso* event, noted that the event is often attended by the same few people and this may be due to the peculiarity of the specific products on which the event is focused on. They suggested that the same peculiarity can represent a limitation, mainly in terms of commercial benefits, but it can be positive from an experiential point of view. One of them explained: "*Lavandaso* is an alternative path, and I consider it as an advantage. Other events, such as the fried fish festival, are attended by one thousand people. However, as Lavandaso is attended by far less people having a common interest (lavender) it is more likely to relate to most of them".

With regard to the role of some particularly enthusiastic and inspirational people acting as promoters, the majority of the interviewees recognize the crucial role of the leader of the association, a retired psychologist, and his charisma contributing to the success of the initiative.

Data therefore point to the conclusion that the experience of hedonic wellbeing (fun, pleasure, sensual gratification, pleasant memories) can be referred mostly to one aspect, that is a widespread feeling of conviviality. Consequently, the most relevant processes outlined in the theoretical framework of this study are participation and communication. The data also show that hedonic pleasure in terms of fun can concern alignment, especially for the organizers and volunteers who enjoy joining shared projects. With regard to these processes, the data suggest that the limited size of the events and the presence of few, particularly active individuals acted as facilitators. Sensorial gratification seems to be associated mainly to the generic environment, the physical stimuli and the food. Pleasure could be experienced both during and after the events, suggesting the importance of reification processes as a way to re-experience.

Engagement and eudaimonic wellbeing

The processes of participation and communication that are commented on in the preceding section in relation to hedonic wellbeing are relevant also for eudaimonic wellbeing. More specifically, they are associated to values that are perceived as particularly important: friendship and willingness to help. The latter concept is referred by the local people to the mutual assistance, viewed as an integral part of the local farmers' lifestyle and ethics. This is clear in the local dialect expression "*Lu rraiutu*", literally "re-help", according to which agricultural practices are shared on a voluntary basis between neighboring farmers (Bertella and Cavicchi, 2018).

Participation, and in particular the relationships developed during the activities, is often described referring to friendship. The data from the interviews and the observation revealed a shared agreement about the events contributing to the development of new friendships or the deepening of already existing ones. The terms "friend(s)", "friendship(s) and "friendly" are recurrent. In this context, conviviality acquires a deeper meaning and the related sense of togetherness, at least for several of the people involved, is not limited to the duration of the events: people enjoyed to cultivate those relations through occasional contacts on social media and with the promise to "meet again next year", which seems to have been fulfilled when considering the loyal presence of some people at the events.

The data regarding the providers, who are small local entrepreneurs, also suggest that the events gave them the opportunity to meet colleagues, something that might be relevant to their professional identity and their role in the local economy. An entrepreneur reported that her participation in the event gave her the opportunity to meet other local entrepreneurs and learn more about the "small and interesting businesses of our area".

The feeling of engagement with and, more precisely, the dedication to the area they belong to is felt quite deeply by most of the entrepreneurs and local people in general, due to the typical challenges connected to the abandoning of rural areas and also to the earthquake that hit the region in 2016 and 2017. The data about the communication during the events make it clear, with some of the conversations being focused on the economic valorisation of the territory, the risk of outmigration, and the job opportunities for the youth. In rural economies, social ties and resources are in fact crucial to job insertion and job creation (Lindsay et al., 2005; Matthews et al., 2009), and the role of volunteering in network building is widely recognised (Beggs and Hurlbert, 1997; Paine et al.,

2013; Hirst, 2011). The earthquake seems to have added some value to the events, as it caused a considerable amount of frustration and confusion but also an emerging willingness to overcome challenges. This willingness is perceived at a collective level, as explained by a local person who referred to the traditional practice of "*Lu rraiutu*".

These aspects of solidarity can also be related to potentially transformative experiences that are somehow embedded in the investigated event. The inclusion of some open meetings to discuss local challenges, goals and opportunities is a proof of it. During the meetings, the process of reflection, characterized by a strong sense of attachment and a genuine concern about the local problems further exacerbated by the earthquake, occurs as a collective process. Moreover, it seems that, through common reflections and discussion, local people are helped to go through rather comprehensive processes of imagination and alignment. In other words, interviewees showed a sense of meaningfulness related to the coordination of the activities, economic as well as recreational ones, aimed at building together a possible future for the local area. The investigated events, implying the involvement of both local and non-local people, are implicitly identified as particularly suitable activities that can contribute to this goal. In the case study, a considerable number of local elders who are retirees but still very active, are included. The data suggest that for those people the engagement in the planning, implementation and also their participation as attendees to the event is a matter of identifying themselves as responsible citizens.

In general, a widespread sense of responsibility could be observed among the participants to the events who are not locals, which is also confirmed by the fact that some of them come back to the event every year.

Discussion

Tourism engagement and wellbeing in a learning perspective

The developed framework, based mainly on the contributions by educationists Jean Lave and Etienne Wenger (1991) and on Coghlan and Gooch (2011), has been an analytical tool useful to uncover important relations between engagement and wellbeing. This can be connected to the relevance assigned to the social aspect, which is something that can be particularly important and to a certain extent peculiar of the type of tourism experiences investigated, that is community-based tourism, small-scale arrangements in rural contexts.

The findings show that the emergence of wellbeing, including personal growth and transformation, develop along the emotional, bodily and cognitive dimensions and can be described through the processes presented in Lave and Wenger (1991). Among those processes, only reification proved to have a limited role. Reification was found to be important, as it played a facilitator role during common activities, was a source of sensory gratification and a key factor with reference to the memories of the tourists. However, collected data do not suggest this process could play a particular important role, especially in terms of eudaimonic wellbeing. On the other hand, some of the other processes investigated were relevant for both forms of wellbeing, and some in particular for eudaimonic wellbeing.

In general, it can be said that participants developed a quite strong sense of belonging related to the experience of conviviality in the community, which will be discussed in the next section. This can be due to the experiential value of tourism as an opportunity to learn through encounters (Ritchie et al., 2003; Richards, 2011; Stone and Petrick, 2013). The case suggests that the social aspect and identity issues are strictly related to engagement understood as participation to the arrangements' activities as an occasion to meet people, communicate and interact with them, and as commitment to common projects and shared goals for the near and distant future.

Reflection and imagination can be regarded as premises for the process of alignment that can be a trigger for eudaimonic wellbeing. Alignment refers to tourism providers and volunteers working together toward the shared goal of organizing pleasant and memorable events, something that can be viewed as relevant to hedonic wellbeing. In addition to this, alignment can also be associated with the revitalization of the economic and socio-cultural life in small villages as it may contribute to the wellbeing of the community. In the case study investigated, alignment proved to be particularly important as it was identified as a sense of a shared willingness to care for the local environment to which the local community is emotionally attached.

Alignment with reference to non-local people also was important, as it was represented by an empathic response to the local challenges and a widespread willingness to help. According to the concept of the transformative potential of tourism experiences as proposed by Coghlan and Gooch (2011), the experience of a tragic episode (the earthquake) can act as a trigger within the community. However, it can be added that the state of confusion can derive from direct experiences, as for the local people, or indirect experiences, as for the tourists.

The findings also suggest that both hedonic and eudaimonic wellbeing develop along several of the identified processes, and, as suggested in the literature, they cannot be considered independent from each other (Henderson and Knight, 2012; Waterman, 2008).

Moreover, the adopted approach deriving from social learning and transformative perspectives highlighted that engagement can play a particularly relevant role not only with reference to sustainability, as suggested by some previous studies (Bertella et al., 2018; Tasci and Severt, 2017), but also to resilience, understood as an active reaction to unpredictable shocks and therefore the quality of life in the community.

Such an approach however did not cover one aspect that, nonetheless, emerged from the case study: the presence of one or few individuals among the community members, in some cases, but not always, directly involved in tourism, whose function is to be inspirational figures and promoters. Interestingly, the case investigated shows that those individuals can belong to the categories of people often viewed as marginal, such as the elders.

Tourism engagement and wellbeing in rural experiences

The case investigated suggests a strong relation between engagement and wellbeing, in particular eudaimonic wellbeing that develops through various processes and dimensions, as discussed in the previous section.

The findings also shed light on the understanding of tourism and tourism engagement, which was defined as a located social practice in the theoretical part of the study. In the observation and the interviews, the material characteristics of the destination proved not to have a key role in making the experience unique for the tourists, as those characteristics are mainly related to individual experience of hedonic wellbeing. Most of the characteristics concern the aesthetic gratification related to the rural landscape, and the way the experience of such a pleasure emerged from the data suggests that this might not be peculiar of the specific destination. In addition to this, the bodily experiences, such as those derived from the weather, do not seem to be so unique as they could be referred to other rural Mediterranean destinations. An exception is food tasting. Although being clearly material, food tasting can also be related to the immaterial aspect of the destination, that is its culinary heritage. A question could therefore be raised about how 'located' the investigated tourism experiences are and to which extent the physicality of the destination is important for engagement and commitment.

On the other hand, when considering the located aspect of the tourism experience as a social space, the data suggest a strong sense of engagement and commitment. The latter element, which is an important component of the adopted learning perspective in relation to identity issues of becoming member of a group, derives from the experience of eudaimonic wellbeing. In particular, data highlight the centrality of values such as friendship, willingness to help and involvement in shared projects for the future of the local area.

Involvement can be related to the concept of "communitas" proposed by Rihova et al. (2013) and the case study suggests a possible integration of this concept with the concept of peripheral participation by Lave and Wenger (1991). In other words, tourists' engagement, although strong, may be seen as peripheral, and directed mainly toward the destination's culture and the specific providers and events. On the other hand, the engagement of local people, especially in its commitment aspect, is stronger and directed more clearly to the local area in all its aspects, both immaterial and material. The group of non-local people could be conceptualized not as a "temporary communitas" but as a "peripheral communitas". The latter can be described as composed by loyal tourists highly engaged with some of the community members of the destination and their culture. In the case study, members of such "peripheral communitas" include traditional tourists and students of the local university coming from other parts of Italy or from abroad. The type of engagement among local and non-local people can be regarded as an elastic bond between these two groups, local community and "peripheral communitas". These are two distinct but related groups and come close occasionally, for example through social media, and overlap during physical interactions.

Finally, the events investigated are quite limited in size and this might be an important aspect to be considered as restricted social groups facilitate communication and interaction with other people, both residents and tourists, and consequently the other relevant processes. Together with the dominant rural culture, such an aspect can promote wellbeing in both hedonic and eudaimonic terms, as suggested by some previous studies (Bertella et al., 2018; Kastenholz et al., 2013).

Conclusion

This study explored tourism engagement by adopting a learning perspective and conducting a case study about a rural event and the related experiences made by tourists and local community members, including but not limited to tourism providers. The adoption of a specific learning perspective centred on tourism as a located social practice of doing, belonging and becoming allowed tourism engagement to be described in relation to wellbeing. With reference to both hedonic and eudaimonic wellbeing, findings suggest that the social aspect of conviviality and the related process of participation, communication and alignment are important in the context investigated. For eudaimonic wellbeing, the process of reflection and imagination and a critical situation, which can become a source of confusion, may play an important role, especially if inspired and coordinated by one or more individuals. The latter aspect emerged from the data although it is not represented in the theoretical framework of the study. The case investigated and the reference to the theoretical framework taken into consideration however helped to conclude that tourism engagement and its relation to wellbeing develop in an intertwined, multidimensional and mainly social way.

The findings also helped to highlight the possibility to reflect further on the conceptualization of tourism engagement as a form of 'elastic relation' among individuals belonging, from one side, to the local community of the destination and, on the other side, to a sort of "peripheral communitas" of loyal tourists. Within such a perspective, tourism engagement seems to be more relevant with reference to the people actively involved and the immaterial aspect of the destination rather than to the physical destination.

Those reflections about tourism engagement have some practical implications. Questions can be raised about what kind of impact this form of tourism engagement, mainly supported by social interactions, may have and although it could be said that there certainly is a positive impact from an experiential point of view, both in relation to pleasure and meaningfulness, it needs to be clear that the economic impacts might be limited on short term. However, exploiting the potential for job creation might provide an increased impact on medium term. On the other hand, it can be argued that loyalty in the long term might be positively affected and, ultimately, very desirable in terms of both sustainability and resilience.

The study clearly shows some limitations as its contributions could be restricted to the type of tourism investigated, that is small-scale and rural tourism. The approach adopted mainly emphasizes the social aspect of various typologies of individuals (tourists, tourism providers and local community members) and this aspect might be very limited in other contexts such as urban tourism in big cities.

References

Andersson, T. D., Getz, D., Vujicic, S., Robinson, R. N., & Cavicchi, A. (2016). Preferred travel experiences of foodies: An application of photo elicitation. *Journal of Vacation Marketing*, *22*(1), 55–67.

Beggs, J., & Hurlbert, J. (1997). The social context of men's and women's job search ties: Membership in voluntary organizations, social resources, and job search outcomes. *Sociological Perspectives*, *40*(4): 601–622.

Bertella, G., & Cavicchi, A. (2018). From sharecroppers to "flying farmers": New forms of tourism entrepreneurship in rural areas. *e-Review of Tourism Research*, *14*(3/4), 133–148.

Bertella, G., Cavicchi, A., & Bentini, T. (2018). The reciprocal aspect of the experience value: Tourists and residents celebrating weddings in the rural village of Petritoli (Italy). *Anatolia*, *29*(1), 52–62.

Bimonte, S., & Punzo, L. F. (2016). Tourist development and host-guest interaction: An economic exchange theory. *Annals of Tourism Research*, *58*, 128–139.

Brodie, R. J., Hollebeek, L. D., Juric, B., & Ilic, A. (2011). Customer engagement: Conceptual domain, fundamental propositions, and implications for research. *Journal of Service Research*, *14*(3), 252–271.

Brown, L. (2009). The transformative power of the international sojourn: An ethnographic study of the international student experience. *Annals of Tourism Research*, *36*(3), 502–521.

Bryce, D., Curran, R., O'Gorman, K., & Taheri, B. (2015). Visitors' engagement and authenticity: Japanese heritage consumption. *Tourism Management*, *46*, 571–581.

Coghlan, A., & Gooch, M. (2011). Applying a transformative learning framework to volunteer tourism. *Journal of Sustainable Tourism*, *19*(6), 713–728.

Crouch, D. (1999). *Leisure/tourism Geographies: Practices and Geographical Knowledge*. Oxon: Routledge.

Crouch, D. (2000). Places around us: Embodied lay Geographies in Leisure and Tourism. *Leisure Studies*, *19*, 63–76.

Crouch, D. (2002). Surrounded by place, embodies encounters. In S. Coleman & M. Crang (Eds.), *Tourism: Between Place and Performance* (pp. 207–218). Oxford: Berghahn Books.

Dewey, J. (1938). *Experience and Education*. New York: McMillan.

Falk, J. H., Ballantyne, R., Packer, J., & Benckendorff, P. (2012). Travel and learning: A neglected tourism research area author links open overlay panel. *Annals of Tourism Research*, *39*(2), 908–927.

Fetterman, D. M. (1998). Ethnography. In L. Bickman & D. J. Rog (Eds.), *Handbook of Applied Social Research Methods* (pp. 473–504). Thousand Oaks, CA: Sage Publications.

Gold, R. L. (1957). Roles in sociological field observations. *Social Forces*, *36*, 217–223.

Grolleau, H. (1987). Rural tourism in the 12 member states of the European economic community. EEC Tourism Unit, DG XXIII.

Henderson, L. W., & Knight, T. (2012). Integrating the hedonic and eudaimonic perspectives to more comprehensively understand wellbeing and pathways to wellbeing. *International Journal of Wellbeing*, *2*(3), 196–221.

Hirst, Λ. (2011). Links between volunteering and employability. *Research Report RR309*, Department for Education and Skills, Cambridge: Cambridge Policy Consultants.

Jaakkola, E., & Alexander, M. (2014). The role of customer engagement behavior in value co-creation: A service system perspective. *Journal of Service Research, 17*(3), 247–261.

Kastenholz, E., Carneiro, M. J., Eusébio, C., & Figueiredo, E. (2013). Host – guest relationships in rural tourism: Evidence from two Portuguese villages. *Anatolia: An International Journal of Tourism and Hospitality Research, 24*(3), 367–380.

Kolb, D. A. (1984). *Experential Learning*. Englewoods Cliffs: Prentice-Hall.

Lave, J., & Wenger, E. (1991). *Situated Learning. Legitimate Peripheral Participation*. Cambridge, MA: Cambridge University Press.

Lindsay, C., Malcolm, G., & McQuaid, R., (2005). Alternative job search strategies in remote rural and peri-urban Markets: The role of social networks. *Sociologia Ruralis, 45*(1/2), 53–70.

Matthews, R., Pendakur, R., & Young, N. (2009). Social capital, labour markets, and job-finding in Urban and Rural Regions: Comparing paths to employment in prosperous cities and stressed rural communities in Canada. *The Sociological Review, 57*(2).

McGladdery, C. A., & Lubbe, B. A. (2017). Rethinking educational tourism: Proposing a new model and future directions. *Tourism Review, 72*(3), 319–329.

Mehmetoglu. M., & Engen, M. (2011) Pine and Gilmore's concept of experience economy and its dimensions: An empirical examination in tourism. *Journal of Quality Assurance in Hospitality & Tourism, 12*(4), 237–255.

Morgan, A. D. (2010). Journey into transformation: Travel to "other" place as a vehicle for transformative learning. *Journal of Transformative Learning, 8*(4), 246–268.

Okazaki, E. (2008). A community-based tourism model: Its conception and use. *Journal of Sustainable Tourism, 16*(5), 511–529.

O'Sullivan, E. V., Morrell, A., & O'Connor, M. A. (2002). *Expanding the Boundaries of Transformative Learning*. New York: Palgrave.

Paine, A. E., McKay, S., & Moro, D. (2013). Does volunteering improve employability? Insights from the British Household Panel Survey and beyond. *Voluntary Sector Review, 9*(4), 355–376.

Pansari, A., & Kumar, V. (2017) Customer engagement: The construct, antecedents, and consequences. *Journal of the Academy of Marketing Science, 45*, 294–311.

Pine, B. J., & Gilmore, J. H. (1998). Welcome to the experience economy. *Harvard Business Review, 76*(6), 176–180.

Pine, B. J., & Gilmore, J. H. (2013). The experience economy: past, present and future. In J. Sundbo & F. Sørensen (Eds.), *Handbook on the Experience Economy* (pp. 21–44). Cheltenham: Edward Elgar Publishing.

Pitman, T., Broomhall, S., McEwan, J., & Majocha, E. (2010). Adult learning in educational tourism. *Australian Journal of Adult Learning, 50*(2), 219–238.

Richards, G. (2011). Creativity and tourism: The state of the art. *Annals of Tourism Research, 38*(4), 1225–1253.

Rihova, I., Buhalis, D., Moital, M., & Gouthro, M. B. (2013). Social layers of customer-to-customer value co-creation. *Journal of Service Management, 24*(5), 553–566.

Ritchie, B. W. (2003). *Managing Educational Tourism*. Clevedon: Channel View Publications.

Ritchie, B. W., Carr, N., & Cooper, C. P. (2003). *Managing Educational Tourism*. Buffalo: Channel View Books.

Ryan, R., M., & Deci, E. (2001). On happiness and human potentials: A review of research on hedonic and eudaimonic well-being. *Annual Review of Psychology, 52*, 141–166.

Sherlock, K. (2001). Revisiting the concepts of host and guests. *Tourist Studies*, *1*(3), 271–295.

Stone, M. J., & Petrick, J. F. (2013). The educational benefits of travel experiences: A literature review. *Journal of Travel Research*, *52*(6), 731–744.

Sundbo, J., & Sorensen, F. (Eds.). (2013). *Handbook on the Experience Economy*. Cheltenham: Edward Elgar Publishing.

Taheri, B., Jafari, A., & O'Gorman, K. (2014). Keeping your audience: Presenting a visitor engagement scale. *Tourism Management*, *42*, 321–329.

Tasci, A. D. A., & Severt, D. (2017). A triple lens measurement of host-guest perceptions for sustainable gaze in tourism. *Journal of Sustainable Tourism*, *25*(6), 711–731.

Towner, J. (1985). The grand tour: A key phase in the history of tourism. *Annals of Tourism Research*, *12*(3), 297–333.

Waterman, A. S. (2008). Reconsidering happiness: A eudaimonist's perspective. *The Journal of Positive Psychology*, *3*(4), 234–252.

Wenger, E. (1998). *Communities of Practice. Learning, Meaning, and Identity*. Cambridge, MA: Cambridge University Press.

Wenger, E. (2000). Communities of Practice and Social Learning Systems. *Organization*, *7*(2), 225–246.

15 Systems, stakeholders, storytelling

Tourism development and
conservation in the peak district and
the Balaton Highlands national parks

Peter Wiltshier and Alan Clarke

Introduction

Through this chapter we explore how the balance between conservation and development is considered in two European national parks; how it is managed and how the stakeholders reflect on their roles. The chapter employs various conceptual approaches that are characterised by socio-cultural lenses of political commentators like Putnam (1995) and Senge (2006), sociologists Hall (2013) and Giddens (1984); an enviro-economic lens of Murphy (1988), Ashworth (1988), Bramwell (2006), Baggio and Cooper (2010), Jamal and Getz (1995), Woodside (1988), Crouch and Brent Ritchie (1999), Moscardo (2014) and Hjalager (2010 and 1997). The ideology we witness in highly developed areas of recreation and conservation is of post-structuralism. Initially we followed the post-structural, power sharing and reductionist philosophy espoused over fifty years of partnership planning. We add to this complexity a nuance from nostalgia, place making and re-interpretation for community-based policy, planning and management. Finally we combine the reductionist with the complex and symbolic in a stakeholder focused management reflective lens. A further philosophical approach that has influenced our practice is that of actor network espoused in the past fifty years to frame the performers in the stories that follow (Latour, 2005; Bianchi, 2003).

Complex, community-based and endogenous discourses have also been studied in the socio-medical context of nealthy, learning communities (Kagan, 2013; Taylor, 2005; Mayo, 1997; Mayo et al., 2013). These approaches broaden the appeal of the socio-economic and socio-cultural that have so often been the touchstone of the sustainable and responsible approaches of tourism and the management of experiences for visitors (and residents). We can recognise the potential for paradigms established in health and well-being, specifically in healthcare, that provide a broad framework for driving the social and cultural capital accrual that will be critical for hosting tourism in the years ahead (O'Meara, 2002). Skills for sustaining community capital and the infrastructure needed to support hosts and, in turn, as development broadens appeal of the destination community, to tourists is a focus. To develop the required skills as hosts and as champions the acquisition of a framework to empower people in communities and to develop notions of partnership and cooperation needs exploration through a social well-being and health lens (Taylor, 2002).

The second part of the chapter considers dyads, discontinuities, paradoxes and contradictions emerging from within the stakeholders' own admissions and insights into positions of power. We take examples of current thinking, how these can now be adapted for paradigms that may only be considered in context beyond national parks and beyond tourism as an activity and series of linked businesses. The literature is used as touchstones throughout the chapter and exemplars are highlighted in each subsection.

In the conclusion we review the trajectory of stakeholders as the conflicts between power and new knowledges are embedded in the territories under exploration. There are some exemplars which we highlight that can be reviewed in the socio-cultural and rational economic modelling that practitioners, academics and theorists will wish to review in future. Our approach also underscores the relative unimportance traditionally assigned to learned lessons, explicit and tacit knowledge retained at the destinations. Previous explorations have clarified that more work needs to be conducted to embed knowledge in stakeholders' repositories to provide evidence of past transgressions in sustainable policies and plans and to amplify for the benefit of current stakeholders the need to avoid repeated errors in establishing management practices for sustainable futures (Clarke et al., 2009).

Literature review

Tourism now has its own pantheon of scholars and a very broad philosophical approach that has recognised the need for integration and interdisciplinarity with mainstream development and sustainability agendas at many levels – micro-business to multinational and public sector responses which should also include the national parks. This chapter accepts and values the contributions made from multiple philosophies and epistemologies but brings the reader back to the need for integration of mainstream public interest and a healthy melding of the public and private sector development agendas with community-predicated endogenous good practices. These good practices must be shared to benefit the learning of stakeholders worldwide. In the context of economic development there are many vested interests. In the public sector sharing intelligence and learning from systems thinking is becoming the norm. The sustainability of any approach is predicated upon the cost-effectiveness of solutions in social, economic and environmental benefits. The approach is satisfying the economics of development foremost. The social and environmental issues are measured in transforming the destinations through partnership. The processes involved in transforming the development sites must allow for the learning to be embedded and articulated through the outcomes before forming a repository agreed by all (McGrath, 2012; Pinho et al., 2012; Sučić, 2009; O'Dell and Essaides, 1998; Mayo, 1997). The codicil is that transformative development is endogenous and furthermore that stakeholders are informed and negotiate perspectives with as representative a group as is possible (Burns et al., 2004).

The economics of sustainable development is foremost seen as cost-effective partnership solutions are going to be core to the outcomes. Framing the actor-network approach with interventions from systems thinking also needs the community bottom-up approaches to be affordable and equitable to avoid power vacuums (Latour, 2005; Checkland, 1981; Heeks, 2013).

Throughout this chapter we identify issues that stakeholders have, through personal communication, considered critical to the success of sustainable development. A balance between expert opinions gleaned through our investigation and the metaphor of discourse, obtained through the literature, is central as well as critical to the outcomes and to the expectations and agenda for future stakeholder consideration.

The list of issues follows, without priority, and in alphabetical order to signify our intention to not cloud judgement for readers with expectations from the various discursive arguments: branding and new identity, capacity constraints, conflict tourism versus production capacity, countryside tourism, destination leadership versus destination management, destination management organisations and strategic issues, food and slow tourism – the importance of localised production and consumption, growth limits, interventions in protected areas, landscapes of power, neo-liberalism and conservation as bed fellows, partnership evolution, place change and development, sharing good practices and intellectual property, sharing resources and finally valorisation management.

Branding and identity

In the United Kingdom legislation was enacted in 1947 to establish national parks for the recreation of all and the conservation of the environment. The very first national park, the Peak District National Park (PDNP) was established in 1951. For more than six decades the Peak District National Park Authority has managed the conservation of the environment and promoted enjoyment of the environment to all. The order in which these two objectives is delivered has some bearing on the success which the PDNP has evaluated its success at achievements. The environment has benefitted immensely in terms of species protection, diversity of species management and environmental indicators of the success stories. In Hungary legislation was later but framed similar responsibilities.

The identity and brand of the Peak is often touted as under-played, under-estimated and largely suffers from an identity crisis with the slightly more attractive identity and brand of the Lake District, located some three hours to the north west of the Peak. Partly this is explained by the terrain; partly this is explained by the integrity of the territory. The Lakes are the location of the highest mountain in England, some breathtaking finger lakes as a result of glacial erosion and largely fall within the confines of the county of Cumbria. Cumbria has an identity and integrity, although established only in 1972 as a county of England, having been formed by an amalgamation of Cumberland, Westmorland and

parts of Lancashire. The Lakes also benefited from early forms of literary promotion with the Lake poets – in fact rumour has it that William Wordsworth
wrote one of the earliest tourist guides to welcome the new arrivals from the
train – and, of course Beatrix Potter had her cottage there. The Peak is an
amalgam of twenty-eight local authorities, some rural and some urban and is
governed by several counties through these urban and rural authorities. Identity
and brand tend to be secondary when the competition is fierce not only between
rural counties (mostly Derbyshire and South and West Yorkshire) but also urban
authorities such as Manchester and Sheffield. These authorities, comprising
highly competitive urban and rural governments and identities have created a
patchwork of brands under the loose destination management organisation of
Visit Peak District. Ultimately the identity and brand strength of the Peak is
lost within the wider context of strong marketing by city and rural DMOs.
The Lakes, North York Moors and Yorkshire Dales do not have this conflicted
identity and confusion between rural and urban and largely not engaging in
the politics of territorial identity with far fewer LTAs to satisfy.

The former CEO of the PDNP has identified that branding, identity and image
are key components of a vibrant destination for social and economic as well as
environmental development. To undertake this development the brand and identity need articulation and a new focus on skills for marketing, distribution and
embedded new knowledge on sustainable perspectives on the objectives of
the park and the objectives of key stakeholders. Excellent analysis of the identity
and learning to be embedded in business opportunities and in managing the
landscape can be seen in Puhakka (2008); Bramwell (2006); Saarinen (2006);
Kernel (2005); Saxena (2005); Dias et al., (2004). These papers all take a
post-structuralist and actor-network approach and are largely European.

Capacity constraints

Upwards of thirty million day visitors come to the PDNP every year. Many stay
for a few hours and spend on average £25 per person. International visitor total
around three million and spend around £250 per person. Residents of central
England's major cities provide the majority of day visitors (with some notable
demand from East Anglia and the South East of England (personal communication, Visit Peak District July 2015). International visitors largely come from
within the EU and North America. Manchester Airport, third busiest in the
UK, has 53% spare capacity (compared to Heathrow running currently at 99%
capacity). It is therefore not difficult to see that the PDNP could benefit economically through expanded international arrivals at Manchester and other central
airports in the future. These international arrivals currently do not have a coordinated tourism visitor offer at Manchester or any of the DMOs located
within fifty miles of the PDNP.

There are concerns over the transport infrastructure and pollution created by
the huge numbers of domestic day visitors, quarry and extractive industries
heavy goods transport and general farming and stock transport. Hill country

farming subsidies have been largely lifted by the UK government. Farming stakeholders are not best positioned to take ownership of the shifting demand from domestic day to international overnight business at present. The maintenance and development landscape of the PDNP is largely the financial burden of the farmer. It seems logical to expect visitors staying for longer periods of time and paying for the services that they receive to become a focus for the PDNP and stakeholders now and in the near future.

As mentioned earlier the key responsibility of the PDNP over the past sixty years has been sustaining the physical environment. To successfully continue with this goal the PDNP should work closely with DMOs and tourism operators to encourage more user-pays options for the future in line with the devolved, empowering UK government policies in place. See examples in the literature that draw our attention to capacity constraints and policy (Dwyer and Edwards, 2010; Liburd and Edwards, 2010; Coles and Church, 2006; Choi and Sirakaya, 2006).

An old dream of the Hungarian nature conservation came true in 1997: a protected ecological system embracing the adjoining area of the Balaton Uplands was established with the connection of the already protected areas which had been separate for a long time. The area of 56, 997 hectares of the Balaton Uplands National Park mainly consists of these six landscape protection areas: Kis-Balaton, Keszthely Hills, Tapolca Basin, Káli Basin, Pécsely Basin and Tihany Peninsula (www.bfnp.hu/en/introduction).

Among its regions Kis-Balaton is also protected by the international Ramsar Convention, serving the protection of wetland habitats. Tihany Peninsula – as a recognition of its outstanding geological values and the work of nature conservation in that region – was awarded of European Diploma in 2003. The Natura 2000 areas, covering partly the national park and going beyond its area ensure the possibility of the conservation of habitats, plant and animal species which are of European importance.

The initiative of the Bakony-Balaton Geopark – the area of which covers partly the national park – sets the aim of interpreting the geological, natural and cultural values and awakening the consciousness of their social significance. The Bakony-Balaton Geopark became a member of the European Geoparks Network and the Global Geoparks Network – assisted by UNESCO in 2012.

The primary objective of the Balaton-felvidéki National Park is the comprehensive conservation and protection of natural assets and areas. Besides protection it is also important to interpret the beautiful landscapes, living and non-living natural values and to provide possibilities for the present and future generations for learning and relaxing in nature. The official Internet site of the Balaton-felvidéki National Park Directorate provides information about the regions, exhibition sites, nature trails and accommodation within the area that belong to the National Park Directorate. The open guided hikes, tours and other programmes, publications, environmental education programmes and the work of nature conservation experts are outlined on this site. These goals can be achieved only with the cooperation of the visitors who demonstrate responsible behaviour in the protected areas.

Conflict tourism versus production capacity

The universities in close proximity to national parks have a universal desire to showcase research engaging the key stakeholders from multiple science and social science perspectives. The exchange opportunity relates to skills development for managing visitor experiences, especially as stakeholders begin to interpret the destination for a wider market share whilst not compromising the integrity of the PDNP as the core attractor for a new offer (Dredge, 2010; Saxena, 2005). The contemporary agenda is the improvements and enhancement of health, well-being and recreation opportunities for host communities within the parks. With this provision as part of policy and planning objectives the offer and narrative for visitors reflects the emergent cultural priority of open access, hill country rights of way and the expectation that greater participation in recreation for health and in walking, climbing, water sports such as kayaking feature enjoyment for both business operators and for local communities in equal shares for visitors from outside of the park (Kagan and Duggan, 2011; O'Meara et al., 2002; Taylor, 2005).

Countryside tourism

The complex components of a stakeholder analysis to increase the vision of sustainable development inherently contain a food, drink and refreshment component. In the current marketplace a focus on local and locally processed goods and services does imply a resource allocation from local farms, local processors and local intermediaries including the entrepreneur within the community. The countryside is increasingly observed to offer these components; the key is to maximise margins and returns for each operator within the supply chain and to maintain a competitive business advantage again without compromising access to the offer made by the rural operators including farmers, processors, restaurants, cafes and a range of retail experiences that feature identifiable offers that have a quality appraisal such as DoC (see Mayo et al., 2009; Garrod et al., 2006; Edwards, 1998).

Destination leadership vs. destination management

Despite the existence of designated national parks we still observe a lack of interpretation by stakeholders with governance responsibilities to assemble, mobilise and reflect on achievements. The notion of leadership is not evident from publicity or from dissemination by the relevant authorities. The notion is much more evident that compliance with legislation and effective methods of regulation are important and inalienable. What is not demonstrable is leadership in a charismatic or even forward-thinking capacity. Recent discussions in news items related to transport, health and consumer welfare in parks, conservation of specific sites within parks, interpretation, photography, fundraising for worthy public causes, consumer appraisals including quality marks, and compliance with historic preservation laws and food. Saarinen (2006) provides a review of the need to create and adapt to existing identity; and to enable transformations we will need to see leadership that is reflective of community aspirations as much as any hegemonic and top-down identity. This implies political change and shifting balance of power amongst the stakeholders (see for example Beritelli and Bieger, 2014; Braden and Mayo, 1999). In Hungary this challenge is beginning to be addressed by the national parks, with the NP establishing networks of visitor centres, for interpretation, education, promotion and branding. In the Balaton there seems to be an eagerness to drive the sustainable development of tourism in the NP forward.

Destination management organisations and strategic issues

Discourses of power and stakeholder engagement are fundamental ideological points of reference for the role, purpose and prospects of DMOs. In this chapter we take an integrative and socio-economic perspective of management and responsibilities for NPs. Whilst acknowledging the core role of environmental protection and safeguarding flora and fauna at the heart of NP role we identify that developing and enhancing the social and economic components of destinations inevitably now devolves to local territorial authorities working alongside NPs. In reality the partnership role is subservient to the marketisation of destinations and accentuating the competitive advantage of landscape, people and built environments in the NP. More attention to the notion of partnership between NP and DMO is at the heart of the discourse. Storytelling, species protection and economic yield are uneasy bedfellows in what must be a driver of the strategy for sustainable development.

Food and slow tourism – the importance of localised production and consumption

At the heart of successful NPs is a thriving agriculture and a supportive governance which has at its heart custodianship of the physical environment whilst leaving the DMO to responsibilities for sharing the outcomes of a thriving farming sector with visitors and communities. Ultimately the partnership between NPs and their communities for a productive food and drink sector is interpreted by farmers, local food and drink processors, with intermediaries such as retailers, agricultural exhibitions and events. The strength of these partnerships and the supply chain is at the centre of the sustainable development agenda and this supply chain is therefore rightly prominent in discourses of power.

Growth limits

We acknowledge the capacity constraints approach created to evaluate impacts on NPs in the twentieth century. In the Balaton Highlands, the NP is actively encouraging more visitors as they have identified only minimal negative impacts from the existing numbers of tourists and visitors. Ideally separating humans from the environment is still preferable to allowing development in specified locations for both flora, fauna and mankind. Realistically human endeavour is essential to the maintenance and health of the physical environment, and keeping communities vital with paid employment and continuous job creation cannot be easily segregated from environmental protection plans. We do see a closer relationship between the world of work and social responsibility as critical. We need to identify a relationship that acknowledges productive capacity and healthy social and economic aspects of NP with the costs of ongoing maintenance and development borne by business and primary production within NP boundaries.

Interventions in protected areas

This is largely split into two components: farming, mining, quarrying, and forestry taking a lead role in managing visitor experiences; education, training taking a lead role in research, and skills development to meet the requirements of triple bottom-line development (Aitchison et al., 2014).

Landscapes of power

We identify stakeholders with special responsibility for community health and well-being and provision of visitor services, welcome, interpretation and storytelling that are constructed on local community-based values and beliefs. This would best be encouraged in a political environment of devolution, empowerment and grass roots acceptance of responsibility for planning, enforcing regulations and further adjustment of policy to reinforce community-based values and beliefs. In this scenario shifting responsibilities from central to local government and in practice from public sector to private sector stakeholders is noted (see Kagan et al., 2013; Ansari et al., 2012; Hung et al., 2011; Castellani and Sala, 2010; Cawley and Gillmor, 2008).

Neo-liberalism and conservation as bedfellows

Marketisation of landscapes and communities has been at the heart of the discussion about responsibility for development and deriving added value for communities from sustainable competitive advantage principles. An uneasy partnership between concept and practice without blueprints from other good practices are apparent from a review of fifty years of European Union experience and evolving policy to protect and enhance landscapes (see for example Agrawal and Gibson, 1999).

Partnership evolution

Conceptual development of relationships and relational ways of looking at managing sustainable tourism have evolved over the past five decades. This is partly for reductionist views on neo-liberal market economies and outsourcing of activities that are not core business and partly because political systems in a reductionist paradigm adhere to regionalism and smaller governance bodies for policy and planning issues within the EU.

Good practices engage supply chain partners in tourism, hospitality, services and communications. Better practices call for cross-sectoral engagement in policy and planning for primary and secondary business, competing and substituting businesses, for tourism. These better practices are not widespread and hardly embedded in knowledge management or knowledge transfer action, which is where they should and could be located (Dalkir, 2013; Casimir et al., 2012; Celino and Concilio, 2010). Barriers to better notions and practices becoming embedded and standard practice include fragmented tourism business structures, intellectual property disputes and under-resourced learning action (in public and private sector partners). Moscardo (2014) identifies basis for partnerships (and new networks) in tourism. Gilchrist and Taylor (2011) and Mayo et al. (2013) and Mayo (1997) all allude to the need for learning partnerships and the significance of the role of the third sector in community development.

Place change and development

In tourism studies and business management a key call to action is through the dynamics of mobility and individualism. Unlike evolution of best practice through understanding systems thinking modelling and structure agency models, development approaches have largely been explored through lifecycles (both destination and business) and some analysis of supply and demand from economic forecasting. NPs can adapt to outcomes of increasing mobility and sophistication in consumer demand by reflexively monitoring the quality, the input-output components and forecasting based upon a wider set of parameters in measuring trends, tastes, fashions and identity created across the chain of suppliers and through the adoption of policy and planning legislation that encompasses the environment, society and business. Simpson (2008) provides some evidence of poor knowledge of consumer behaviour and the need for greater evaluation of the contemporary situation in NPs prior to, and in support of, further decision making.

Sharing good practices and intellectual property

There are two areas for investigation here. The first is the attitude to a competitive quality of service and product and adoption in space, time and place at micro-business level and at macro-regional or community level. The second is the willingness to place innovation and success stories in the public domain (rather than maintain a copyright and intellectual ownership approach). See examples in discussions by Clark and Clarke (2011) and Hjalager (1997 and 2010).

Sharing resources

In NP context we are focused here on the public-private partnership network becoming established so that best practices can be freely exchanged at business and community levels. This has seldom occurred outside of academic research for IP reasons and for competitive advantage opportunity as we have already outlined. The political will and environment for adopting changes in sharing resources is emerging in new structures at political and environmental levels but slow to emerge in the economic perspective. For further illustrations from the literature please see Timur and Getz (2008), Beaumont and Dredge (2010).

Valorisation management

Consumers are driven by technological advances to reflect frequently on the fitness for purpose of products and services through social media. This low-cost option is an irreversible trend in tourism and in managing perceptions versus expectations in the NP context. Some suppliers that may be considered dinosaurs, or luddites, will allow consumers to assess and communicate satisfaction and dissatisfaction without comment or engaging the shifting demand that mobility and individualism have surely engendered in the contemporary consumer. Learning about satisfaction indicators, monitoring feedback and trends across the market, at micro-business and macro-community level have started but are not widespread enough to allow tourism a coherent approach to valorising visitor services and products. Dredge (2010) implies we need a participatory approach from core stakeholders if we are to accept diverse opinions, collective interests, varying scenarios and a process of development and evaluation that makes sense to us all.

Discussion

The landscapes of power in NPs are inevitably requiring multidisciplinary solutions. These solutions are sought from the ground-up; from local communities that can acknowledge feelings of being empowered and accept devolved offer of power to provide solutions informed by knowledge that has been generated from a wide variety of backgrounds, case studies and scenarios and often involving experimentation in developed and developing destinations. In the second decade of the twenty-first century we observe the increased demands made by all stakeholders on the burden of public sector bodies for funding. The traditional answer in our examples is to encourage management teams to outsource some core activities and tourism appears to be an activity that public sector funds should not be used (Moscardo, 2014; Hjalager, 2010; Beaumont and Dredge, 2010; Clarke et al., 2009). Effectively the private sector stakeholders have been inadvertently or obliquely sought to take ownership of tourism as a series of connected business opportunities. These opportunities are represented as interpretation, education, information dissemination and signposting primarily. Private sector business is actively encouraged through European Union regional growth and structure funds to apply for start-up grants to 'sweeten the pill' of devolution and empowerment. This thinking and operationalising has not often been successful as private sector business seldom possess skills and capacities to navigate policy and planning barriers. Would some of these barriers present as enablers but that is not yet the case or opportunity.

Were we to acknowledge a structure agency discourse we would see the need, as we indeed do, for storytelling and narratives that underpin beliefs and values that are inherited and a significant part of the cultural legacy in our case of NPs. To manage changes in destinations, place change management, needs decisions supported and systems thinking that is driven by the widest access to repository of knowledge on best practices. To re-interpret stories and navigate lifecycle models we need to forecast trends and anticipate behaviour responses. Key to this, as we observe, are interventions in protection of landscapes and their biota. We have enjoyed fifty years of marketised landscapes so there are inevitably stories to share around. We observe and document through various disciplinary lenses representations of power, individualism, mobility, fixity and the role of communications now through social media. To create outcomes from a discourse of change management we review practices through a lens of valorisation. We propose that storytelling and interpretation are still very much the stakeholders' most obvious and critical capacity to provide the private sector with the necessary support to work effectively with the new devolved political landscape around NPs (Aitchison et al., 2000). To monitor and manage the visitor experience we have these stories and we acknowledge a central role for sharing them and good practices in other landscapes. We must consider resources allocated in these practices and create new structures and complex networks designed in good practices and identify whether we can replicate them.

A healthy economy builds social and environmental capacity to manage change to mitigate negative effects on carrying capacity and growth limits. Again partnerships must evolve around healthy economic destinations linking good practices, many in our examples, from within the European Union with similar systems of devolved governance at local community level. Stakeholders and actor-network approaches are core to deciding the strategy and policy and enabling the planning and practices derived from evolving partnerships. Fundamentally leadership and management capacity will drive new economic models so new forms and ways of consultation at micro, meso and macro levels are necessary and should be funded accordingly at those levels. Leadership needs to help inculcate into a competitive advantage landscape a series of innovations that both meets the outcomes of ongoing debate over socio-economic and environmental constraints.

Endogeny is at the core therefore of the devolved and empowered discourse of power. We see examples of leadership in culturally embedded and valued food and drink; such explorations in slow food tourism have a long history in Italy and Spain. Our productive capacity should not undermine the principles of conservation and recreation underpinning the 1947 legislation in the UK. Similar value statements underpin the Hungarian environmental legislation as well as that of many other countries. Cross-sectoral partnerships help avoid conflict in the rural environment that presents a threat to the integrity of the countryside as we value it. Food, agriculture, our natural and man-made heritage all reinforce the storytelling that can help reinforce farming and other cross-sectoral partners in mining and forestry.

Finally, branding and destination management organisations will help secure co-ordination across competing sectors and provide support for learning across sectors. These activities in branding and identity will secure a stronger position in the market to permit ongoing synergistic product promotion without compromising substitute activity.

Conclusion

In Table 15.1 we have illustrated ways in which discourse analysis can support sustainable development in our case studies. Now we can prioritise issues and factors through those discourses. There is a need to prioritise as certain of these issues and their discourses serve as pre-conditions for the solutions that may be offered to complex, post-structural situations and the associated planning.

Landscapes where power is shared and communities are empowered to lead and manage must be critical to success. We acknowledge that solutions will be multi- and inter-disciplinary in the way that systems approaches require inputs and scenarios from not only sociology and geography but also from politicians, academics, practitioners in all manner of declared roles in a supply chain. These linkages in the disciplinary approach have emerged from all the literature and related discourses. There is a sense in which partners and networks are the products of our learning to understand and negotiate the landscape of power. These views are espoused in the work of Hannam and Knox (2005) from a tourism critical studies lens. The interdisciplinarity is also demanded of the Bianchi (2003), and latterly Heeks and Stanforth (2013, 2014) development studies approach. Mol, writing in 2010, also confirms our need to take multiple perspectives to produce resolution for complex scenarios of the future. Pritchard and Morgan in 2001, writing from a marketing perspective, also confirmed the need to obtain consensus from partners before moving to sustain tourism. Identity and culture must be agreed before stakeholders can move forward. As Bramwell and Cox discussed in 2009, it is the re-prioritising of stakeholders' perspectives to accommodate varying stages in service and product lifecycle and partnership that helps to define where we should like to be in the present and how we could forecast for the future.

A structure and agency approach, as predicated by Latour (2005), and demonstrated in Finland by the likes of Puhakka et al. (2009) and Saarinen (2006), lies at the heart of the contemporary and dynamic perspectives. During the past decade, in an era of continuous flux and review of change management brought about partly through questioning the new-liberal marketised approach to visitor economies at destination, the emergent discourse is of ever-increasing

Table 15.1 Power discourse and systems thinking (after Checkland, 1981)

Concept	Application	Practice	Sample
Mobility – at regional level – cooperation in approaching new markets	Becken et al. (2012) understanding regional influences and importance of interdependencies	Baltic Sea examples	North and Midlands of England with focus on walking, climbing, trekking (Cath Lee as example in PDNP). The BHNP has focussed on promoting cycling through a multi-stakeholder approach but there is no built route in the Highlands. Cyclists are challenged to find their ways through the Balaton hinterlands, though the visitor centres offer them the opportunity to park their bicycles. There are strong regional pressures to develop this and some of the forestry routes have been marked for cycling. However cyclists complain that the routes are poorly maintained and the conditions vary greatly from region to region.
Marketisation, Valorisation and Relational approaches	Rytteri et al. (2012) hotels in West Finland Hall and Campos (2014) Principles of democracy, equity, transparency and interactivity from Nordic countries Orellana et al. (2012) Netherlands Understanding Dutch visitor flows and spatial distribution	Local political reality coupled to smart marketing. Monitoring and managing visitor experiences. Behaviour patterns in protected areas	National Parks Week July–August 2015 Photography competition Nikon August 2015 (Peak DNP rated 3rd) Environmental Quality Mark New product: Peak District Cycle Shuttle Matlock and Bakewell rail Special events – Tour de France, L'eroica. To make the BHNP more attractive and therefore valuable include educational paths and trails with detailed interpretation signage. The Arboretum in Zirc has a 'how far can you jump area' which shows how nature can outperform the civilised humans.

| Stakeholder | Haukeland (2011) safeguarding conservation and recreation Norway
Van Riper and Kyle (2014) USA
Beliefs, moral norms, supportive, conservation behaviours encouraged | Practical steps to increase awareness of environmental issues and suggest ways of adjusting visitor behaviour | The Observatory – the Pannon Csillagda – has special events and themed presentations both within the Week of the national parks and during what the Hungarians called Shooting Stars week.
The NPs are promoting multi-site visits with videos and publications that encourage the visitor to try a different park next time, collect stamps and receive 15% discounts. The Hungarian NPs are committed to awareness campaigns, focussing on the work in and around the Visitor Centres and the educational paths which have been introduced. There are now erdei iskola or forest schools lasting two or three days aimed at children between the ages of 7–14.
Endogeny is seen most clearly with the promotion of local produce, both foods and crafts, including ceramics, under the umbrella of the Liveable Balaton. Tourinform offices – the Hungarian Tourism Information Centres – have dedicated shelves for these products. | Hope Valley Quarry
Provision of heritage tours and nascent corporate social responsibility annual campaign.
The university has been involved in promoting the NP, not only with research and skills training but also |

Table 15.1 (Continued)

Concept	Application	Practice	Sample
			with hosting exhibitions along our corridors from the photography competitions organised in the NP. Other stakeholders have also adopted a partnership approach in the Highlands area. In Bakonybél, for instance, there was a joint office housing Tourinform and the BHNP. Student visits are also encouraged from around the country. Tihany offers the opportunity to meet the local potter: talking and working with clay in an interactive experience.
Endogeny	Stanford (2014) Lake District	Encouraging people to use different and more sustainable modes of transport	Buxton Little Red Tram Enterprise culture.
Actor Network	Sandström et al. (2014) creation of co-management through social networks	Legitimacy in co-management to a variety of key actors in content and actor roles	Rewarding frequent visitors at Stanage-North Lees. 12 months free parking for £15 one-off donation subsidising the site maintenance. Macmillan Cancer Support fundraising walks. Protection of the villages and heritages cf the NP has been a particular focus. Even properties on the fringes of the Park cannot be developed without approval and proof that they are connected to the sewage system. The use of septic tanks has now been effectively outlawed around the Lake.

			The NP's regional Farmers' Market which began without a licence around five years ago to produce a market for the unemployed and underemployed producers of the region has become so successful that it attracts over 2000 people every Sunday. Some of the producers were even travelling over 200 kilometres from the Great Plain to take part but the number of vendors has now been limited and priority has been given to the local producers.
Structure	McGreavy (2015) Maine	Reinforcing messages amongst key decision makers	Planning road tunnel beneath NP. Finding ways to engage visitors with
Agency	Puhakka et al. (2014) Finnish examples	Several approaches to socio-cultural sustainability Knowledge transfer of the visitor experience	diverse lifestyles and expectations in the honeypots including Stanage-North Lees, Edale and Dovedale. Engage enterprise partners like Beechenhill Farm, Ilam.

criticality of functionalism and rationalism, even resource-based approaches (Jamal and Everett, 2004) to a more critical social perspective where analysis of problematisation (changed priorities and substitution of supply and demand resources), social regularities (between stakeholders from micro- to macro-governance levels) and knowledge production (an amalgam of stakeholder agendas) is now dominant (Dredge and Jamal, 2015; Kauppila et al., 2011, Klein et al., 2011).

McCool, writing in 2009, talks of the post-structuralist as being 'messy'. This messiness inevitably requires readers and analysts to understand benefits of new structures, with organisations producing benefits for partners in achieving some sort of consensus over development.

In the Venn diagram of new discourse on solutions we see the space and place overlapping the development agendas and the new identities being forged through complex change (Saarinen, 2006). At the intersection of these three domains we see the machinations of complex simulations using what is effectively systems thinking by stakeholders. Our numerous personal and team worldviews are informed by actor networks interests, involvement, engagement and numerous experiments and explorations through many different existing disciplines. All these lenses from social science and physical science are needed to produce a resolution.

Ultimately the key principles of NPs are to retain benchmarking of good practices and more widely disseminate findings and process. We agree that community rights are inalienable from development agendas and conservation is at the heart of the argument in 2015, as it was in 1947 in the United Kingdom or in Hungary some fifty years later.

References

Agrawal, A., & Gibson, C. C. (1999). Enchantment and disenchantment: The role of community in natural resource conservation. *World Development, 27*(4), 629–649.

Aitchison, C., MacLeod, N. E., Macleod, N. E., & Shaw, S. J. (2014). *Leisure and tourism landscapes: Social and cultural geographies.* London: Routledge.

Aitchison, C., McLeod, N. E., & Shaw, S. J. (2000). *Leisure and tourism landscapes: Social and cultural geographies.* London: Routledge.

Ansari, S., Munir, K., & Gregg, T. (2012). Impact at the 'bottom of the pyramid': The role of social capital in capability development and community empowerment. *Journal of Management Studies, 49*(4), 813–842.

Ashworth, G. J. (Ed.). (1988). *Marketing in the tourism industry: The promotion of destination regions.* London: International Thomson Publishing Services.

Baggio, R., & Cooper, C. (2010). Knowledge transfer in a tourism destination: The effects of a network structure. *The Service Industries Journal, 30*(10), 1757–1771.

Beaumont, N., & Dredge, D. (2010). Local tourism governance: A comparison of three network approaches. *Journal of Sustainable Tourism, 18*(1), 7–28.

Becken, J., Brandt, J., Hansen, A. C., Holmes, E., Wagner, P., & Laube, M. (2012). *Natural heritage in the Baltic Sea region: Challenges and solutions for sustainable transport to and within protected areas.* Berlin: Verkehrsclub Deutschland.

Beritelli, P., & Bieger, T. (2014). From destination governance to destination leadership – Defining and exploring the significance with the help of a systemic perspective. *Tourism Review, 69*(1), 25–46.

Bianchi, R. V. (2003). Place and power in tourism development: Tracing the complex articulations of community and locality. *Pasos: Revista de turismo y patrimonio cultural, 1*(1), 13–32.

Braden, S., & Mayo, M. (1999). Culture, community development and representation. *Community Development Journal, 34*(3), 191–204.

Bramwell, B. (2006). Actors, power, and discourses of growth limits. *Annals of Tourism Research, 33*(4), 957–978.

Bramwell, B., & Cox, V. (2009). Stage and path dependence approaches to the evolution of a national park tourism partnership. *Journal of Sustainable Tourism, 17*(2), 191–206.

Burns, D., Heywood, F., & Wilde, P. (2004). *What works in assessing community participation?* Bristol: Policy Press.

Casimir, G., Lee, K., & Loon, M. (2012). Knowledge sharing: influences of trust, commitment and cost. *Journal of Knowledge Management, 16*(5), 740–753.

Castellani, V., & Sala, S. (2010). Sustainable performance index for tourism policy development. *Tourism Management, 31*(6), 871–880.

Cawley, M., & Gillmor, D. A. (2008). Integrated rural tourism: Concepts and Practice. *Annals of Tourism Research, 35*(2), 316–337.

Celino, A., & Concilio, G. (2010). Participation in environmental spatial planning: Structuring-scenario to manage knowledge in action. *Futures, 42*(7), 733–742.

Checkland, P. (1981). *Systems thinking, systems practice.* Chichester: John Wiley & Sons.

Choi, H. C., & Sirakaya, E. (2006). Sustainability indicators for managing community tourism. *Tourism Management, 27*(6), 1274–1289.

Clark, J. R. A., & Clarke, R. (2011). Local sustainability initiatives in English National Parks: What role for adaptive governance? *Land Use Policy, 28*(1), 314–324.

Clarke, A., Raffay, Á., & Wiltshier, P. (2009). Losing it: Knowledge management in tourism development projects. *Tourismos: An International Multidisciplinary Journal of Tourism, 4*(3), 149–166.

Coles, T., & Church, A. (2006). Tourism, politics and the forgotten entanglements of power. In *Tourism, power and space* (pp. 15–56). London: Routledge.

Crouch, G. I., & Ritchie, J. B. (1999). Tourism, competitiveness, and societal prosperity. *Journal of Business Research, 44*(3), 137–152.

Dalkir, K. (2013). Knowledge management in theory and practice. London: Routledge.

Dias, E., Rhin, C., Haller, R., & Scholten, H. (2004). Adding value and improving processes using location-based services in protected areas: The WebPark experience. *e-Environment: Progress and Challenge Special edition on e-Environment Instituto Politécnico Nacional Mexico, Mexico City*, 291–302.

Dredge, D. (2010). Place change and tourism development conflict: Evaluating public interest. *Tourism Management, 31*(1), 104–112.

Dredge, D., & Jamal, T. (2015). Progress in tourism planning and policy: A post-structural perspective on knowledge production. *Tourism Management, 51*(C), 285–297.

Dwyer, L., & Edwards, D. (2010). Sustainable tourism planning. In *Understanding the sustainable development of tourism.* Oxford: Goodfellow Publishers Limited.

Edwards, B. (1998). Charting the discourse of community action: Perspectives from practice in rural Wales. *Journal of Rural Studies, 14*(1), 63–77.

Garrod, B., Wornell, R., & Youell, R. (2006). Re-conceptualising rural resources as countryside capital: The case of rural tourism. *Journal of rural studies*, *22*(1), 117–128.

Giddens, A. (1984). *The constitution of society: Outline of the theory of structuration*. Berkeley: University of California Press.

Gilchrist, A., & Taylor, M. (2011). *The short guide to community development*. Bristol: Policy Press.

Hall, C. M., & Campos, M. J. Z. (2014). Public administration and tourism – International and Nordic perspectives. *Scandinavian Journal of Public Administration*, *18*(1), 3–17.

Hall, S., Massey, D., & Rustin, M. (2013). After neoliberalism: Analysing the present. *Soundings: A Journal of Politics and Culture*, *53*(1), 8–22.

Hannam, K., & Knox, D. (2005). Discourse analysis in tourism research: A critical perspective. *Tourism Recreation Research*, *30*(2), 23–30.

Haukeland, J. V. (2011). Tourism stakeholders' perceptions of national park management in Norway. *Journal of Sustainable Tourism*, *19*(2), 133–153.

Heeks, R., & Stanforth, C. (2013). Technological change in developing countries: Opening the black box of process using Actor-Network Theory. Working Paper no. 5.

Heeks, R., & Stanforth, C. (2014). Understanding development project implementation: An actor-network perspective. *Public Administration and Development*, *34*(1), 14–31.

Hjalager, A. M. (1997). Innovation patterns in sustainable tourism: An analytical typology. *Tourism Management*, *18*(1), 35–41.

Hjalager, A. M. (2010). A review of innovation research in tourism. *Tourism Management*, *31*(1), 1–12.

Huck, J., Al, R., & Rathi, D. (2011). Finding KM solutions for a volunteer-based non-profit organization. *Vine*, *41*(1), 26–40.

Hung, K., Sirakaya-Turk, E., & Ingram, L. J. (2011). Testing the efficacy of an integrative model for community participation. *Journal of Travel Research*, *50*(3), 276–288.

Jamal, T. B., & Everett, J. (2004). Resisting rationalisation in the natural and academic lifeworld: Critical tourism research or hermeneutic charity? *Current Issues in Tourism*, *7*(1), 1–19.

Jamal, T. B., & Getz, D. (1995). Collaboration theory and community tourism planning. *Annals of Tourism Research*, *22*(1), 186–204.

Kagan, C. (2006). *Making a difference: Participation and well-being*. Liverpool: New Start Publishing.

Kagan, C., & Duggan, K. (2011). Creating community cohesion: The power of using innovative methods to facilitate engagement and genuine partnership. *Social Policy and Society*, *10*(3), 393–404.

Kagan, C., Micallef, M., Siddiquee, A., Fatimilehin, I., Hassan, A., Santis, C., . . . Bunn, G. (2013). Intergenerational work, social capital and wellbeing. *Global Journal Community Psychology Practice*, *3*(4), 286–293.

Kauppila, O. P., Rajala, R., & Jyrämä, A. (2011). Knowledge sharing through virtual teams across borders and boundaries. *Management Learning*, 1350507610389685.

Kernel, P. (2005). Creating and implementing a model for sustainable development in tourism enterprises. *Journal of Cleaner Production*, *13*(2), 151–164.

Klein, P., Fatima, M., McEwen, L., Moser, S. C., Schmidt, D., & Zupan, S. (2011). Dismantling the ivory tower: Engaging geographers in university – community partnerships. *Journal of Geography in Higher Education*, *35*(3), 425–444.

Latour, B. (2005). *Reassembling the social: An introduction to actor-network-theory* (Clarendon Lectures in Management Studies).

Liburd, J. J., & Edwards, D. (Eds.). (2010). *Understanding the sustainable development of tourism.* Oxford: Goodfellow.

Mayo, M. (1997). Partnerships for regeneration and community development. Some opportunities, challenges and constraints. *Critical Social Policy, 17*(52), 3–26.

Mayo, M., Blake, G., Diamond, J., Foot, J., Gidley, B., Shukra, K., & Yamit, M. (2009). Community empowerment and community cohesion: Parallel agendas for community building in England? *Journal of Social Intervention: Theory and Practice, 18*(1), 23–43.

Mayo, M., Mendiwelso-Bendek, Z., & Packham, C. (2013). Community development, community organising and third sector – University research partnerships. *Community Research for Community Development,* 1.

McCool, S. F. (2009). Constructing partnerships for protected area tourism planning in an era of change and messiness. *Journal of Sustainable Tourism, 17*(2), 133–148.

McGrath, S. (2012). Vocational education and training for development: A policy in need of a theory? *International Journal of Educational Development, 32*(5), 623–631.

McGreavy, B. (2015). Resilience as discourse. *Environmental Communication,* (ahead-of-print), 1–18.

Moscardo, G. (2014). Tourism and community leadership in rural regions: Linking mobility, entrepreneurship, tourism development and community well-being. *Tourism Planning & Development,* (ahead-of-print), 1–17.

Murphy, P. E. (1988). Community driven tourism planning. *Tourism Management, 9*(2), 96–104.

O'Dell, C. S., & Essaides, N. (1998). *If only we knew what we know: The transfer of internal knowledge and best practice.* New York: Simon and Schuster.

O'Meara, K. (2002). Uncovering the values in faculty evaluation of service as scholarship. *The Review of Higher Education, 26*(1), 57–80.

Orellana, D., Bregt, A. K., Ligtenberg, A., & Wachowicz, M. (2012). Exploring visitor movement patterns in natural recreational areas. *Tourism Management, 33*(3), 672–682.

Pinho, I., Rego, A., & e Cunha, M. P. (2012). Improving knowledge management processes: A hybrid positive approach. *Journal of Knowledge Management, 16*(2), 215–242.

Pritchard, A., & Morgan, N. J. (2001). Culture, identity and tourism representation: Marketing Cymru or Wales. *Tourism Management, 22*(2), 167–179.

Puhakka, R. (2008). Increasing role of tourism in Finnish national parks. *Fennia-International Journal of Geography, 186*(1), 47–58.

Puhakka, R., Cottrell, S. P., & Siikamäki, P. (2014). Sustainability perspectives on Oulanka National Park, Finland: Mixed methods in tourism research. *Journal of Sustainable Tourism, 22*(3), 480–505.

Puhakka, R., Sarkki, S., Cottrell, S. P., & Siikamäki, P. (2009). Local discourses and international initiatives: Sociocultural sustainability of tourism in Oulanka National Park, Finland. *Journal of Sustainable Tourism, 17*(5), 529–549.

Putnam, R. D. (1995). Bowling alone: America's declining social capital. *Journal of Democracy, 6*(1), 65–78.

Rytteri, T., & Puhakka, R. (2012). The art of neoliberalizing park management: Commodification, politics and hotel construction in Pallasyllästunturi National Park, Finland. *Geografiska Annaler: Series B, Human Geography, 94*(3), 255–268.

Saarinen, J. (2006). Traditions of sustainability in tourism studies. *Annals of Tourism Research, 33*(4), 1121–1140.

Sandström, A., Crona, B., & Bodin, Ö. (2014). Legitimacy in co-management: The impact of pre-existing structures, social networks and governance strategies. *Environmental Policy and Governance, 24*(1), 60–76.

Saxena, G. (2005). Relationships, networks and the learning regions: Case evidence from the Peak District National Park. *Tourism Management, 26*(2), 277–289.

Senge, P. M. (2006). *The fifth discipline: The art and practice of the learning organization.* New York: Broadway Business.

Simpson, M. C. (2008). Community benefit tourism initiatives – A conceptual oxymoron. *Tourism Management, 29*(1), 1–18.

Stanford, D. J. (2014). Reducing visitor car use in a protected area: A market segmentation approach to achieving behaviour change. *Journal of Sustainable Tourism, 22*(4), 666–683.

Sučić, M. (2009). Public Private Partnership – Postulate for Competitive Tourism Development. In *Proceedings of 7th International Conference "Economic Integration, Competition and Cooperation* (pp. 2–3). *University of Rijeka,* Opatija.

Taylor, M. (2005). The new public management and social exclusion: Cause or response? In *New public management* (pp. 121–140). London: Routledge.

Taylor, M., Purdue, D., Wilson, M., & Wilde, P. (2005). Evaluating community projects. *Joseph Rowntree Foundation.* www. jrf. org. uk.

Timur, S., & Getz, D. (2008). A network perspective on managing stakeholders for sustainable urban tourism. *International Journal of Contemporary Hospitality Management, 20*(4), 445–461.

Van Riper, C. J., & Kyle, G. T. (2014). Understanding the internal processes of behavioral engagement in a national park: A latent variable path analysis of the value-belief-norm theory. *Journal of Environmental Psychology,* 38: 288–297.

Woodside, A. G., & Carr, J. A. (1988). Consumer decision making and competitive marketing strategies: Applications for tourism planning. *Journal of Travel Research, 26*(3), 2–7.

Index

Page numbers in italics indicate figures; page numbers in bold indicate tables.